21世纪英语专业系列教材

英语泛读教程

(第二版)

第3册

主　编　李正栓　宋德文　姜亚军
副主编　郭淑青　杨丽华　赵翠华

编　者　葛文词　李海云　彭鲁迁　李金英

图书在版编目(CIP)数据

英语泛读教程.第3册/李正栓,宋德文,姜亚军主编.—2版.—北京:北京大学出版社,2014.7

(21世纪英语专业系列教材)

ISBN 978-7-301-22700-8

Ⅰ.①英⋯　Ⅱ.①李⋯ ②宋⋯ ③姜⋯　Ⅲ.英语—阅读教学—高等学校—教材　Ⅳ.①H319.4

中国版本图书馆CIP数据核字(2013)第139498号

书　　名：	英语泛读教程(第二版)第3册
著作责任者：	李正栓　宋德文　姜亚军　主编
责 任 编 辑：	郝妮娜
标 准 书 号：	ISBN 978-7-301-22700-8/H·3329
出 版 发 行：	北京大学出版社
地　　　址：	北京市海淀区成府路205号　100871
网　　　址：	http://www.pup.cn　新浪官方微博:@北京大学出版社
电 子 信 箱：	bdhnn2011@126.com
电　　　话：	邮购部 62752015　发行部 62750672　编辑部 62759634　出版部 62754962
印 刷 者：	北京大学印刷厂
经 销 者：	新华书店
	787毫米×1092毫米　16开本　15.5印张　490千字
	2008年11月第1版
	2014年7月第2版　2016年4月第2次印刷
定　　　价：	39.00元

未经许可,不得以任何方式复制或抄袭本书之部分或全部内容。
版权所有,侵权必究
举报电话:010-62752024　电子信箱:fd@pup.pku.edu.cn

《21世纪英语专业系列教材》
编写委员会

（以姓氏笔画排序）

王立非	王守仁	王克非
王俊菊	文秋芳	石 坚
申 丹	朱 刚	仲伟合
刘世生	刘意青	殷企平
孙有中	李 力	李正栓
张旭春	张庆宗	张绍杰
杨俊峰	陈法春	金 莉
封一函	胡壮麟	查明建
袁洪庚	桂诗春	黄国文
梅德明	董洪川	蒋洪新
程幼强	程朝翔	虞建华

总 序

北京大学出版社自2005年以来已出版《语言与应用语言学知识系列读本》多种,为了配合第十一个五年计划,现又策划陆续出版《21世纪英语专业系列教材》。这个重大举措势必受到英语专业广大教师和学生的欢迎。

作为英语教师,最让人揪心的莫过于听人说英语不是一个专业,只是一个工具。说这些话的领导和教师的用心是好的,为英语专业的毕业生将来找工作着想,因此要为英语专业的学生多多开设诸如新闻、法律、国际商务、经济、旅游等其他专业的课程。但事与愿违,英语专业的教师们很快发现,学生投入英语学习的时间少了,掌握英语专业课程知识甚微,即使对四个技能的掌握也并不比大学英语学生高明多少,而那个所谓的第二专业在有关专家的眼中只是学到些皮毛而已。

英语专业的路在何方?有没有其他路可走?这是需要我们英语专业教师思索的问题。中央领导关于创新是一个民族的灵魂和要培养创新人才等的指示精神,让我们在层层迷雾中找到了航向。显然,培养学生具有自主学习能力和能进行创造性思维是我们更为重要的战略目标,使英语专业的人才更能适应21世纪的需要,迎接21世纪的挑战。

如今,北京大学出版社外语部的领导和编辑同志们也从教材出版的视角探索英语专业的教材问题,从而为贯彻英语专业教学大纲做些有益的工作,为教师们开设大纲中所规定的必修、选修课程提供各种教材。《21世纪英语专业系列教材》是普通高等教育"十一五"国家级规划教材和国家"十一五"重点出版规划项目《面向新世纪的立体化网络化英语学科建设丛书》的重要组成部分。这套系列教材要体现新世纪英语教学的自主化、协作化、模块化和超文本化,结合外语教材的具体情况,既要解决教学内容、教学方法和教育技术的时代化,也要坚持弘扬以爱国主义为核心的民族精神。因此,今天北京大学出版社在大力提倡专业英语教学改革的基础上,编辑出版各种英语专业技能、英语专业知识和相关专业知识课程的教材,以培养具有创新性思维和具有实际工作能力的学生,充分体现了时代精神。

北京大学出版社的远见卓识,也反映了英语专业广大师生盼望已久的心愿。由北京大学等全国几十所院校具体组织力量,积极编写相关教材。这就

领导、各位编辑和工作人员为本套教材的成长所提供的关爱与支持。

英语专业教学任重道远,教材建设永无止境。本套教材旨在适应新形势下的英语专业教学,探索教学新路,缺点与不足之处在所难免,衷心希望得到专家学者的批评指正,听到广大师生的改进意见。

编　者
2014年5月

第二版前言

国家级规划教材《英语泛读教程》自2008年问世以来，受到了全国英语专业老师和学生的一致好评。过去六年的教材使用与教学实践证明，本教材选材方向正确，既兼顾语言表达与人文知识的相得益彰，又注重西方文化传统与现代文化的融会贯通，既注重经典传承，也关注时代变迁。

《英语泛读教程》第二版基本保持了第一版的编写思想。修订内容之一是更换了部分课文，以求选材的时代性、内容的丰富性、文本的趣味性和文体的多样性。在筛选文章的过程中，我们既考虑提升学生的英语水平与人文知识基础，也注重整套教材内容的前后衔接。

第二版对课文后面的练习也做了调整。具体的考量有三：第一，注重从具体课文到所涉及领域之间的递进关系，通过具体的课文使学生对相关领域的知识有所了解。第二，注重学生对篇章结构的理解。第三，注重课内阅读与课外阅读之间的配合。具体修订内容如下：

一、为了提高学生的学习兴趣，本次修订替换了约30%的课文，新的课文内容多启发人文思考，更能体现通过文化思考来带动语言习得，同时注重学生思辨能力的提升。

二、移除各单元练习中的翻译部分，加入了词汇题，有助于学生进一步掌握和复习课文中的重点词汇。

三、新增命题拓展。通过此题的延伸，可以引导学生有意识地进行批评性阅读，从而使其更深刻地领会和理解西方文化的内涵与实质。

四、新设一个引导性的课外拓展题，让学生自己学会如何围绕课本提供的主题进行拓展学习，从大学基础学习阶段就培养良好的自主深入学习的习惯，更有利于学生知识面的扩展。

五、每个单元后面新增二十分钟的阅读材料，材料选自历年英语专业四级阅读真题，以提高学生的限时阅读水平，提升学生阅读的有效性。

我们相信，通过此次修订，这套泛读教材将更好地服务于英语人才的培养。借此机会，感谢为本套教材改版而默默奉献的老师们，也感谢北京大学出版社的

是说，这套教材是由一些高等院校有水平有经验的第一线教师们制定编写大纲，反复讨论，特别是考虑到在不同层次、不同背景学校之间取得平衡，避免了先前的教材或偏难或偏易的弊病。与此同时，一批知名专家教授参与策划和教材审定工作，保证了教材质量。

  当然，这套系列教材出版只是初步实现了出版社和编者们的预期目标。为了获得更大效果，希望使用本系列教材的教师和同学不吝指教，及时将意见反馈给我们，使教材更加完善。

  航道已经开通，我们有决心乘风破浪，奋勇前进！

胡壮麟
北京大学蓝旗营

第一版前言

本教材是为了适应新时期高等学校英语专业教学的需要，根据《高等学校英语专业英语教学大纲》的要求而编写的英语专业阅读教材，可供高校英语专业阅读教学使用，也可作为中高级英语学习者的自学书籍。

在前两册的基础上，本册进一步突出英语专业阅读教材的特点，广泛收录英美名家在各个时期的作品，旨在扩大学生词汇量，培养英语语感，拓宽学生视野，增强人文素养，提高学生的鉴赏能力和思辨能力。在选择文章时，编者兼顾典藏性和时代性，既有文学巨擘的传世佳作，又不乏颇具前瞻性的商界杂谈；在题材上，力求涵盖社会生活的方方面面，有对生命的考问，有对艺术的追寻，有对爱情的缅怀，也有闪耀智慧光芒的机巧思辨；在体裁上，时评时叙，亦庄亦谐，有的古雅隽永，有的灵异怪诞，有的铺排绚丽，有的朴实无华，于犀利中见幽默，在淡定中显温情，充分体现了本书在选材上时代跨度大，题材范围广，文体多样化的宗旨，从而使学生在徜徉英语语言殿堂的同时，体验中西文化的碰撞，品味跌宕起伏的哲理人生。

本书在编排上沿袭了前两册的体例，每个单元有 Text A 和 Text B 两篇阅读材料，对生词、难词加以注释，在注释中编者有意识地给读者提供一定的选择空间，要求学生作出正确的词义选择。为了帮助学生深入理解原文，编者对文中出现的文化现象单独加以注释。考虑到本书是英语专业的基础课教材，编者在每篇文章后都配以阅读练习题，针对性极强，训练学生的略读、寻读、细读、评读等阅读技巧，引导学生去解读、思考、分析和批评。所有练习都围绕阅读展开，回答问题和正误判断部分检测了学生对原文内容的理解程度，解释原文和英汉翻译是对学生的理解能力的更深层次的测试，阅读评述部分旨在训练学生口头和笔头的发挥能力及思维拓展能力，是对原文阅读的进一步延伸。

作为英语专业的阅读教材，本书与国内传统的泛读教材有所不同，是一次新的尝试。由于时间仓促以及编者水平有限，纰漏和不周之处在所难免，欢迎使用本书的社会各界人士加以批评指正。

编者
2008年5月

Contents

Unit One 1
- **Text A** Successful New Year 1
- **Text B** A Winning Way to Handle New Ideas 9
- **Twenty Minutes' Reading** 17

Unit Two 21
- **Text A** Language and Culture Differences in Daily Life 21
- **Text B** Different Ethical Values in Chinese and American Cultures 29
- **Twenty Minutes' Reading** 38

Unit Three 42
- **Text A** Universality of the Folktale 42
- **Text B** I Am Cinderella's Stepmother and I Know My Rights 50
- **Twenty Minutes' Reading** 57

Unit Four 61
- **Text A** What Is True Freedom? 61
- **Text B** I'm Too Busy for Me 68
- **Twenty Minutes' Reading** 75

Unit Five 79
- **Text A** On Photography I 79
- **Text B** On Photography II 87
- **Twenty Minutes' Reading** 93

Unit Six 97
- **Text A** The Bridges of Madison County 97
- **Text B** Letter in the Wallet 105
- **Twenty Minutes' Reading** 113

Unit Seven 117
- **Text A** The Dream-work 117
- **Text B** Group Psychology and the Analysis of the Ego 124
- **Twenty Minutes' Reading** 131

Unit Eight 135
- **Text A** The Oval Portrait 135
- **Text B** A Diagnosis of Death 144
- **Twenty Minutes' Reading** 152

Unit Nine 156
- **Text A** The Allegory of the Cave 156
- **Text B** Utopia 165
- **Twenty Minutes' Reading** 172

Unit Ten 176
- **Text A** How to Escape out of Thought Traps? 176
- **Text B** Motivated by All the Wrong Reasons 183
- **Twenty Minutes' Reading** 190

Unit Eleven 194
- **Text A** On Life 194
- **Text B** The Rhythm of Life 202
- **Twenty Minutes' Reading** 210

Unit Twelve 214
- **Text A** Love 214
- **Text B** Of Friendship 221
- **Twenty Minutes' Reading** 230

Unit One

Text A

Successful New Year
Anonymous

《成功的新年》如何安排好生活？如何过好新的一年？本文将试图给您一个建议，希望对您或有裨益。

Now that the Christmas festivities are over, the next order of Business is the New Year. That means resolutions.

Frankly, I'm tired of New Year's resolutions. I make them every year. I break them every year, often forgetting the resolutions by Martin Luther King Day. On the other hand, there are plenty of bad habits I'd like to get rid of before my next birthday in September. So here I am, finalizing my New Year's resolutions strategy. Let's see if we can break the losing streak in naught seven.

I have two lofty goals for 2007:

* Get some exercise

* Quit smoking

I agonized before typing those words. I'm an introvert, super lazy and smoke like a chimney. Trust me when I tell you I'm scared as hell sharing these resolutions. Given my track record of not finishing what I start, there's a good chance of failure.

But if I'm serious about growing as a person, not smelling like Uncle Joe's burnt ribs

streak /stri:k/ *n.* **a.** a long stripe or mark on a surface which contrasts with the surface; **b.** a particular type of behaviour of a person; **c.** a continuous series of successes or failures in gambling or sport

lofty /ˈlɒ(:)fti/ *adj.* **a.** (of thoughts, aims, etc.) noble; **b.** high; **c.** (derog.) seeming to be proud or superior

agonize /ˈæɡənaɪz/ *v.* to suffer great anxiety or worry intensely

introvert /ˌɪntrəˈvɜːt/ *n.* person who is shy, quiet and unable to make friends easily cf. extrovert

as hell (*infml*) used after adjectives or some adverbs to emphasize the adjective or adverb

all the time, and not having to sit down every 10 feet, putting these resolutions out in public is the best thing I can do.

So here's the game plan.

> sure-fire (infml) sure to succeed
> factor in include a particular thing in the calculations about how long sth will take, how much it will cost, etc.
> consecutive /kənˈsekjʊtɪv/ adj. following in regular unbroken order

Smokey's 8 sure-fire tips for successful New Year's resolutions:

(If you have tips to make New Year's resolutions more sure-firely successful, please share in the comments!)

1. Aim for something you can track

"Lose weight" or "get more exercise" are nice resolutions and all, but without specifics to focus on, they're doomed from the get-go.

Can you aim for a number or other measurable goal? The more focused the resolution, the easier it is to succeed.

Instead of "be healthier", how about one of these more specific resolutions?

* Take a 20-minute walk everyday after lunch.

* Run a 7-minute mile.

* Finish the company 10k in an hour.

* Lose 20 pounds.

For the exercising resolution, my trackable goal is 120 days in the gym. I want to be generally healthier, get more exercise, and have more energy. Factoring in my schedule and overall laziness, an average of 3 times a week at the gym is a hard, but achievable goal.

For the quit-smoking resolution, my trackable goal is to have 30 consecutive smoke-free days within 3 months.

2. Set a deadline, the sooner the better

A deadline far off in the distance is quickly forgotten. Without a deadline, you may find yourself making the same resolutions year after year.

For my goal of exercising at least 3 days a week, I need to get 120 days in the gym in a whole year (365 days). Hmm, looking at that big 1-2-0 number is <u>kinda</u> scary and having a deadline so far away (Dec 31, 2007) makes it easy to ignore the resolution for just another day.

That really increases my chances of failure. I think I need to add a 3-month milestone of 30 days in the gym by April 1. Doesn't seem so hard now, and hopefully by April, getting some exercise has become an indispensable habit that I'll continue for the rest of the year and beyond.

3. Be <u>accountable</u> to someone you don't want to let down

Having to tell someone whose opinion you respect when you've succeeded (or failed) is a big incentive.

Remember that deadline. You can combine tips 2 and 3 into one "I finally accomplished a resolution!" party. Make that date at the beginning of the year!

For me, I'm being accountable to you, the Internet. I figure you, dear Internet, are the scariest person I can be accountable to. God help me.

Health Top Tips Nutrition Lifestyle

4. Use the <u>buddy</u> system

The buddy system works for keeping us safe. It also works for keeping us motivated.

Find a friend who wants what you want. Both of you now have a fighting chance of keeping this year's resolution.

I have a buddy for both resolutions. There're plenty of people looking to quit smoking and/or get more exercise.

5. Do a 30-day challenge

I learned about the 30-day challenge from Steve Pavlina. "It's a way to trick yourself into not being scared of the <u>commitment</u>." Steve says.

---

kinda /ˈkaɪndə/ kind of
accountable /əˈkaʊntəbəl/ *adj.* responsible; having to justify one's actions
buddy /ˈbʌdi/ *n.* companion, partner
commitment /kəˈmɪtmənt/ *n.* **a.** an obligation, responsibility, or promise that restricts freedom of action; **b.** dedication to a cause or principle

It seems too overwhelming to think about making a big change and sticking with it every day for the rest of your life when you're still habituated to doing the opposite. The more you think about the change as something permanent, the more you stay put.

That summarizes how I feel about the quit-smoking challenge. I love smoking. It's great after a meal. Or in the mornings with a soy latte and the *New York Times*. Trade that in for mood swings and cravings so strong I want to claw my eyes out. That's crazy talk.

> **soy latte** latte is a strong coffee with frothy steamed milk. soy latte is one type of coffee beverage which is combined with soy milk.
> **chunk** /tʃʌŋk/ **a.** a roughly cut lump; **b.** (*infml*) a part, esp. a large part
> **No biggie.** (*AmE*) not particularly important or serious
> **adulation** /ˌædjʊˈleɪʃən/ *n.* praise and admiration for someone that is more than they really deserve
> **velvety** /ˈvelvɪti/ *adj.* soft and smooth in a way that suggests the feel of velvet
> **filet** /fɪˈleɪ/ *n.* a piece of meat or fish without bones
> **splurge** /splɜːdʒ/ *v.* to spend more money than one can usually afford

I'm using the 30-day challenge to track the nicotine intake. To break it down into a manageable chunk. I'm not going to be smoke-free every day, but 30 consecutive smoke-free days within the first 3 months is doable. 1 month, 4 weeks, 30 days. No biggie.

6. Visualize the result

Why are you making this resolution? It's not because you suddenly hate chocolate and all things sugary. It's because you want to fit into those jeans. More than that, it's because you want the sweet ego-boosting adulation from all those around. Think about the sweet adulation, not the velvety sweetness of cheesecake.

For me, the goal is to not be out of breath walking from my car up the stairs to my apartment. That's not a very sexy goal to visualize, so I imagine myself chasing down a purse snatcher and being everybody's hero. And not coughing up a lung every morning.

7. Reward yourself

Ruth's Chris Filet gives you something awesome to look forward to.

If you're quitting smoking, calculate how much money you saved and splurge on yourself.

I spent roughly $700 on cigarettes a year. At the end of the year, I'm going to take that money and buy my friends a nice meal. (I seem to have Andrea's selfish need to be selfless.)

I'm picturing a fat, juicy Filet, medium rare, and a side of sweet potato casserole (with pecan crust) at Ruth's Chris.

8. Start right away

If you don't start on January 1, your chance of success drops from 74% to 37%. (source: Bureau of Fake Statistics) So start immediately!

I think starting on the 2nd is okay. We'll need a day off to recover from the hangover. Don't put it off too long, or you'll be making the same resolution next year.

I have a sneaking suspicion I have some kind of attention deficit disorder, though never formally diagnosed. If I put something off for a couple of days, forget about it. Seriously, just forget about it. It's gone forever.

If you need some ideas, here are the Top 10 New Year's Resolutions, according to 10 Million Resolutions.

1. Lose Weight and Get in Better Physical Shape

2. Stick to a Budget

3. Debt Reduction

4. Enjoy More Quality Time with Family & Friends

5. Find My Soul Mate

6. Quit Smoking

7. Find a Better Job

8. Learn Something New

medium rare medium (of meat) partly cooked but still slightly pink inside, cf. rare, well-done
casserole /ˈkæsərəʊl/ *n.* **a.** a dish made by cooking meat, vegetables or other foods in liquid inside a heavy container at low heat; **b.** the heavy, deep container with a lid used in cooking such dishes
pecan /pɪˈkæn/ *n.* a long thin sweet nut with a dark red shell
crust /krʌst/ *n.* a hard outer covering of sth
sneaking /ˈsniːkɪŋ/ *adj.* **a.** secret, not openly expressed; **b.** (of a feeling or belief) not proved but probably right
attention deficit disorder (*AmE*) attention deficit hyperactivity disorder (*BrE*) a condition in which someone, esp. a child, is often in a state of activity or excitement and unable to direct their attention towards what they are doing
quality time the time that one focuses on or dedicates oneself to a cherished person or activity
soul mate a person with whom one has a strong affinity

9. Volunteer and Help Others

10. Get Organized

Cultural Notes

1. **Martin Luther King Day**—Martin Luther King Day is a national holiday observed each year in the United States on the third Monday in January, commemorating the birthday (Jan.15) of Martin Luther King, Jr. Dr. King (1929—1968) was an African-American clergyman who shaped the American civil rights movement. His nonviolent demonstrations against racial inequality led to civil rights legislation. King was an eloquent speaker and delivered his famous speech "I Have a Dream" at 1963 march on Washington. He was awarded the Nobel Peace Prize in 1964 and became not only the symbolic leader of American blacks but also a world figure. On the evening of April 4, 1968, he was assassinated while leading a protest march in Memphis, Tennessee.

2. **Joe**—Some common names in English sometimes have special meanings. For example, "By George" means "Oh, dear". The name "Joe" means an ordinary man or sometimes it refers to the typical person who can represent a group of people of the same kind. One of the other expressions concerning the name is "a Joe job", which is a boring task.

3. **Smokey**—a. Smokey Bear, fictional character, whose mission is to raise public awareness to protect America's forests. Smokey's message now is "Only You Can Prevent Wildfires." b. The word "Smokey" also refers to "the highway police (slang)".

4. **God help me**—May God help me. It is used to give force to a statement of the danger or seriousness of a situation or action.

5. **The New York Times**—The flagship publication of the New York Times Company, *the New York Times* is one of the most influential newspapers in the world. The New York Times Company got its start in 1851 when Henry Jarvis Raymond and George Jones produced their first paper, *the New York Daily Times*, which quickly became a success. The word Daily was dropped in 1857. Now the company has become a major newspaper publisher and media company, which owns newspapers, television and radio stations, and electronic information services.

Comprehension Exercises

I. Answer the following questions based on the text.

1. Why does the author write the article?
2. What does the author intend to achieve in the coming new year?
3. Why does he put his resolutions out in public this time?
4. Who is Smokey here?
5. What resolutions are easier to be carried out according to the author?

II. Write T for true and F for false in the brackets before each of the following statements.

1. (   ) The author is tired of New Year's resolutions because he doesn't think it significant.
2. (   ) The author doesn't think he will have a big change after a chain of failure in the past.
3. (   ) In comparison with "Lose 20 pounds", the resolution of "Lose weight" is not bad.
4. (   ) "Run a 7-minute mile" is equal to "Run a mile in 7 minutes".
5. (   ) Working out in the gym about 4 weeks before April is acceptable for the author.
6. (   ) The Internet won't let down the author.
7. (   ) The author has a very bad cough.
8. (   ) The author will have a meal with his friends at Ruth's Chris at the end of the year.
9. (   ) Many people are careful in spending money.
10. (   ) People are most concerned about their weight and physical shape.

III. Select the most appropriate word or phrase and use its proper form to complete each of the following sentences.

agonize	resolution	lofty	factor	consecutive
indispensable	accountable	incentive	figure	track
overwhelm	boost	habituate	craving	company
adulation	splurge	hangover	sneak	introvert

1. Smoking is a causative _____ in several major diseases.
2. Why do you _____ yourself with the thought of your failure?
3. Employees receive a certain number of shares of stock each year, which provides

employees an _____ to help the company succeed.
4. There may be certain times of day when smokers _____ their cigarette.
5. How did he _____ off in the middle of the meeting without being noticed?
6. He was reelected for four _____ terms.
7. Don't hesitate to _____ on domestic delights that afford long-term pleasure, like expensive cookware, fluffy towels and designer sheets.
8. Philosophers earn public respect when they contribute to the _____ of practical problems of public importance.
9. He had a terrible _____ after the New Year's party.
10. Walking is the best possible exercise. _____ yourself to walk very fast.
11. He is mentally ill and cannot be held _____ for his actions.
12. Too much detail can _____ even the most meticulous planner.
13. It is universally acknowledged that trees are _____ to us.
14. After receiving the _____ of his friends, he gradually believed it to be the gospel truth and was overcome with self-admiration.
15. No one could _____ out how he got to be so wealthy.

IV. Paraphrase the underlined words or expressions in each sentence.

1. Let's see if we can break the losing streak in naught seven.
   _____
   _____

2. Given my track record of not finishing what I start, there's a good chance of failure.
   _____
   _____

3. I think I need to add a 3-month milestone of 30 days in the gym by April 1.
   _____
   _____

4. It's a way to trick yourself into not being scared of the commitment.
   _____
   _____

5. The more you think about the change as something permanent, the more you stay put.
   _____
   _____

V. **Discuss with your partner about each of the following statements and write an essay in no less than 200 words about your understanding of one of them.**

1. Be clear about what you really want before setting goals.

2. Confidence, commitment and patience ensure success.

3. Failure is your friend.

VI. **List four websites where we can learn more about New Year resolution and provide a brief introduction to each of them.**

1.
2.
3.
4.

Text B

A Winning Way to Handle New Ideas
Azriel Winnett

《处理新想法的成功之路》改变一种思维和行为的习惯,从另一个角度看待同一个问题,这是我们对于新的观念所应该持有的态度,也是我们面对未来应该持有的态度。观念指导我们的行为,因此处理好这些新的想法就显得尤为重要。

Janet DiClaudio, who was in charge of medical records at two large American hospitals, had an unusual problem. But, the past master in finding creative solutions to work related problems that she was, she found an equally unusual solution.

Of course, proper record keeping is critically important in any hospital. Moreover, if it is run on a commercial basis, medical records will determine how and what the institution gets paid. On the other hand, filling out medical records is not the most exciting pastime in the world. It can be a big pain, in fact. Doctors would prefer to do other things with their time.

But records have to be completed, properly and promptly. So what do you do about it? Janet DiClaudio got down to work and developed a highly "sophisticated system".

Janet called her system "Tootsie Roll Pops". Every time a doctor completed a medical record on time, he or she was awarded a Tootsie Roll Pop—apparently a cheap candy you buy by the bagful—and his or her name went into a drawing for a magnum of champagne.

Now, you don't have to feel sorry for most of these worthy doctors, thanks very much. Some of them can afford to buy a Tootsie Roll Pop factory. Many have case loads of the best champagne in the world back Home in their cellars.

Yet Janet's system worked like a charm. The "Tootsie Roll Pop" campaign led to a doubling in record-completion productivity at the General Hospital in Buffalo, New York, where Janet was working.

She then took a new position at a hospital in Savannah, Georgia, and found that her new institution had a backlog of about 300 medical records. No problem! In Savannah, she rewarded each doctor who completed a record from the backlog with a handful of animal crackers.

magnum /ˈmæɡnəm/ *n.* a large wine bottle that holds approximately 1.5 liters
champagne /ʃæmˈpeɪn/ *n.* an expensive white or pink fizzy wine made in the Champagne area of Eastern France, or, more generally, any similar wine. Champagne is often drunk to celebrate sth
case load caseload the number of cases handled (as by a court or clinic) usu. in a particular period
cellar /ˈselə/ *n.* a room under the ground floor of a building, usually used for storage
backlog /ˈbæklɒɡ/ *n.* a large amount of things that one should have done before and must do now
animal crackers animal-shaped cookies

Two weeks later, the hospital had gone through twenty pounds of animal crackers, but the record backlog had been all but eliminated. As a result, the hospital was able to collect more than four million dollars. For that return, I hardly think the accounts department would have complained about the expenditure on the crackers!

> **saga** /ˈsɑːɡə/ *n.* **a.** a long and complicated series of events, or a description of this; **b.** a long story about events that happen over many years
> **doughty** /ˈdaʊti/ *adj.* resolute and without fear
> **measly** /ˈmiːzli/ *adj.* very small and disappointing in size, quantity, or value
> **goody** /ˈɡʊdi/ *n.* **a.** sth that is nice to eat; **b.** sth attractive, pleasant, or desirable
> **amongst** /əˈmʌŋst/ among
> **landmark** /ˈlændmɑːk/ *n.* **a.** sth prominent that identifies location; **b.** important new development; **c.** sth preserved for historic importance; **d.** boundary marker
> **altogether** /ˌɔːltəˈɡeðə/ *adv.* **a.** completely or in total; **b.** with everything included
> **live up to** fulfill the requirements or expectations of

A basic need moves the most sophisticated. Roger Firestien recounts this delightful medical saga in his *Leading on the Creative Edge* which I quoted in a previous article. What has it do with us? Well, I bring it here not only because it is such a beautiful illustration of creativity in problem solving, but also—and this is what really concerns us—it forcefully demonstrates the power of praise and recognition.

After all, the doughty physicians in our story weren't children; it couldn't have been the handout of a few measly goodies that motivated them. There's a more basic need, however, that apparently doesn't fail to move even the most sophisticated amongst us.

In a landmark work *In Search of Excellence* researchers Tom Peters and Robert Waterman ask readers to imagine that they are sales assistants in a store who are being punished for failing to treat a customer well.

If you are in this situation, you might feel yourself to be in a frustrating dilemma, because you still don't know what to do to receive approval. In fact, you might well react by avoiding customers altogether, since you have come to associate customers with punishment.

Now, supposes a manager would tell you that a "mystery shopper" has complimented you on your outstanding courtesy and helpfulness. What would you do now? Most likely, you'd rush back to the floor to find more customers to treat well, for now you have associated them with praise and recognition. Your self-esteem has been enhanced immeasurably, and you want to keep living up to expectations of you.

I would have thought that you don't need to be a university professor to work this one out, but Peters and Waterman report:

"Our general observation is that most managers know very little about the value of positive reinforcement. Many either appear not to value it at all, or consider it beneath them, undignified, or not very macho. The evidence from the excellent companies strongly suggests that managers who feel this way are doing themselves a great disservice..."

But positive reinforcement should be dispensed not only when someone whom we lead does something we wanted him to do. Encouragement is also the appropriate response when someone suggests a novel idea or solution to a problem. And this brings me back to a subject we have discussed before.

Inhibitions to the winds...

About 30 years ago, a creativity consulting firm on the American East Coast was conducting creativity seminars for large corporations. The leaders urged participants to throw inhibitions to the winds, unleash the power locked up in their minds, and to throw up all the ideas they could manage, however wild they might appear to be. Their peers were then asked to evaluate the proposals and see if they could be used to solve company problems.

Inevitably, seminar participants could only see negative aspects in most of the suggestions, and swiftly tore them to pieces. As the sessions ended, the more discerning amongst them sometimes confided in the organizers: "You know, we had the beginnings of some pretty powerful ideas in this session. But by the time we got done evaluating them, all we had left was the same worn-out, old concepts."

Then it happened that at one seminar, several people from the same company noticed the idea slaughtering. They approached the two leaders conducting the session and suggested they talk to the president of their company.

"This man," they explained, "has a unique way of dealing with ideas. And it seems to pay off. Our company is growing by leaps and bounds, has excellent relationships with customers and suppliers, and is

macho /ˈmætʃəʊ/ *adj.* having or showing characteristics conventionally regarded as male, esp. physical strength and courage, aggressiveness, and lack of emotion
disservice /ˌdɪsˈsɜːvɪs/ *n.* an action that causes harm or difficulty
inhibition /ˌɪnhɪˈbɪʃən/ *n.* a feeling of fear or embarrassment that stops one from behaving naturally
to the winds to the wind aside, away
discerning /dɪˈsɜːnɪŋ/ *adj.* showing the ability to make good judgments, esp. about art, music, beauty, style, etc.
confide /kənˈfaɪd/ *v.* to tell sth secret or personal to someone whom you trust not to tell anyone else
by leaps and bounds in leaps and bounds, extremely rapidly

a great place to work."

Of course, the two consultants were intrigued. They asked for a meeting with the company president. "I obviously must be doing something right," he told them, "but I'm darned if I know what it is... I'd love to find out."

> **darned** /dɑːnd/ *adj.* (*infml*) used instead of a swearword to express annoyance, surprise, or refusal
>
> **spin-off** /ˈspɪnɒf/ a product made during the manufacture of sth else
>
> **prophecy** /ˈprɒfɪsi/ *n.* a prediction uttered under divine inspiration

In short, the consultants shadowed the president for a week. They sat in on meetings and strategic conversations and walked through the plant with the president.

The visitors soon realized that when someone approached the president with a new idea, the latter became very conscious of what was about to occur. Someone in the company was about to present an idea they thought might improve the organization, smooth out the work flow, or make more money. The president became all ears. In contrast to his counterparts in many other companies who perceived new ideas as threats, he saw them as opportunities. He knew that this was the stuff that made his Business better.

When someone proposed an idea, the president would respond by enumerating the PLUSES (strengths or advantages) of the idea. He would then discuss its POTENTIALS (possible spin-offs or future gains which could be realized if the idea were implemented). Finally, he would address CONCERNS posed by the idea.

Even when addressing concerns, however, instead of saying: "This idea will cost too much", he would throw out a challenge by asking: "How might you reduce the cost?" or "How might you raise the money to develop this idea?" Instead of offering a prophecy of doom by saying: "Management will never accept this idea" he would inquire: "How might you get management's support?"

The seed which was planted in the minds of this corporate president's "shadows" that week led to the development and fine-tuning of a tool that was to have far reaching effects in the Business and organizational world. The PPC (Pluses, Potentials, Concerns) Technique was developed by Dr. Firestien and two colleagues, Dianne Foucar-Szocki and Bill Shepard.

If you were to propose an idea to this company president, and he evaluated it together with you in the manner outlined above, how would you react? Wouldn't you be inspired by the friendly challenge thrown out at you to find a way of overcoming even the smallest concerns?

It makes you think, doesn't it?

Cultural Notes

1. **Azriel Winnett**—A writer, editor and the creator of Hodu.com—Your Communication Skills Portal, a free website helping people improve their communication and relationship skills in their business or professional life, in the family unit and on the social scene. Most of the publications in the website are his works. A former South African, Mr. Winnett presently lives in Israel.

2. **Tootsie Roll Pop**—A hard candy lollipop with a Tootsie Roll filling at its center. The Tootsie Pop was invented in 1931 by The Sweets Company of America, which changed its name to Tootsie Roll Industries, Inc. in 1966. In addition to chocolate (the original flavor), Tootsie Pops come in a variety of flavors including raspberry, cherry, orange and grape, etc.

Comprehension Exercises

I. Answer the following questions based on the text.

1. What distinguishes Janet DiClaudio from others?
2. Why does the author tell her story here?
3. What problem do most managers share according to Waterman?
4. Why did the two consultants shadow the president of the company?
5. How did the president respond to the idea proposed by his men?

II. Write T for true and F for false in the brackets before each of the following statements.

1. (　) If a doctor keeps the medical records properly, he can get a good pay.
2. (　) Many doctors working at the Buffolo General Hospital possess great wealth.
3. (　) The accounts department of the hospital in Savannah, Georgia, where Janet worked was not satisfied with the large expenses for the animal crackers.
4. (　) Simple methods may possibly be the most effective.

5. (　　) Janet knew the magic of the positive reinforcement very well.
6. (　　) Peterson and Waterman points out that many managers don't value praise and recognition because it doesn't have much influence on their work.
7. (　　) The seminar participants were expected to raise constructive ideas.
8. (　　) To acquire sound advice, the president invited the two leaders of the session to his company.
9. (　　) Many managers suffer from fear of novel ideas.
10. (　　) The creativity seminars held 30 years ago inspired Dr. Firestien and his colleagues to develop the PPC technique.

III. Select the most appropriate word or phrase and use its proper form to complete each of the following sentences.

amongst	backlog	charm	compliment	confide
dilemma	disservice	dispense	enumerate	eliminate
expenditure	illustration	intrigue	inhibition	landmark
measly	prophecy	reinforcement	sophisticated	discerning

1. Tools are becoming more _____ and everything seems to be getting faster, more efficient, more compact or hands-free.
2. However, on the question of how to deal with the _____ products, financial analysis cannot answer.
3. The Sex Discrimination Act has not _____ discrimination in employment.
4. Agriculture is linked to industry through rural _____ on manufactures.
5. _____ is often more useful than definition for showing what words mean.
6. Muttering among themselves for hours, the men developed a deepening sense of _____ and of brotherhood。
7. The average British bathroom measures a _____ 3.5 square meter.
8. The conference discussed, _____ other things, the problem of environmental protection.
9. Try to formulate your own position as you read these _____ statements on the problem.
10. Mercifully some one arrived upon the scene to extricate him from the _____ and assume the responsibility.
11. He tried to _____ the pianist upon the accuracy of his pedaling.
12. The use of steel _____ with structures of this type greatly increases their strength.

13. When the identical experiment was performed with mature segments of roots, no _____ was observed.
14. She returned to the charge the next evening, and requested her niece to _____ in her.
15. The heroic deeds of the people's soldiers are too numerous to _____ .

IV. Paraphrase the underlined words or expressions in each sentence.

1. But, the past master in finding creative solutions to work related problems that she was, she found an <u>equally unusual solution</u>.

2. There's a more basic need, however, that apparently doesn't <u>fail to move even the most sophisticated</u> amongst us.

3. Your self-esteem has been <u>enhanced immeasurably</u>, and you want to keep living up to expectations of you.

4. Then it happened that at one seminar, several people from the same company noticed the idea <u>slaughtering</u>.

5. Finally, he would <u>address CONCERNS</u> posed by the idea.

V. Discuss with your partner about each of the following statements and write an essay in no less than 200 words about your understanding of one of them.

1. Healthy relationships help us enjoy a happier and more productive life.

2. Lack of recognition can have a profoundly negative impact on productivity.

3. The solutions are within ourselves to reduce the stress in our workplace.

VI. List four websites where we can learn more about planning and provide a brief introduction to each of them.

1. _____
   _____
   _____.

2. _____
   _____
   _____.

3. _____
   _____
   _____.

4. _____
   _____
   _____.

Twenty Minutes' Reading

You are required to read the following sections within 20 minutes.

 SECTION A

The American economic system is organized around a basically private-enterprise, market-oriented economy in which consumers largely determine what shall be produced by spending their money in the marketplace for those goods and services that they want most. Private businessmen, striving to make profits, produce these goods and services in competition with other businessmen; and the profit motive, operating under competitive pressures, largely determines how these goods and services are produced. Thus, in the American economic system it is the demand of individual consumers, coupled with the desire of businessmen to maximize profits and the desire of individuals to maximize their incomes that together determine what shall be produced and how resources are used to produce it.

An important factor in a market-oriented economy is the mechanism by which consumer demands can be expressed and responded to by producers. In the American economy, this mechanism is provided by a price system, a process in which prices rise and fall in response to relative demands of consumers and supplies offered by seller-producers. If the product is in short supply relative to the demand, the price will bid up and some consumers will be eliminated from the market. If, on the other hand, producing more of a commodity results in reducing its cost, this will tend to increase the supply offered by seller-producers, which in turn will lower the price and permit more consumers to buy the product. Thus, price is the regulating mechanism in the American economic system.

The important factor in a private-enterprise economy is that individuals are allowed to own productive resources, and they are permitted to hire labor, gain control over natural resources, and produce goods and services for sale at a profit. In the American economy, the concept of private property embraces not only the ownership of productive resources but also certain rights, including the right to determine the price of a product or to make a free contact with another private individual.

1. In the first paragraph, "the desire of individuals to maximize their incomes" means _____.
   A. Americans are never satisfied with their incomes
   B. Americans tend to overstate their incomes
   C. Americans want to have their incomes increased
   D. Americans want to increase the purchasing power of their incomes
2. The first two sentences in the second paragraph tell us _____.
   A. producers can satisfy the consumers by mechanized production
   B. consumers can express their demands through producers
   C. producers decide the prices of products
   D. supply and demand regulate prices
3. According to the passage, a private-enterprise economy is characterized by _____.
   A. private property and rights concerned
   B. manpower and natural resources control
   C. ownership of productive resources
   D. free contacts and prices
4. The passage is mainly about _____.
   A. how American goods are produced
   B. how American consumers buy their goods
   C. how American economic system works
   D. how American businessmen make their profits
5. The phrase "bid up" in the second paragraph probably means _____.
   A. offered   B. made higher
   C. stated   D. tried to get

SECTION B

According to sociologists, there are several different ways in which a person may become recognized as the leader of a social group. In the family, traditional cultural patterns confer leadership on one or both of the parents. In other cases, such as friendship groups, one or more persons may gradually emerge as leaders, although there is no formal process of selection. In larger groups, leaders are usually chosen formally through election or recruitment.

Although leaders are often thought to be people with unusual personal ability, decades of research have failed to produce consistent evidence that there is any category of "natural leaders". It seems that there is no set of personal qualities that all leaders have in common; rather, virtually any person may be recognized as a leader if the person has qualities that meet the needs of that particular group.

Research suggests that there are typically two different leadership roles that are held by different individuals. Instrumental leadership is leadership that emphasizes the completion of tasks by a social group. Group members look to instrumental leaders to "get things done". Expressive leadership, on the other hand, is leadership that emphasizes the collective well-beings of a social group's members. Expressive leaders are less concerned with the overall goals of the group than with providing emotional support to group members and attempting to minimize tension and conflict among them.

Instrumental leaders are likely to have a rather secondary relationship to other group members. They give others and may discipline group members who inhibit attainment of the group goals. Expressive leaders cultivate a more personal or primary relationship to others in the group. They offer sympathy when someone experiences difficulties and try to resolve issues that threaten to divide the group. As the difference in these two roles suggest, expressive leaders generally receive more personal affection from group members; instrumental leaders, if they are successful in promoting group goals, may enjoy a more distant respect.

6. What does the passage mainly discuss?
   A. The problems faced by leaders.
   B. How leadership differs in small and large groups.
   C. How social groups determine who will lead them.
   D. The role of leaders in social groups.
7. The passage mentions all of the following ways by which people can become leaders EXCEPT _____.
   A. recruitment
   B. formal election process

C. specific leadership training

D. traditional cultural patterns

8. Which of the following statements about leadership can be inferred from the second paragraph?

   A. A person who is an effective leader of a particular group may not be an effective leader in another group.

   B. Few people succeed in sharing a leadership role with another person.

   C. A person can best learn how to be an effective leader by studying research on leadership.

   D. Most people desire to be leaders but can produce little evidence of their qualifications.

9. In mentioning "natural leaders" in the second paragraph, the author is making the point that _____.

   A. few people qualify as "natural leaders"

   B. there is no proof that "natural leaders" exist

   C. "natural leaders" are easily accepted by the members of a group

   D. "natural leaders" share a similar set of characteristics

10. The passage indicates that instrumental leaders generally focus on _____.

    A. ensuring harmonious relationships

    B. sharing responsibility with group members

    C. identifying new leaders

    D. achieving a goal

Unit Two

Text A

Language and Culture Differences in Daily Life
Anonymous

语言和文化的差异在世界全球化的今天日益凸现出来,了解这些已经成了当务之急。

In many aspects of our life, we often divide the world into two parts: the eastern one and the western one. The former usually refers to Asia and the latter includes mainly Europe, North Africa and America. We divide like this not only because of the geographical location differences, but also due to the cultural differences to a large extent. In the following parts, you'll see such differences, from the causes to the customs of the two sides nowadays.

Part I What leads to the cultural difference?

The cultures of the East and the West really distinguish each other a lot. This is because the culture systems are two separate systems on the whole.

The origin of the eastern cultures is mainly from two countries: China and India. Both of the two cultures are gestated by rivers. In China, the mother river is the Yellow River while the Indian one is the Hindu River. These two cultures were developed for several thousand years and formed their own styles. Then in the Tang Dynasty of China, the Chinese culture gradually went overseas to Japan, mixed into the Japanese society and shaped the Japanese culture. Though a bit different from the

geographical /ˌdʒiəˈɡræfikəl/ *adj.* of geography (science of the earth's surface, physical features, divisions, climate, products, population, etc.)
location /ləʊˈkeɪʃən/ *n.* **a.** position or place; **b.** place, not a film studio, where (part of) a film is photographed
origin /ˈɒrɪdʒɪn/ *n.* starting-point
gestate /ˈdʒesteɪt/ *v.* **a.** to carry in the uterus during pregnancy; **b.** to conceive and gradually develop in the mind

Chinese one, it belongs to the same system.

When the two mother rivers gave birth to the eastern culture, another famous culture was brought up on the Mesopotamian Plain—the Mesopotamian Civilization. This civilization later on developed into the cultures of the Ancient Greece and Ancient Rome. And these two are well-known as the base of the European culture. Like the Chinese culture, the European one also crossed waters. When the colonists of England settled down in America, their culture went with them over the Atlantic Ocean. So the American culture doesn't distinguish from the European one a lot.

Mesopotamian Civilization ancient civilization developed in Mesopotamian Plain
distinguish /dɪsˈtɪŋgwɪʃ/ v. **a.** see, hear, recognize, understand well the difference; **b.** make out by looking, listening, etc.; **c.** be a mark of character, difference; **d.** behave so as to bring credit to oneself
pictographic /ˌpɪktəˈgræfɪk/ adj. **a.** consisting of an ancient or prehistoric drawing or painting on a rock wall; **b.** consisting of one of the symbols belonging to a pictorial graphic system
count /kaʊnt/ v. **a.** say or name (e.g. numerals) in order; **b.** find the total of; **c.** include; be included; in the reckoning; consider (sb or sth) to be
interference /ˌɪntəˈfɪərəns/ n. (of persons) breaking in upon (other persons' affairs) without right or invitation
typical /ˈtɪpɪkəl/ adj. **a.** serving as a type; **b.** representative or characteristic

At the same time, the difference of the language systems adds to the cultural differences. In the East, most languages belong to the pictographic language while the Western languages are mostly based on the Latin system, for example, the one I'm using to write this paper.

Other factors like human race difference count as well. But what's more, due to the far distance and the steep areas between the East and West, the two cultures seldom communicate until in recent centuries. So they grew up totally in their own ways with almost no interference from the other.

Part II How differently do people behave in daily life?

The differences are everywhere. They affect people's ways of thinking and their views of the world. Even in everyday life, the cultural differences show up from the moment the eyes are opened to the minute the dreams are invited.

In the following, I'll give some typical example of the differences.

Section 1: Greeting

Greeting is the first step to form a culture, because people begin to communicate with others. The individuals become a community.

How do Chinese greet each other? Informally, if we meet an friend in the street, we are used to say: "Hi, have you had your meal?" or "Where are you going?" When it is the case of two gentlemen, they tend to shake hands.

However, in the western countries, the above questions are just questions, not greeting at all. They may think you're inviting them to dinner if you ask about their meals. Usually, they'll just give each other a smile or greet with a "Hi." They 'll shake hands only in some formal situations. By the way, Westerners can leave a party or meeting halls without a formal conge, nor should they shake hands with every attendee as most of us will do in China.

Section 2: Expressing gratitude

Think of the situations below. Your mother is busy in the kitchen. She suddenly asks you to fetch a bowl for her. You do so. What'll your mother's response be? Probably she'll just continue doing the cooking. After a while, the dinner is ready. Your mother hands you your bowl of rice. What's your response? Probably just begin to eat.

That's what I want to say. In Chinese families, we rarely say "Thank you" to other family members for receiving help or service. Neither will we say so between good friends. It's such an unpopular response that if you say it, the counterpart will think you are treating him as a stranger, otherwise you are lacking of intimacy.

But in the West, "thank you" is one of the most frequently used sentences. Teachers will thank a student for answering a question; husbands will thank his wife for making a coffee.

However, as an interesting phenomenon, it's a custom to say "thank you" in Japan. Whether in family or among friends, Japanese chronically use it all the day. This is

individual /ˌɪndɪˈvɪdjuəl/ **a.** *adj.* (*opp. of general*)special for one person or thing; **b.** *n.* characteristic of a single person, animal, plant or thing; **c.** *n.* any one human being (contrasted with society)
community /kəˈmjuːnɪti/ *n.* **a.** the people living in one place, district or country, considered as a whole; **b.** group of persons having the same religion, race, occupation, etc, or with common interests; **c.** condition of sharing, having things in common, being alike in some way
conge /ˈkɔːnʒeɪ/ *n.* **a.** formal permission to depart; **b.** abrupt and unceremonious dismissal
attendee /əˌtenˈdiː/ *n.* a person who is present on a given occasion or at a given place
gratitude /ˈɡrætɪtjuːd/ *n.* thankfulness; being grateful
counterpart /ˈkaʊntəpɑːt/ *n.* person or thing exactly like, or closely corresponding to another
intimacy /ˈɪntɪməsi/ *n.* **a.** the state of being intimate; close friendship or relationship; (*euphemism*) sexual relations; **b.** (*pl.*) intimate actions, e.g. caresses or kisses
chronically /ˈkrɒnɪkəli/ *adv.* (of a disease or condition) continually, lasting for a long time

probably the aberrance of the culture.

Section 3: Dining

The ways people eat, that is, the table manner, really distinguish a lot. The reason for this is probably because of the different dining tools and menus.

Easterners use chopsticks, or sometimes even grasp rice straightly with hands as Indians do. The thin and long chopsticks cannot be used to cut food, so we usually use our teeth to act as knives. We hold our food, meat or vegetable, with the chopsticks, send them to the mouths, bite off a part of it and remain the other part on the chopsticks. That's the usual way we eat. We are also used to hold up our bowls when having rice or soup. Japanese hold bowls to have miso soup without spoons. But all these habits are considered rude in the Western countries.

The etiquette in the West requests that when eating, bowls and plates cannot leave the tables. Food should be cut by knives to fit into the mouths. Of course your mouth cannot touch the plates or bowls. So the regular process is like this. You cut your steak on the plate with fork and knife, send the meat cube into the mouth with fork and nothing will be returned back but the fork alone.

Section 4: Symbolizing

Symbolization is how people imagine or regard something. It actually reflects the way people think. Here I'll only discuss some symbolization that frequently appears in daily life.

The first is about the colors. We often give each color some meanings, because we feel differently when facing different colors. So people always have preference when choosing colors of clothes, decorations, etc. In the APEC summit held in Shanghai several years ago, on the last day, the presidents from all over the world wore the traditional Chinese Tang suits and took a photo together. The colors of the suits were chosen by themselves freely. However, it's quite interesting to find that most Easterners chose red while most of the westerners preferred blue. To explain

---

aberrance /æˈberəns/ *n.* straying away from what is normal, expected or usual; being not true to type

chopsticks /ˈtʃɔpstɪks/ *n.* (*pl.*) pair of tapering sticks (wood, ivory, etc.) used by the Chinese and Japanese for lifting food (placed on the thinnest ends) to the mouth

miso soup Japanese soup made of a high-protein fermented paste consisting chiefly of soybeans, salt, and usually grain (as barley or rice) and ranging in taste from very salty to very sweet

etiquette /ˈetɪket/ *n.* rules for formal relations or polite social behavior among people, in a class of society or profession

symbolize /ˈsɪmbəlaɪz/ *v.* **a.** be a symbol of; **b.** make use of a symbol or symbols for

preference /ˈprefərəns/ *n.* **a.** act of preferring; **b.** that which is preferred; the favoring of one person, country, etc. esp. by admitting imports at a lower import duty

this, it's easy to realize that what red means is almost opposite in the East and the West. Red means luck, fortune here. We Chinese often use this color to decorate in festivals, such as red lanterns, red Chinese nodes, and red bangers. But red stands for blood, revolutions in the West. So the presidents avoided wearing this unlucky color.

> **lantern** /'læntən/ *n.* case (usu. metal and glass) protecting a light from the wind, etc., outdoors
> **node** /nəʊd/ *n.* **a.** (*bot.*) point on the stem of a plant where a leaf or bud grows out; **b.** (*phy.*) point or line of rest in a vibrating body; **c.** (*fig.*) point at which the parts of something begin or meet
> **banger** /'bæŋə/ *n.* **a.** (*sl.*) sausage; **b.** noisy firework; **c.** old dilapidated car

Cultural Notes

1. **Mesopotamian Plain**—It is a region in west Asia between the River of Tigris and the River of Euphrates extending from the mountains of east Asia Minor to the Persian Gulf.

2. **Ancient Rome**—In the early half of the first century BC, the rise of Rome, from provincial settlement to imperial power, is an epic story that reads like fiction rather than fact. A fable goes like this: Romulus is said to have slain his twin brother Remus and founded the future city-state, both infants having survived abandonment on the banks of the Tiber thanks to the nurturing milk of a she-wolf. Ancient Rome traces all facets of one of the world's greatest civilizations, from the legends surrounding Rome's foundation to the strife that precipitated the Empire's collapse. It describes a remarkable imperial power that left an indelible mark on the lands it occupied. The face of Europe today would be radically different, were it not for the rich cultural, technological, linguistic, and administrative legacy bequeathed it by the Romans.

3. **Ancient Greece**—The ancient Greece civilization lasted from about 800 BC, when the Greeks began to set up city states, to 146 BC when the Romans invaded and conquered Greece.

4. **Latin system**—It is the italic language of ancient Latium and of Rome and until modern times. It is still the dominant language of school, church, and state in Western Europe.

5. **APEC summit**—Ninth Asia-Pacific Economic Cooperation summit was held on October 20 to 21, 2001, in Shanghai. The theme of the conference was "New Century, New Challenge: participation, cooperation, and promote common prosperity".

In April 1992, the Australian Prime Minister first advocated APEC summit for the time, the Asia-Pacific region to hold a summit meeting. On November 19—20, 1993, the first informal summit meeting was held in Seattle in the United States of Black Island. Apart from Malaysia, the other 14 members of the Organization attended the meeting. There are 21 member countries (or districts) now: Australia, Brunei, Canada, Chile, China, Chinese Hong Kong, Indonesia, Japan, Korea, Malaysia, Mexico, New Zealand, Papua New Guinea, Peru, Philippines, Russia, Singapore, Chinese Taipei, Thailand, United States and Vietnam.

Cultural Notes

I. Answer the following questions based on the text.

1. What has caused the division of eastern and western worlds in your opinion?
2. Please tell the role China or Chinese culture plays in eastern cultures.
3. What is the part of language in culture? Please give some examples.
4. Do you insist your mother should say thank you as a western mother does when you have done something for her?
5. Do any two eastern countries (or western countries) have the same tradition or cultural characteristics?

II. Write T for true and F for false in the brackets before each of the following statements.

1. (   ) The division of east and west concerns both the location and cultural aspects in countries.
2. (   ) Chinese culture is longer than that of India as everybody can see.
3. (   ) Japanese develops more rapidly because its culture is splendid by itself.
4. (   ) Western and eastern cultures are different also because European culture originates from a plain, not along rivers like eastern ones.
5. (   ) Language systems exert significant influence on the difference of culture.
6. (   ) The author has given a thorough statement of the different aspects in the two cultural traditions.
7. (   ) Greeting is the first step to communicate with others, thus its role is not to be neglected.
8. (   ) Both in Chinese and English families, people have different ways to express their gratitude.

9. (　　) Rudeness and politeness are not to be divided according to a certain tradition only, to some extent it is only something conventional.
10. (　　) Color is something most natural which has nothing to do with cultures.

III. Select the most appropriate word or phrase and use its proper form to complete each of the following sentences.

aberrance	attendee	count	counterpart	chronically
community	distinguish	etiquette	gestate	gratitude
interference	individual	intimacy	node	origin
preference	steep	summit	typical	conge

1. In analyzing a situation, it's essential to _____ the main aspect from the minor one.
2. Many words in the English language are French in _____.
3. Identical twins are in fact more similar to each other than a clone would be to his or her original, since twins _____ simultaneously in the same womb and are raised in the same environment at the same time, usually by the same parents.
4. You can _____ on him for a truthful report of the accident.
5. You have to shift down when you climb up _____ hills.
6. These demands sometimes also take the form of political _____ in the educational system and distortion of its governing policies.
7. The following example will illustrate a _____ method for solving such problems.
8. There are 96 pieces and they are worth, _____ and collectively, a lot of money.
9. A supportive house for eight to ten older people, each with his or her own room, provides privacy and a sense of _____.
10. He felt _____ and admiration for those who rescued his country from such peril.
11. The U.S. Congress is the _____ of the British Parliament.
12. The affection that had followed marriage, the love that followed _____, the understanding that followed time together filled her life.
13. People born in the autumn live longer than those born in the spring and are less likely to fall _____ ill when they are older, according to an Austrian scientist.
14. It has been proved that nuclear radiation will lead to genetic _____.

15. As in Chinese _____, the hostess tries to keep eating as long as the slowest guest.

IV. Paraphrase the underlined words or expressions in each sentence.

1. The cultures of the East and the West really <u>distinguish</u> each other a lot.

2. Whether in family or among friends, Japanese <u>chronically</u> use it all the day. This is probably the <u>aberrance</u> of the culture.

3. The <u>etiquette</u> in the West requests that when eating, bowls and plates cannot leave the tables.

4. This is because the culture systems are two separate systems <u>on the whole</u>.

5. Even in everyday life, the cultural differences <u>show up</u> from the moment the eyes are opened to the minute <u>the dreams are invited</u>.

V. Discuss with your partner about each of the following statements and write an essay in no less than 200 words about your understanding of one of them.

1. Cultural differences are there definite and sure even though sometimes we don't feel it strongly.

2. No matter how hard one could try, the influence of culture couldn't be so easily rooted out from one's life.

3. Respecting difference in cultures will be our best choice when we are communicating with people from other cultures or touring in other countries.

VI. List four websites where we can learn more about culture differences and provide a brief introduction to each of them.

1. _____
   _____.
2. _____
   _____.
3. _____
   _____.
4. _____
   _____.

Text B

Different Ethical Values in Chinese and American Cultures

Anonymous

《中美文化中的不同伦理观》对于不同民族的伦理观念的对比,初步确立一个较为明晰的印象。

I. Cases across Chinese and American cultures

A young American woman went to Hong Kong to work, and at the time of her arrival she knew nothing about the Chinese culture or language. On her way to school one day, she went to the bank to get some money. Unexpectedly, the bank clerk asked her if she had had her lunch. She was extremely surprised at such a question because in the American culture it would be regarded as an indirect invitation to lunch. Between unmarried young people it can also

ethical /ˈeθɪkəl/ *adj.* of morals or moral questions
unexpectedly /ˌʌnɪkˈspektɪdli/ *adv.* unseen, not expected

indicate the young man's interest in dating the girl. Since this bank clerk was a complete stranger to the girl, she hastily commented that she had eaten already. After this she proceeded to school and was even more surprised when one of the teachers asked her the same question. In the following days she was asked the same question again and again, and she spent many hours trying to work out why so many people kept asking her this. Eventually she came to a conclusion: the people must be concerned about her health. She was somewhat underweight at the time, and so she concluded they must worry that she was not eating properly! Only much later did she discover that the question had no real significance at all—it was merely a greeting.

Misunderstanding like this can easily occur. Some more cases are given below:

1) In Chinese greetings, you will often hear "Have you eaten yet/had your lunch" (asked after meal time), "What have you done", "Where have you been", "Where are you going" (asked on the way), "Are you going to work", "Are you going home", "Are you taking a walk" (asked when meeting a neighbor), "Are you full / hungry" (asked around meal time), "Are you going shopping / doing sport" (asked when a certain thing is being done). In America, people usually greet each other by saying "Hi / Hello", "Good morning / afternoon / evening", "How are you", "How do you do".

2) In Chinese partings, the Chinese way of leave-taking is relatively brief or even seems too abrupt. "Chinese visitors often stand up suddenly and say 'I'm leaving now'. As they move to the door, they use phrases like 'I'm sorry to have wasted your time' or 'I'm sorry to have taken up so much of your time'". When the guest is about to leave, it is polite for the host to insist on the guest's staying a little longer. Moreover, the host generally sees his guest off to the door and usually even further. When the host is not going to accompany the guest for a distance, he may say to the guest, "I'm not going to see you off afar" or "Please walk slowly". And the guest will respond as "Don't see me off" or "Please go back". In American partings, a guest must hint several times that he is leaving as the preparation for leaving. Then, just before he leaves, he must say something like "Thank you for a lovely afternoon"

---

indicate /ˈɪndɪkeɪt/ *v.* point to; point out; make known; be sign of; show the need of; state briefly
hastily /ˈheɪstɪlɪ/ *adv.* said, made or done quickly
proceed /prəˈsiːd/ *v.* **a.** go forward, go on; **b.** come, arise from; **c.** take legal action; **d.** go on from a lower university degree
eventually /ɪˈventjuəlɪ/ *adv.* in the end
significance /sɪɡˈnɪfɪkəns/ *n.* meaning; importance
relatively /ˈrelətɪvlɪ/ *adv.* comparatively; in proportion to
abrupt /əˈbrʌpt/ *adj.* **a.** unexpectedly sudden; **b.** (of speech, writing, behavior) rough; brusque; disconnected

or "Thank you, I enjoyed this beautiful evening". After saying goodbye to each other, the host usually shows the guest to the door and sees him off there.

3) As for compliment responses, when being complimented by "Your shoes are very pretty", a Chinese may reply with "No, they are not as pretty as yours" or "Really? I got them very cheap", while an American may reply with a simple "Thanks" or "Oh, they are ancient. I've had them for years". When being complemented by "You have done a great job", a Chinese may respond with "Oh, that is the result of joint efforts of my leaders and colleagues", while an American with a simple "Thank you for your compliment".

compliment /ˈkɒmplɪmənt/ *n.* **a.** expression of admiration, approval, etc., either in words or by action, e.g. by asking sb for his advice or opinions, or by imitating him; **b.** (*formal*) greetings

joint /dʒɔɪnt/ **a.** *adj.* (*attrib only*) held or done by, belonging to, two or more persons together; **b.** *n.* place, line or surface at which two or more things are joined; **c.** *n.* device or structure by which things, e.g. lengths of pipe, bones are joined together; **d.** *n.* (*sl.*) place visited by people for gambling, drinking or drug-taking; **e.** *n.* (*sl.*) cigarette containing a drug; **f.** *v.* provide with a joint or joints; **g.** *v.* divide at a joint or into joints

considerate /kənˈsɪdərɪt/ *adj.* thoughtful (of the needs, etc., of others)

maintain /meɪnˈteɪn/ *v.* **a.** keep up; remain; continue; **b.** support; **c.** assert as true; **d.** keep in good repair or working order; **e.** defend

interfere /ɪntəˈfɪə/ *v.* **a.** (of person) break in upon (other persons' affairs) without right or invitation; **b.** (of person) meddle; tamper (with); **c.** (of events, circumstances, etc.) come into opposition; hinder or prevent

illustrate /ˈɪləstreɪt/ *v.* **a.** explain by examples, pictures, etc.; **b.** supply a book, article, lecture, etc. with pictures, diagrams, etc.

amicability /ˌæmɪkəˈbɪlɪtɪ/ *n.* peaceability; being done in a friendly way

modesty /ˈmɒdɪstɪ/ *n.* state of being modest

II. Different ethical values

When a Chinese speaker makes such greetings as those in Case 1 on meeting, he is not really concerned about or interested in whether you have eaten, what you have done, where you have been, and whether you are really doing a certain thing, but intends to make you feel that he is considerate and thoughtful towards you and to maintain a good relationship with you. These greetings are not to be answered, you may nod or smile and then pass; moreover, he will always go away before you answer. Such Chinese greetings sound very strange to Americans and often make them feel very uncomfortable. They feel that their own privacy is interfered with. To them, it has nothing to do with others whether they have eaten, what they have done, where they have been, and whether they are really doing a certain thing.

It is well illustrated in Chinese parting expressions that Chinese always keep in mind friendship, familiarity and amicability, and tend to show consideration and concern for others. But Americans never do so. Even they may think "Why did you bother yourself wasting my time since you think it was a waste of my time".

With regard to compliment responses, Chinese always show modesty and value solidarity, and emphasize co-operation among group members. They believe that individual success is due to the collective effort of the staff in a unit, an organization or a community, and they belittle their own efforts by owing successes to others just to keep the harmonious world going. But Americans always show pride and value independence, and emphasize personal happiness and achievements. They believe that individual success is due to personal effort. That is why most American heroes (in art or history) are independent and tend to accomplish their goals with little or no assistance from others, which can be illustrated from Abraham Lincoln's endeavor (to be a president) to make himself an idol of most Americans.

Chinese people value family so much that they always try to be amicable and show much concern for others just as they do within a family. Not surprisingly, in their conversations they always talk of personal stuffs like age, income, marriage and so on. Americans worship privacy so much that they would like to be able to do certain things unobserved by others. They believe that each person has his own separate identity and personality, which should be recognized and reinforced. Therefore, conversations with others' personalstuffs and activities involved are not advocated.

As far as social ethical value is concerned, Chinese people do value and emphasize the interests of the people, the community and the whole nation. They even sacrifice the interests of individuals for those of the collective, as is sufficiently and clearly incarnated in those like "Serve the people" (from Mao Zedong), "Common wealth" (from Deng Xiaoping) and "Power for the people" (from Jiang Zemin). Unlike Chinese, Americans emphasize and focus on the interests of the individual rather than those of the collective. They even believe that there must be something wrong with someone who fails to demonstrate individualism, which can be seen from

solidarity /ˌsɒlɪˈdærɪti/ *n.* unity resulting from common interests or feelings
emphasize /ˈemfəsaɪz/ *v.* put emphasis on; give emphasis to
belittle /bɪˈlɪtl/ *v.* cause to seem unimportant or of small value
harmonious /hɑːˈməʊniəs/ *adj.* **a.** pleasingly or satisfactorily arranged; **b.** in agreement; free from ill feeling; **c.** sweet-sounding; tuneful
amicable /ˈæmɪkəbəl/ *adj.* peaceable; done in a friendly way
reinforce /ˌriːɪnˈfɔːs/ *v.* make stronger by adding or supplying more men or material; increase the size, thickness, of sth so that it supports more weight, etc.
involve /ɪnˈvɒlv/ *v.* **a.** (sb or sth) to be caught or mixed up (in trouble, etc.); get (sb or sth) into a complicated or difficult condition; **b.** have as a necessary consequence
advocate /ˈædvəkeɪt/ **a.** *n.* person who speaks in favor of sb or sth (esp. a cause); **b.** *n.* (*legal*) person who does this professionally in a court of law in Scotland (=barrister in England and Wales) **c.** *v.* to suppovt or recommend publicly
sacrifice /ˈsækrɪfaɪs/ **a.** *n.* the offering of sth precious to a god; instance of this; the thing offered; **b.** *n.* the giving up of sth of great value to oneself for a special purpose, or to benefit sb else; sth given up in this way; **c.** *v.* make a sacrifice; **d.** *v.* give up as a sacrifice
sufficiently /səˈfɪʃəntli/ *adv.* enough
incarnate /ˈɪnkɑːnɪt/ **a.** *adj.* having a body; (esp.) in human form; **b.** *adj.* (of an ideal, ideal, etc.) appearing in human form; **c.** *v.* make incarnate; **d.** *v.* put (an idea, etc.) into a real or material form; **e.** *v.* (of a person) be a living form of (a quality)

American Grand Elections and some sayings like "God helps those who help themselves" and "He travels the fastest who travels alone."

Through the above case studies, we can see that what obviously attracts our attention to differences in values between Chinese culture and American culture is the emphasis on whether to perform individualism or collectivism. Chinese stress the importance of the whole nation and community, tend to emphasize the interests and welfare of the collective over those of the individual, value considerations, concerns and thoughtfulness for others, attach much importance to co-operation and collective efforts, and think much of friendship and amicability and hospitality, which we call collectivism. Americans, on the contrary, emphasize the importance of human individuals in contrast to the social wholes, such as families, classes or societies, to which they belong, stress the priority of individual needs, interests and welfare over those of a group, value individual rights and freedom, prefer the virtue of self-reliance and personal independence and loosely knit social relationships and think more of individual roles than of collective efforts, which we call individualism.

> **individualism** /ɪndɪˈvɪdjuəlɪzəm/ *n.* **a.** social theory that favors the free action and complete liberty or belief of individuals (contrasted with the theory favoring the supremacy of the state); **b.** feeling or behavior of a person who puts his own private interests first; egoism
>
> **collectivism** /kəˈlektɪvɪzəm/ *n.* **a.** a political or economic theory advocating collective control especially over production and distribution; also a system marked by such control; **b.** emphasis on collective rather than individual action or identity
>
> **welfare** /ˈwelfeə/ *n.* **a.** condition of having good health, comfortable living and working conditions, etc; **b.** (US) social security
>
> **thoughtfulness** /ˈθɔːtfulnɪs/ *n.* given to or chosen or made with heedful anticipation of the needs and wants of others
>
> **hospitality** /hɒspɪˈtælɪti/ *n.* friendly and generous reception and entertainment of guests, esp. in one's own home
>
> **priority** /praɪˈɒrɪti/ *n.* **a.** right to have or do sth before others; **b.** claim to consideration; high place among competing claims
>
> **self-reliance** /ˈselfriˈlaɪns/ *n.* having or showing confidence in one's own powers, judgment, etc.

Cultural Notes

1. **Privacy**—Privacy has no definite boundaries and it has different meanings for different people. It is the ability of an individual or group to keep their lives and personal affairs out of public view, or to control the flow of information about themselves. Privacy can be seen as an aspect of security—one in which trade-offs between the interests of one group and another can become particularly clear.

   The right against unsanctioned invasion of privacy by the government, corporations or individuals is part of many countries' privacy laws, and in some cases, constitutions. Almost all countries have laws which in some way limit privacy; an example of this would be law concerning taxation, which normally require the sharing of information about personal income or earnings. In some countries individual privacy may conflict with freedom of speech laws and some laws may require public disclosure of information which would be considered private in other countries and cultures.

Countries such as France protect privacy explicitly in their constitution (France's *Declaration of the Rights of Man and of the Citizen*), while the Supreme Court of the United States has found that the US constitution contains "penumbras" that implicitly grant a right to privacy against government intrusion, for example in *Griswold v. Connecticut* (1965). Other countries without constitutional privacy protections have laws protecting privacy, such as the United Kingdom's *Data Protection Act 1998* or Australia's *Privacy Act 1988*. The European Union requires all member states to legislate to ensure that citizens have a right to privacy, through directives such as *Directive 95/46*.

2. **American Grand Elections**—It is the US presidential election campaign. American presidents are elected every four years in the Election Day, the first Tuesday after the first Monday in November in even years, which is legally chosen for national election.

3. **Individualism**—It is a term used to describe a moral, political, or social outlook that stresses human independence and the importance of individual self-reliance and liberty. Individualists promote the exercise of individual goals and desires. They oppose most external interference with an individual's choices—whether by society, the state, or any other group or institution. The concept of "individualism" was first used by the French Saint-Simonian socialists to describe what they believed was the cause of the disintegration of French society after the 1789 Revolution. The term was however already used (pejoratively) by reactionary thinkers of the French Theocratic School, such as Joseph de Maistre, in their opposition to political liberalism. In the English language, the word was first introduced in the English translation of the second volume of *Alexis de Tocquevilles Democracy in America*, which was published in 1835. A more positive use of the term in Britain came to be used with the writings of James Elishama Smith.

4. **Collectivism**—It is a term used to describe any moral, political, or social outlook, which stresses human interdependence and the importance of a collective, rather than the importance of separate individuals. Collectivists focus on community and society, and seek to give priority to group goals over individual goals. The philosophical underpinnings of collectivism are for some related to holism or organicism, the view that the whole is greater than the sum of its parts. Specifically, a society as a whole can be seen as

having more meaning or value than the separate individuals that make up that society. Collectivism is widely seen as the antipole of individualism.

Comprehension Exercises

I. Answer the following questions based on the text.

1. Do you think Hong Kong should be more English or American rather than Chinese since English has long been their daily usage?
2. Do you think Chinese leave-taking is abrupt when your visitors stand up and go?
3. Which way of seeing the guests off is better in your opinion, the Chinese way or the American one?
4. What is the bigger difference—the difference in understanding or expressing?
5. Do you think American independence is so great as to dwarf the Chinese cooperation?

II. Write T for true and F for false in the brackets before each of the following statements.

1. (　　) People care about the young American woman's health so they asked about her lunch.
2. (　　) All Chinese people will insist their guests stay longer when they are to take leave.
3. (　　) The Chinese are always sincere when they say that is the joint efforts of their leaders and colleagues.
4. (　　) Chinese people tend to show more consideration and concerning about others in daily addressing.
5. (　　) Abraham Lincoln's endeavor was an idol of most Americans because of his heroic independence.
6. (　　) Chinese people are inclined to extend their concern for family members to others because they value family as a tradition.
7. (　　) The Chinese have many ways of greetings which have no significant meaning.
8. (　　) Not all Americans worship privacy very much and they don't want others to know much of their life and personal affairs.
9. (　　) Americans would think the demonstrating of individualism is very important.
10. (　　) In the text, the word individualism has a negative meaning, which is quite same with the meaning in Chinese.

III. Select the most appropriate word or phrase and use its proper form to complete each of the following sentences.

advocate	amicability	abrupt	belittle	considerate
endeavor	hastily	hospitality	indicate	illustrate
incarnate	idol	merely	maintain	modesty
occur	proceed	solidarity	sacrifice	welfare

1. The abundant remnants of wild game _____ that the people who lived here had not yet domesticated animals or farmed.
2. Lee alerted his compatriots to _____ prepare for reunification of the Korean peninsula.
3. Safety rests on a complex system of signals that tell drivers when they can _____.
4. Giving these events a lot of media coverage _____ perpetuates the problem.
5. This _____ event shows how a relatively small occurrence—such as a slight slide in rainfall—may have a tremendous impact.
6. Revolution can only _____ at a time when both internal and external conditions of a country are ripe enough.
7. The country is meant to rise with a _____ government concerning about the benefit of its people rather than its own pockets.
8. The company has struggled to _____ its domination in the marketplace.
9. When people have an _____ relationship, they are pleasant to each other and solve their problems without quarrelling.
10. Someone who shows _____ does not talk much about their abilities or achievements.
11. If a group of people show _____, they show support for each other or for another group, especially in political or international affairs.
12. It is apparent that the author is diligent in finding every reason to _____ and criticize this remarkable deal.
13. It is an _____ that raises the opportunity to treat disease early but also raises the fear of genetic discrimination.
14. Mr Williams is a conservative who _____ fewer government controls on business.
15. His strong left-wing views make him the devil _____ to more extreme Conservatives.

IV. Paraphrase the underlined words or expressions in each sentence.

1. She was <u>somewhat underweight</u> at the time, and so she concluded they must worry that she was not eating properly!

2. With regard to compliment responses, Chinese always <u>show modesty and value solidarity,</u> and emphasize co-operation among group members.

3. Chinese people value family so much that they always try to <u>be amicable</u> and show much concern for others just as they do within a family.

4. Only much later did she discover that the question <u>had no real significance</u> at all—it was <u>merely a greeting</u>.

5. Americans, on the contrary, emphasize the importance of human individuals in contrast to <u>the social wholes</u>, such as families, classes or societies.

V. Discuss with your partner about each of the following statements and write an essay in no less than 200 words about your understanding of one of them.

1. Individualism is an impressive characteristic of the Americans.

2. Sometimes too much hospitality will bring trouble to people.

3. Self-reliance doesn't conflict with collectivism, and emphasis on both aspects is necessary in our culture.

VI. List four websites where we can learn more about Ethical Values and provide a brief introduction to each of them.

1. _____

2. _____

3. _____

4. _____

Twenty Minutes' Reading

You are required to read the following sections within 20 minutes.

SECTION A

Racket, din clamor, noise, whatever you want to call it, unwanted sound is America's most widespread nuisance. But noise is more than just a nuisance. It constitutes a real and present danger to people's health. Day and night, at home, at work, and at play, noise can produce serious physical and psychological stress. No one is immune to this stress. Though we seem to adjust to noise by ignoring it, the ear, in fact, never closes and the body still responds—sometimes with extreme tension, as to a strange sound in the night.

The annoyance we feel when faced with noise is the most common outward symptom of the stress building up inside us. Indeed, because irritability is so apparent, legislators have made public annoyance the basis of many noise abatement programs. The more subtle and more serious health hazards associated with stress caused by noise traditionally have been given much less attention. Nevertheless, when we are annoyed or made irritable by noise, we should consider these symptoms fair warning that other thing may be happening to us, some of which may be damaging to our health.

Of many health hazards to noise, hearing loss is the most clearly observable and measurable by health professionals. The other hazards are harder to pin down.

For many of us, there may be a risk that exposure to the stress of noise increases susceptibility to disease and infection. The more susceptible among us may experience noise as a complicating factor in heart problems and other diseases. Noise that causes annoyance and irritability in health persons may have serious consequences for these already ill in mind or body.

Noise affects us throughout our lives. For example, there are indications of effects on the unborn child when mothers are exposed to industrial and environmental noise. During infancy and childhood, youngsters exposed to high noise levels may have trouble falling asleep and obtaining necessary amounts of rest.

Why, then, is there not greater alarm about these dangers? Perhaps it is because the link between noise and many disabilities or diseases has not yet been conclusively demonstrated. Perhaps it is because we tend to dismiss annoyance as a price to pay for living in the modern world. It may also be because we still think of hearing loss as only an occupational hazard.

1. The author's attitude toward noise would best be described as _____.
    A. unrealistic
    B. traditional
    C. concerned
    D. hysterical
2. In Paragraph 1, the phrase "immune to" are used to mean _____.
    A. unaffected by
    B. hurt by
    C. unlikely to be seen by
    D. unknown by
3. Which of the following best states the main idea of the passage?
    A. Noise is a major problem; most people recognize its importance.
    B. Although noise can be annoying, it is not a major problem.
    C. Noise is a major problem and has not yet been recognized as such.
    D. Noise is a major problem about which nothing can be done.
4. The author condemns noise essentially because it _____.
    A. is against the law
    B. can make some people irritable
    C. is a nuisance
    D. in a danger to people's health

5. The author would probably consider research about the effects noise has on people to be _____.
   A. unimportant
   B. impossible
   C. a waste of money
   D. essential

SECTION B

Yet, according to one authority on the subject, we can each probably recognize more than 1,000 faces, the majority of which differ in fine details. This, when one comes to think of it, is a tremendous feat, though, curiously enough, relatively little attention has been devoted to the fundamental problems of how and why we acquire this gift for recognizing and remembering faces. Is it an inborn property of our brains, or an acquired one? As so often happens, the experts tend to differ.

The gift of being able to describe a face accurately is a rare one, as every experienced police officer knows to his cost. As the Lancet put it recently, " when we try to describe faces precisely words fail us, and we resort to identikit（拼脸型图）procedures."

Thus, some argue that it is inborn, and that there are "special characteristics about the brain's ability to distinguish faces". In support of this they note how much better we are at recognizing a face after a single encounter than we are, for example, in recognizing an individual horse. On the other hand, there are those, and they are probably in the majority, who claim that the gift is an acquired one.

But of all these, sight is predominant. Formed at the very beginning of life, the ability to recognize faces quickly becomes an established habit, and one that is, essential for daily living, if not necessarily for survival. How essential and valuable it is we probably do not appreciate until we encounter people who have been deprived of the faculty.

The arguments in favor of this latter view, it must be confessed, are impressive. It is a habit that is acquired soon after birth. Watch, for instance, how a quite young baby recognizes his mother by sight. Granted that his other senses help—the sound of her voice, his sense of smell, the distinctive way she handles him.

This unfortunate inability to recognize familiar faces is known to all, but such people can often recognize individuals by their voices, their walking manners or their spectacles. With typical human ingenuity many of these unfortunate people overcome their handicap by recognizing other characteristic features.

6. It is stated in the passage that _____.
   A. it is unusual for a person to be able to identify a face satisfactorily
   B. the ability to recognize faces unhesitatingly is an unusual gift
   C. quit a few people can visualize faces they have seen
   D. few people can give exact details of the appearance of a face
7. What is the first suggested explanation of the origin of the ability?
   A. It is one of the characteristics peculiar to human beings.
   B. It is acquired soon after birth.
   C. It is something we can do from the very moment we are born.
   D. It is learned from our environment and experiences.
8. What the author feels strange about is that _____.
   A. people have the tremendous ability to recognize more than 1,000 faces
   B. people don't think much of the problem of how and why we acquire the ability to recognize and remember faces
   C. people don't realize how essential and valuable it is for them to have the ability to recognize faces
   D. people have been arguing much over the way people recognize and remember faces
9. According to the passage, how important is the ability to recognize faces?
   A. It is useful in daily life but is not necessarily essential.
   B. It is absence would make normal everyday life impossible.
   C. Under certain circumstances we could not exist without it.
   D. Normal social life would be difficult without it.
10. This passage seems to emphasize that _____.
    A. the ability to recognize individuals is dependent on other senses as well as sight
    B. sight is indispensable to recognizing individuals
    C. the ability to recognize faces is a special inborn ability of the brain
    D. the importance of the ability of recognizing faces is fully appreciated by people.

Unit Three

Text A

Universality of the Folktale
Stith Thompson

The teller of stories has everywhere and always found eager listeners. Whether his tale is the mere report of a recent happening, a legend of long ago, or an elaborately contrived fiction, men and women have hung upon his words and satisfied their yearnings for information or amusement, for incitement to heroic deeds, for religious edification, or for release from the overpowering monotony of their lives. In villages of central Africa, in outrigger boats on the pacific, in the Australian bush, and within the shadow of Hawaiian volcanoes, tales of the present and of the mysterious past, of animals and gods and heroes, and of men and women like themselves, hold listeners in their spell or enrich the conversation of daily life. So it is also in Eskimo igloos under the light of seal-oil lamps, in the tropical jungles of Brazil, and by the totem poles of the British Columbian coast. In Japan too, and China and India, the priest and the scholar, the peasant and the artisan all join in their love of a good story and their honor for the man who tells it well.

When we confine our view to our own occidental world, we see that for at least three or four thousand years, and doubtless for ages before, the art of the story-teller has been cultivated in every rank of society. Odysseus entertains the court of Alcinous with the marvels of his adventures. Centuries later we find the long-haired page reading nightly from interminable chivalric romances to entertain his lady while her lord is absent on his crusade. Medieval priests illustrate sermons by anecdotes old and new, and only sometimes edifying. The old peasant, now as always, whiles away the winter evening with tales of wonder and adventure and the marvelous workings of fate. Nurses tell children of Goldilocks or the House that Jack Built. Poets write epics and novelists novels. Even now the

contrive /kənˈtraɪv/ *v.* **a.** to form or think of (a plan, method, etc.); **b.** to form or make (something) in a skillful or clever way; **c.** to make (something) happen in a clever way or with difficulty
artisan /ˈɑːtɪzən, -sən/ *n.* a worker who practices a trade or handicraft
occidental /ˌɒksɪˈdentl/ *adj.* denoting or characteristic of countries of Europe and the Western Hemisphere
interminable /ɪnˈtɜːmɪnəbl/ *adj.* **a.** having or seeming to have no end; **b.** continuing for a very long time
chivalric /ˈʃɪvəlrɪk/ *adj.* of or relating to the knights who fought in the Middle Ages
sermon /ˈsɜːmən/ *n.* **a.** a speech about a moral or religious subject that is usually given by a religious leader; **b.** a serious talk about how someone should behave
edify /ˈedɪfaɪ/ *v.* to teach (someone) in a way that improves the mind or character

cinemas and theaters bring their stories directly to the ear and eye through the voices and gestures of actors. And in the smoking-rooms of sleeping cars and steamships and at the banquet table the oral anecdote flourishes in a new age.

> anecdote /ˈænɪkdəʊt/ n. a usually short narrative of an interesting, amusing, or biographical incident
> bard /bɑːd/ n. a tribal poet-singer skilled in composing and reciting verses on heroes and their deed
> legitimate /lɪˈdʒɪtɪmət/ adj. a. allowed according to rules or laws; b. real, accepted, or official; c. fair or reasonable
> dispel /dɪˈspel/ v. to make (something, such as a belief, feeling, or idea) go away or end
> foist /fɔɪst/ v. to force someone to accept (something that is not good or not wanted)

In the present work we are confining our interest to a relatively narrow scope, the traditional prose tale—the story which has been handed down from generation to generation either in writing or by word of mouth. Such tales are, of course, only of the many kinds of story material. For, in addition to them, narrative comes to us in verse as ballads and epics, and in prose as histories, novels, dramas, and short stories. We shall have little to do with the songs of bards, with the ballads of the people, or with poetic narrative in general, though stories themselves refuse to be confined exclusively to either prose or verse forms. But even with verse and all other forms of prose narrative put aside, we shall find that in treating the traditional prose tale—the folktale—our quest will be ambitious enough and will take us to all parts of the earth and to the very beginnings of history.

Although the term "folktale" is often used in English to refer to the "household tale" or "fairy tale" (the German Marchen), such as "Cinderella" or "Snow White", it is also legitimately employed in a much broader sense to include all forms of prose narrative, written or oral, which have come to be handed down through the years. In this usage the important fact is the traditional nature of the material. In contrast to the modern story writer's striving after originality of plot and treatment, the teller of a folktale is proud of his ability to hand on that which he has received. He usually desires to impress his readers or hearers with the fact that he is bringing them something that has the stamp of good authority, that the tale was heard from some great story-teller or from some aged person who remembered it from old days.

So it was until at least the end of the Middle Ages with writers like Chaucer, who carefully quoted authorities for their plots—and sometimes even invented originals so as to dispel the suspicion that some new and unwarranted story was being foisted on the public. Though the individual genius of such writers appears clearly enough, they always depended on authority, not only for their basic theological opinions but also for the plots of their stories. A study of the sources of Chaucer or Boccaccio takes one directly into the stream of traditional narrative.

The great written collections of stories characteristic of India, the Near East, the classical world, and Medieval Europe are almost entirely traditional. They copy and recopy. A tale which gains favor in one collection is taken over into others, sometimes intact and sometimes with changes of plot or characterization. The history of such a story, passing it may be from India to Persia and Arabia and Italy and France and finally to England, copied and changed from manuscript to manuscript, is often exceedingly complex. For it goes through the hands of both skilled and bungling narrators and improves or deteriorates at nearly every retelling. However well or poorly such a story may be written down, it always attempts to preserve a tradition, an old tale with the authority of antiquity to give it interest and importance.

If use of the term "folktale" to include such literary narratives seems somewhat broad, it can be justified on practical grounds if on no other, for it is impossible to make a complete separation of the written and the oral traditions. Often, indeed, their interrelation is so close and so inextricable as to present one of the most baffling problems the folklore scholar encounters. They differ somewhat in their behavior, it is true, but they are alike in their disregard of originality of plot and of pride of authorship.

Nor is complete separation of these two kinds of narrative tradition by any means necessary for their understanding. The study of the oral tale will be valid so long as we realize that stories have frequently been taken down from the lips of unlettered taletellers and have entered the great literary collections. In contrary fashion, fables of Aesop, anecdotes from Homer, and saints' legends, not to speak of fairy tales read from Perrault or Grimm, have entered the oral stream and all their association with the written or printed page has been forgotten. Frequently a story is taken from the people, recorded in a literary document, carried across continents or preserved through centuries, and then retold to a humble entertainer who adds it to his repertory.

It is clear then that the oral story need not always have been oral. But when it once habituates itself to being passed on by word of mouth it undergoes the same treatment as all other tales at the command of the raconteur. It becomes something to tell to an audience, or

intact /ɪnˈtækt/ *adj.* **a.** not broken or damaged; **b.** having every part
bungle /ˈbʌŋgl/ *v.* **a.** to make mistakes in doing (something); **b.** to not do (something) well or successfully
antiquity /ænˈtɪkwətɪ/ *n.* **a.** ancient times; **b.** very great age
inextricable /ˌɪnɪkˈstrɪkəbl/ *adj.* **a.** impossible to separate; **b.** closely joined or related
baffle /ˈbæfl/ *v.* to confuse (someone) completely
repertory /ˈrepətrɪ/ *n.* an organized group of actors that performs many kinds of plays with each play being performed for only a short time
raconteur /ˌrækɔnˈtɜː/ *n.* someone who is good at telling stories

at least to a listener, not something to read. Its effects are no longer produced indirectly by association with words written or printed on a page, but directly through facial expression and gesture and repetition and recurrent patterns that generations have tested and found effective.

> **gratify** /ˈgrætɪfaɪ/ v. **a.** to make (someone) happy or satisfied; **b.** to do or give whatever is wanted or demanded by (someone or something)
> **cosmology** /kɒzˈmɒlədʒi/ n. the scientific study of the origin and structure of the universe
> **tangible** /ˈtændʒəbl/ adj. **a.** easily seen or recognized; **b.** able to be touched or felt
> **ubiquity** /juːˈbɪkwəti/ n. presence everywhere or in many places especially simultaneously

This oral art of tale telling is far older than history, and it is not bounded by one continent or one civilization. Stories may differ in subject from place to place, the conditions and purposes of taletelling may change as we move from land to land or from century to century, and yet everywhere it ministers to the same basic social and individual needs. The call for entertainment to fill in the hours of leisure has found most peoples very limited in their resources, and except where modern urban civilization has penetrated deeply they have found the telling of stories one of the most satisfying of pastimes. Curiosity about the past has always brought eager listeners to tales of the long ago which supply the simple man with all he knows of the history of his folk. Legends grow with the telling, and often a great heroic past evolves to gratify vanity and tribal pride. Religion also has played a mighty role everywhere in the encouragement of the narrative art, for the religious mind has tried to understand beginnings and for ages has told stories of ancient days and sacred beings. Often whole cosmologies have unfolded themselves in these legends, and hierarchies of gods and heroes.

Worldwide also are many of the structural forms which oral narrative has assumed. The hero tale, the explanatory legend, the animal anecdote—certainly these at least are present everywhere. Other fictional patterns are limited to particular areas of culture and act by their presence or absence as an effective index of the limits of the area concerned. The study of such limitations has not proceeded far, but it constitutes an interesting problem for the student of these oral narrative forms.

Even more tangible evidence of the ubiquity and antiquity of the folktale is the great similarity in the content of stories of the most varied peoples. The same tale types and narrative motifs are found scattered over the world in most puzzling fashion. A recognition of these resemblances and an attempt to account for them brings the scholar closer to an understanding of the nature of human culture. He must continually ask himself, "why do some peoples borrow tales and some lend? How does the tale serve the needs of the social group?" when he adds to his task an appreciation of the aesthetic and practical urge toward storytelling, and some knowledge of the forms and devices, stylistic and histrionic, that belong to this ancient and widely practiced art, he finds that he must bring to his work more talents than one man can easily possess. Literary critics, anthropologists, historians, psychologists, and aestheticians are all needed if we are to hope to know why folktales are made, how they are invented, what art is used in their telling, how they grow and change and occasionally die.

histrionic /ˌhɪstrɪˈɒnɪk/ too emotional or dramatic

Cultural Notes

1. **Stith Thompson** (1885—1976) —He led a distinguished life as an American educator, folklorist, editor, and author. Between 1921 and 1955, he was a professor of folklore and English, and later dean of the graduate school and distinguished service professor at Indiana university, Bloomington. Five institutions have awarded Thompson honorary doctorates for his work in folklore studies. He published numerous books on the subject, including European tales among north American Indians (1919), the types of the folktales (1928), and tales of the north American Indian (1929). He is best known for his six-volume motif index of folk literature (1932—1937; 1955—1958, 2 nd ed.)

2. **Odysseus**—He was a legendary Greek king of Ithaca and a hero of Homer's epic poem the *Odyssey*. Odysseus also plays a key role in Homer's *Iliad* and other works in that same Epic Cycle.

3. **Alcinous**—He was, in Greek mythology, a son of Nausithous, or of Phaeax (the son of Poseidon and Corcyra), and father of Nausicaa, Halius, Clytoneus and Laodamas with Arete. His name literally means "mighty mind". He married his brother Rhexenor's daughter after Rhexenor was killed.

4. **Geoffrey Chaucer**—He was born circa 1340 in London, England. In 1357 he became a public servant to Countess Elizabeth of Ulster. He continued to work as a public servant to the British court throughout his lifetime. *The Canterbury Tales* became his best known and most acclaimed work. He died October 25, 1400 of in London, England and was the first to be buried in Westminster Abbey's Poet's Corner.

5. **Boccaccio** (1313—1375)—Italian poet and scholar, best remembered as the author of the earthy tales in the *Decameron*. With Petrarch he laid the foundations for the humanism of the Renaissance and raised vernacular literature to the level and status of the classics of antiquity.

Comprehension Exercises

I. Answer the following questions based on the text.
1. What's the difference between modern story writers and folktale tellers?
2. What do folktales attempt to do by copying and recopying old stories?
3. Does a folktale have to be oral?
4. What's the importance of folktale?
5. What's the relationship between religion and folktale?

II. Write T for true and F for false in the brackets before each of the following statements.
1. (   ) People have always honored storytellers.
2. (   ) Fairy tales are for children only.
3. (   ) Most of medieval European stories are traditional.
4. (   ) The effects of folktale are produced through words written instead of facial expression or gesture when being told.
5. (   ) Different cultures have totally different folktales.

III. Select the most appropriate word or phrase and use its proper form to complete each of the following sentences.

antiquity	baffling	chivalric	cosmology	dispel
enrich	evolve	gratify	habituate	histrionic
inextricable	interminable	intact	legitimate	monotony
occidental	penetrate	repertory	tangible	yearning

1. He lay all that night sleepless, and _____ to go home.
2. The cheerless _____ was sometimes enlivened with a little innocent merriment.
3. Both are offering proposals to _____ retirement accounts, improve the educational system, and reduce taxes for working people.
4. In some respects the African mind works rather differently from the _____ one.
5. Perpetual irritation of his mucous membranes by _____ inhalations of cigarette smoke had not yet begun.
6. Slight and graceful still, he affected the _____ and courtly in gesture.
7. Their works bear the same relation to the _____ drama which a transparency bears to a painting.

8. Meanwhile, no one can legally do anything to _____ the eagles and prevent them from eating rare birds.
9. Fish are served whole, head and tail _____, symbolizing a good beginning and end in the coming year.
10. Searching for or removal of any object of _____ including arrowheads, pottery or other artifacts is prohibited.
11. The challenge for advertisers is to make sure that their advertising messages are _____ from the content.
12. Wolves and dogs evaluate and _____ to humans to varying extents, to their own and other species as well as others.
13. They trample the developing plants and allow frost to _____ the rhizomes.
14. Superbugs _____ when common bacterial infections develop resistance to the drugs used to treat them.
15. Motivation deficiency occurs when an individual is completely frustrated in attempting to _____ a specific need.

IV. Paraphrase the underlined words or expressions in each sentence.

1. Whether his tale is the mere report of a recent happening, a legend of long ago, or an <u>elaborately contrived fiction</u>, men and women have <u>hung upon his words</u> and satisfied their yearnings for information or amusement, for incitement to heroic deeds, for <u>religious edification</u>, or for release from <u>the overpowering monotony of their lives</u>.

   _____

   _____

2. In contrast to the modern story writer's <u>striving after originality of plot and treatment</u>, the teller of a folktale is proud of his ability to hand on that which he has received.

   _____

   _____

3. For it goes through the hands of both skilled and <u>bungling narrators</u> and improves or deteriorates <u>at nearly every retelling</u>.

   _____

   _____

4. Legends grow with the telling, and often a great heroic past evolves to <u>gratify vanity and tribal pride</u>.

   _____

   _____

5. Even more tangible evidence of the <u>ubiquity and antiquity of the folktale</u> is the great similarity in the content of stories of the most varied peoples.

V. Discuss with your partner about each of the following statements and write an essay in no less than 200 words about your understanding of one of them.
1. They differ somewhat in their behavior, it is true, but they are alike in their disregard of originality of plot and of pride of authorship.

2. However well or poorly such a story may be written down, it always attempts to preserve a tradition, an old tale with the authority of antiquity to give it interest and importance.

3. It is clear then that the oral story need not always have been oral.

VI. List four websites where we can learn more about folktale and provide a brief introduction to each of them.
1.
2.
3.
4.

Text B

I Am Cinderella's Stepmother and I know My Rights
Judith Rossner

I've been often asked to explain why I never sued the brothers Grimm or took public exception to the ugly little tale people think is about me and my daughters, yet have chosen to sue Mr. Disney over his loathsome movie. It's fair to guess that if I hadn't won the lawsuit, no one would care a bit about us or about the damages we've sustained. Having succeeded in getting the movie out of circulation, and in discouraging new editions of the story as well, I am besieged by hostile queries and comments, usually masquerading as concern for the storyteller's freedom.

First, it's essential to say I didn't look forward to pressing the suit and had hoped the whole matter would simply go away. If the picture the Grimms painted was distorted beyond belief, at least the name Cinderella—a name not bequeathed to my daughter by her parents or used by anyone who ever knew her—seemed to afford us some protection. Between scholars explicating the text and psychiatrists relating it to the events of our lives, not to speak of reporters investigating us for some gossip magazine, the story has not blown over. In fact, I have felt hostile eyes upon me all the time.

One of the defense attorneys claimed it wasn't the restoration of my good name I was after, but only attention. I was jealous, he said, of the unending spotlight on my stepdaughter Cinderella. I can only wish that he be locked in a room with the Grimms for eternity. He deserves the company of two men who constantly rewrite reality to make it bearable to themselves, no matter what havoc they create for those around them.

I have never claimed my girls were easy. Their father, my first husband, a remote and undemonstrative man, tended to

---

sue /su:/ *v.* **a.** to use a legal process by which you try to get a court of law to force a person, company, or organization that has treated you unfairly or hurt you in some way to give you something or to do something; **b.** to bring a lawsuit against someone or something

loathsome /ˈləʊðsəm/ *adj.* **a.** causing feelings of hatred or disgust; **b.** very bad

besiege /bɪˈsiːdʒ/ *v.* **a.** to surround a city, building, etc., with soldiers and try to take control of it; **b.** to gather around (someone) in a way that is aggressive, annoying, etc.; **c.** to overwhelm (someone) with too many questions or requests for things

query /ˈkwɪəri/ *n.* a question or a request for information about something

masquerade /ˌmæskəˈreɪd/ *n.* **a.** a party at which people wear masks and often costumes; **b.** a way of appearing or behaving that is not true or real

bequeath /bɪˈkwiːð/ *v.* **a.** to say in a will that (your property) will be given to (a person or organization) after you die; **b.** to give (ideas, knowledge) to (young people) as part of their history

explicate /ˈeksplɪkeɪt/ *v.* to explain or analyze (something, such as an idea or work of literature)

attorney /əˈtɜːni/ *n.* one who is legally appointed to transact business on another's behalf

havoc /ˈhævək/ *n.* a situation in which there is much destruction or confusion

undemonstrative /ˌʌndɪˈmɒnstrətɪv/ *adj.* **a.** not showing emotion or feelings in a free and open way; **b.** not demonstrative

show affection by lavishing gifts of clothing and jewelry upon them. When he died suddenly, leaving a legacy of debt and an estate in disorder, the girls were denied, not only the token protection of his presence, but also those material compensations he had provided. They became anxious and moody and worried that their prospects for decent marriages had been ruined.

At that time, Cinderella—as I shall call her to avoid confusion—was 14. Her father was a man of no particular ability or ambition who had made a good deal of money on a stock-market fluke. When he began to court me he was floundering, incapable of mobilizing himself or controlling his strong-willed daughter. She would not go to school. She had a foul mouth. She would not dress decently for any occasion. And she was filthy.

The notion of anyone's being forced to sweep the cinders in a household that can afford help is ludicrous except in certain circumstances. Cinderella spent her waking time at home, sitting at the fire, poking at the cinders and getting covered with ash, which she did not mind in the least! Since she neither kept her own room neat or helped in other household tasks, tending the fireplace seemed a perfect job for her. Nor did she appear to mind! That is one of the ironies of the charming little tale she later told people who relayed it to the people who told the Grimms. She would starve before she'd cook a meal and let her clothing get stiff with dirt before she'd wash it, but tending the fireplace was a task she appeared to enjoy!

Allow me to move to the tale of her father's bringing home from town (as requested by them respectively) fine clothing and jewelry for my daughters, the branch of a hazelnut tree for Cinderella. As the Gimms told it, Cinderella planted the branch in memory of her mother and proceeded to weep over it such copious tears as to cause it to sprout into a tree.

I promise you that her mother would not have done the same for Cinderella, who, she'd often said, would be the death of her. And her father, if he let her come close, was usually rewarded by a slap in the face. What I am saying is that those tears that watered the hazelnut tree were tears not of mourning but of jealously and guilt. The girl had ample reason for both. One of the qualities that

lavish /ˈlævɪʃ/ *adj.* giving or using a large amount of something
fluke /fluːk/ *n.* a stroke of luck
flounder /ˈflaʊndə(r)/ *v.* **a.** to move in an awkward way with a lot of difficulty and effort; **b.** to be unsure about what to do or say; **c.** to have a lot of problems and difficulties
foul /faʊl/ *adj.* very unpleasant to taste or smell
filthy /ˈfɪlθɪ/ *adj.* very dirty
cinder /ˈsɪndə(r)/ *n.* a very small piece of burned material (such as wood or coal)
ludicrous /ˈluːdɪkrəs/ *adj.* very foolish
copious /ˈkəʊpiəs/ *adj.* very large in amount or number

made the Grimms' tale less objectionable to us than Mr. Disney's was that in their own way, the Grimms showed the suffering my girls endured. Those birds that pecked the beans from the fireplace and brought Cinderella the gown, and were thus clearly seen to be in her service, also pecked out my daughters' eyes. Mr. Disney, of course, gives us a saint incapable of thoughts of revenge, a portrait which, in its deep untruth, is much more unsettling to us.

Let us pass on to the matter of the Prince, who and what he was (a Prince, of course), and who he most distinctly was not (a responsible young man). Even if the rumors of drink and seductions and shoplifting were true, time might have turned him into a responsible adult. On the other hand, such escapades would worry any parent and were strikingly similar to our experiences with Cinderella. I've always found it peculiar that people failed to wonder why the prince should have wanted this one pretty young girl of all the pretty young girls, including my two daughters, who lived in his kingdom.

To make a long story short, they were two of a king. Those same stores in the village that locked the doors when they saw Cinderella approaching (do we need to deal, at all, with the nonsense of fairy godmothers and/or mice who provide her with clothes?) had, obviously, a much greater problem in dealing with our little Prince, who could buy whatever he wanted but chose to rip it off instead. If Cinderella didn't drink it was only because she liked to be in full control of everyone around her; if she was not promiscuous, it was because her filth discouraged advances (though it has always amused me that people swallowed whole the notion of a girl's being unrecognizable because she took a bath, combed her hair and put on a new dress).

In any event, my daughters were as eager as all the other young girls in the kingdom to be chosen by the prince. Even in the modern era, when television has given an idea of the boredom of royalty's daily life, many girls might say they would give an arm or a leg to be a princess. Surely the Grimms knew the difference between using such an expression and actually cutting off one's big toe so one's foot will fit a glass slipper! Just as surely, any sane girl who thought of performing such a lunatic act would have been afraid of losing the prince

peck /pek/ *v.* **a.** (of a bird) to strike sharply at something with the beak; **b.** to kiss lightly and quickly
saint /seɪnt/ *n.* a person who is officially recognized by the Christian church as being very holy because of the way he or she lived
unsettling /ʌnˈsetlɪŋ/ *adj.* making you upset, nervous, worried, etc.
escapade /ˌeskəˈpeɪd/ *n.* an exciting, foolish, or dangerous experience or adventure
promiscuous /prəˈmɪskjuəs/ *adj.* **a.** having or involving many sexual partners; **b.** including or involving too many people or things; **c.** not limited in a careful or proper way
lunatic /ˈluːnətɪk/ *n.* **a.** a person who behaves in a very foolish way; *adj.* **b.** not sane

stump /stʌmp/ *n.* **a.** a part that remains after something has been broken off, removed, worn down; **b.** the part of an arm or leg that remains after most of it has been cut off

caricature /ˈkærɪkətʃʊə(r)/ *n.* **a.** a drawing that makes someone look funny or foolish because some part of the person's appearance is exaggerated; **b.** someone or something that is very exaggerated in a funny or foolish way

hideous /ˈhɪdɪəs/ *adj.* very ugly or disgusting

dread /dred/ *v.* to be afraid or scared of, be frightened of

recrimination /rɪˌkrɪmɪˈneɪʃn/ *n.* an angry statement in which you accuse or criticize a person who has accused or criticized you

entail /ɪnˈteɪl/ *v.* to have (something) as a part, step, or result

vindicate /ˈvɪndɪkeɪt/ *v.* **a.** to show that (someone) should not be blamed for a crime, mistake, etc.; **b.** to show that (someone or something that has been criticized or doubted) is correct, true, or reasonable

conjure /ˈkʌndʒə/ *v.* **a.** to make (something) appear or seem to appear by using magic; **b.** to create or imagine (something)

upon his discovery that she had a stump where her big toe had been! This is one of the few places where Mr. Disney's story is less objectionable than the Grimms'.

Which returns us to the matter of my motive in bringing this suit. Simply put, I owed it to my daughters. As you have seen, I have never claimed they were perfect. But beautiful they were. We knew it, everyone in town knew it, the Grimms knew it! It is the only quality allowed them in a tale that is otherwise a nightmare of caricature. Yet Mr. Disney chose to send them into history via the movies—which are seen in one theatrical showing by more people than read the Grimms' tales in the decade after they were written—as not only unhappy, but hideously ugly! Still, I was reluctant to sue. If dreaded each release of the movie, I dreaded more the revelation and recrimination trying to stop it would entail.

Then video stores began to open near my home. I couldn't pass them without wondering if they stocked The Movie. I'd feel a change in some neighbor and sense she'd seen it and connected me and my girls to the story for the first time. Nightmares made sleep increasingly difficult. I entered therapy with a man I thought was being king because he felt sorry for me. Finally, I talked to a lawyer who urged that I bring suit, with the results that you know. I FEEL vindicated by the court's decision, almost as pleased that certain bookstores have ceased to carry the Grimms. I think my life would now be pleasant and "normal" were I not being subjected to all sorts of pressures from disturbed children and misguided parents who are angry when they can't find "Cinderella" at their book or video stores.

I'm sick of the argument that a child's imagination conjures stories more frightening than anything in Grimm, and that the stories offer deep consolation for the difficulties of the real world. It is my own feeling that children will be better rather than worse off if confined to a diet of after-school specials and quiz shows. I wish that both had been available when I was raising my girls. They have a variety of problems that might never have arisen had they not been exposed, too young to the ugly fantasies of the Brothers Grimm.

The other day a little girl and her mother got on the elevator in my building and the little girl shrieked "Mommy, is that the witch who killed 'Cinderella'?" Nobody can tell me that this idea came from a child's mind, and when I find out where she got that one, I'll sue him, her or them, too.

Cultural Notes

The Brothers Grimm—Jacob (1785—1863) and Wilhelm Grimm (1786—1859) were German academics, linguists, cultural researchers, lexicographers and authors who studied German folklore and oral traditions. They are among the best-known storytellers of folktales, publishing a collection of stories eventually known as *Grimms' Fairy Tales* which includes narratives like *Briar Rose* and *Little Red Riding Hood*. *Grimms' Fairy Tales* have been told in a wide variety of media formats over the past several decades, and as such, the storylines have often been tweaked to fit varying ideas of what's appropriate for children.

Comprehension Exercises

I. Answer the following questions based on the text.

1. Why did the stepmother sue Disney instead of the Brothers Grimm?
2. Was it out of jealousy when the stepmother sued Disney?
3. How was Cinderella described by her stepmother?
4. What did Cinderella like to do in her daily life according to her stepmother?
5. To what extent do you find the stepmother to be sympathetic in the passage?

II. Write T for true and F for false in the brackets before each of the following statements.

1. (   ) Cinderella's two stepsisters were as pretty as her.
2. (   ) Cinderella cried because of jealousy and guilt according to her stepmother.
3. (   ) The prince was responsible young man.
4. (   ) No girl would rather sacrifice a lot to become a princess.
5. (   ) The stepmother didn't sue the Brothers Grimm because she liked them.

III. Select the most appropriate word or phrase and use its proper form to complete each of the following sentences.

attorney	bequeath	besiege	caricature	compensation
conjure	copious	dread	explicate	filthy
hideous	loathsome	lavish	ludicrous	lunatic
query	revenge	sue	undemonstrative	vindicate

1. He tried to _____ the retailer for profiteering in a local court last month, presenting a picture of the melon plus the receipt.
2. The last named place he says pen or speech cannot describe, as it contained so many _____ and sickening horrors.
3. If soldiers _____ a place, they surround it and wait for the people in it to stop fighting or resisting.
4. You never answered my _____ as to whether English is your native language.
5. The best legacy the king could _____ his subjects is a state where everyone is subject to the law—including the king.
6. My analysis will be mostly an attempt to _____ what the Cox Report would have said if they had been able to properly weigh the conflicting arguments.
7. On his refusal to appear in person or by his _____, he was pronounced contumacious.
8. With their bland, _____ looks and their inner unease, both performers are in peak form.
9. They fly in a private jet, have a personal physician on staff and maintain multiple _____ residences.
10. The Court ordered Dr Williams to pay £300 _____ and £100 costs after admitting assault.
11. Soon you'll be doing _____ tricks that you once dreamed were insurmountable.
12. There is something delightfully and liberatingly _____ about parading higgledy-piggledy in a line of walkers of all shapes and sizes.
13. Long before Altamont's arrival, he had done justice to a _____ breakfast.
14. In other words their support for terrorism stemmed in a _____ way from a smothered understanding that terrorism might be wrong.
15. She is incensed that people get horrible illnesses and die _____, random deaths.

IV. Paraphrase the underlined words or expressions in each sentence.

1. First, it's essential to say I didn't look forward to pressing the suit and had hoped the whole matter would simply go away.

2. Between scholars explicating the text and psychiatrists relating it to the events of our lives, not to speak of reporters investigating us for some gossip magazine, the story has not blown over.

3. I can only wish that he be locked in a room with the Grimms for eternity.

4. Their father, my first husband, a remote and undemonstrative man, tended to show affection by lavishing gifts of clothing and jewelry upon them.

5. That is one of the ironies of the charming little tale she later told people who relayed it to the people who told the Grimms.

V. Discuss with your partner about each of the following statements and write an essay in no less than 200 words about your understanding of one of them.

1. Let us pass on to the matter of the Prince, who and what he was (a Prince, of course), and who he most distinctly was not (a responsible young man).

2. Even in the modern era, when television has given an idea of the boredom of royalty's daily life, many girls might say they would give an arm or a leg to be a princess.

3. They have a variety of problems that might never have arisen had they not been exposed, too young to the ugly fantasies of the Brothers Grimm.

VI. List four websites where we can learn more about different versions of Cinderella and provide a brief introduction to each of them.

1. _____
   _____
   _____ .
2. _____
   _____
   _____ .
3. _____
   _____
   _____ .
4. _____
   _____
   _____ .

Twenty Minutes' Reading

You are required to read the following sections within 20 minutes.

SECTION A

A scientific panel convened by the World Health Organization recommended guidelines on Friday for doctors conducting clinical studies of SARS patients. The panel urged doctors to apply the guidelines in analyzing the masses of potentially useful information about various therapies that were collected in this year's epidemic. Much of that information has not been published or analyzed.

"It is a matter of urgency to get better analysis and review," said Dr. Simon Mardel, a WHO official who led the two-day meeting that ended on Friday. He said thousands of potential therapies and compounds had been tested so far as researchers try to determine treatments for SARS, or severe acute respiratory syndrome. "We recognize that having no treatment for SARS is hindering our ability to control an epidemic in so many ways." He said.

In the epidemic earlier this year, various treatments, like drugs to fight the virus or strengthen the immune system, as well as traditional Chinese medicine, were delivered under emergency conditions, in widely different settings and countries to patients suffering from varying stages of the illness. Those conditions—generally without standardized measurements or controlled situations—have made it hard to interpret results.

Standard supportive therapy like nursing, and in severe cases the use of mechanical respirators(呼吸器)to help patients breathe, is the mainstay(主要支持) of SARS care, and helped many patients survive. But doctors still do not know how best to treat SARS patients who have breathing difficulties. Dr. Mardel said. One method is invasive ventilation. A second method involves blowing oxygen into the lungs through a mask. Both carry the risk of transmitting the virus to hospital employees. Without proper analysis, the panel was unable to say definitively which treatment worked best, or which caused the most harm. "There is a lack of shared information," Dr. Mardel said, noting that a lot of data have not been published.

The panel also agreed on guidelines that would allow doctors to conduct quick and safe clinical trials, a process that generally takes years to complete. The world Health Organization, a United Nations agency did not release the guidelines. Dr. Mardel said they were flexible because no one knew where, when and in what setting SARS would return. Experts in many countries have already listed the treatments they want to test, and the health agency is leaving these decisions to individual nations.

1. Guidelines recommended by the scientific panel can be used for _____.
   A. gathering potentially useful information about various therapies collected
   B. conducting clinical studies of SARS patients
   C. determining treatment for SARS
   D. publishing all the information about SARS
2. According to the passage, it is difficult to interpret the results of certain treatments for SARS because _____.
   A. patients were in different countries
   B. patients were given medicines in widely different settings
   C. patients were at different stages of the illness
   D. these conditions had no standardized measurements or controlled situations
3. According to doctors, the two methods to treat SARS patients who have breathing difficulties both _____.
   A. carry the risk of infecting hospital employees
   B. are effective in curing patients
   C. don't run the risk of transmitting the virus to hospital employees
   D. prove to work effectively and cause no harm
4. According to a WHO official, Dr. Mardel, the guidelines were flexible because _____.
   A. SARS would reemerge in poor countries
   B. no one knew where, when and in what setting SARS would return

C. SARS would not appear in developed countries

D. no one knew whether SARS would return or not

5. Which of the following can be the best title of the passage?

   A. SARS, a Dreadful Disease

   B. No Good Methods to Treat SARS

   C. SARS Will Return One Day

   D. Health Panel Recommends New Guidelines on SARS

SECTION B

In recent years, teachers of introductory courses in Asian American studies have been facing a dilemma nonexistent a few decades ago, when hardly any texts in that field were available. Today, excellent anthologies（文选）and other introductory texts exist, and books on individual Asian Americans are published almost weekly. Even professors who are experts in the field find it difficult to decide which of these to assign to students; non-experts who teach in related areas and are looking for writings for and by Asian American to include in survey courses are in an even worse position.

A complicating factor has been the continuing lack of specialized one-volume reference works on Asian Americans, such as biographical dictionaries or desktop encyclopedias. Such works would enable students taking Asian American studies courses (and professors in related fields) to look up basic information on Asian American individuals, institutions, history, and culture without having to wade through（费力的阅读冗长或艰深的材料）mountains of primary source material. In addition, given such works. Asian American studies professors might feel more free to include more challenging Asian American material in their introductory reading lists, since good reference works allow students to acquire on their own the background information necessary to interpret difficult or unfamiliar material.

6. The author is primarily concerned with _____.

   A. responding to a criticism

   B. describing a course of study

   C. discussing a problem

   D. evaluating a past course of action

7. The "dilemma"(Line 2, Para.1) can best be characterized as being caused by the necessity to make a choice when faced with a _____.

   A. lack of acceptable alternatives

   B. lack of strict standards for evaluating alternatives

C. preponderance of bad alternatives as compared to good

D. multitude of different alternatives

8. Biographical dictionaries and desktop encyclopedias are _____.

   A. primary source materials

   B. introductory texts

   C. excellent anthologies

   D. reference materials

9. Which of the following is implied about the introductory courses in Asian American studies a few decades ago?

   A. The range of different textbooks that could be assigned for such courses was extremely limited.

   B. The texts assigned as readings in such courses were often not very challenging for students.

   C. Students often complained about the texts assigned to them in such courses.

   D. Such courses were offered only at schools whose libraries were rich in primary sources.

10. According to the passage, the existence of good one-volume reference works about Asian Americans could result in _____.

    A. increased agreement among professors of Asian American studies regarding the quality of the sources available in their field

    B. an increase in the number of students sighing up for introductory courses in Asian American studies

    C. increased accuracy in writings that concern Asian American history and culture

    D. the inclusion of a wider range of Asian American material in introductory reading lists in Asian American studies

Unit Four

Text A

What Is True Freedom?

Ashok Kumar Gupta

《什么是真正的自由》自由是一个热点甚至敏感的话题，因此认清什么是真正的自由就显得愈发重要。本文着意论述什么是真正的自由。

Freedom is the cherished goal of humanity throughout its history.

No society has ever been happy under the rule of people of some other society. History, from one perspective, is nothing but a struggle between two groups—one attempting to enslave or keeping enslaved the other and the other fighting incessantly to ward off this slavery. All wars are nothing but a manifestation of this ancient phenomenon. It seems we cannot tolerate losing our freedom and at the same time we cannot allow others to be free. When we are under the rule of someone else we fight to throw off the shackles and when we are free we strive to enslave others.

It is true not only for political or social groups but also for individuals. Just have a look at the kind of relationships we have built. Don't we try to dominate all persons we come across? We can see parents trying to dominate children, husbands trying to dominate wives, bosses trying to dominate subordinates and vice versa. Even friends try to dominate each other. It seems life is nothing but a struggle to dominate the other.

It can be said that there are nations, societies, groups or individuals who are free. Today, in the modern world, autonomy seems to be the norm. We can see autonomous entities all around, but this autonomy is superficial. Such

ward off prevent from happening
shackle /'ʃæk ə l/ *n.* **a.** metal band on prisoner; **b.** U-shaped fastener **c.** restraint on freedom
autonomy /ɔː'tɒnəmi/ *n.* **a.** the right of a group of people to govern itself, or to organize its own activities; **b.** personal independence and the capacity to make decisions and act on them
norm /nɔːm/ *n.* **a.** a standard or model or pattern regarded as typical; **b.** the usual or normal situation, way of doing sth, etc.

autonomy remains in existence only till such a time when a more powerful entity decides to take it away. A behind-the-scene power struggle is going on everywhere. Human beings are not left untouched by all this. They can feel it subconsciously. As a result, modern man is continuously trying to defy authority or any force which makes him feel bound in any sense. To take a small example, individual human beings, these days, are preferring not to marry at all. Even after marriage, the moment one feels that his/her freedom is being curtailed, one walks away. Religious, legal or social pressures are proving inadequate in preserving the institution of marriage.

> **entity** /ˈentɪti/ *n.* sth that exists as a single and complete unit
> **defy** /dɪˈfaɪ/ *v.* **a.** openly resist sb or sth; **b.** challenge sb
> **curtail** /kɜːˈteɪl/ *v.* **a.** to cut short; **b.** to restrict
> **encroach** /ɪnˈkrəʊtʃ/ *v.* **a.** to intrude gradually or stealthily, often taking away sb's authority, rights, or property; **b.** exceed proper limits
> **inkling** /ˈɪŋklɪŋ/ *n.* a slight suggestion or vague understanding
> **mirage** /ˈmɪrɑːʒ/ *n.* **a.** an optical illusion in which atmospheric refraction by a layer of hot air distorts or inverts reflections of distant objects; **b.** sth that appears to be real but is unreal or merely imagined
> **mire** /ˈmaɪə/ *v.* **a.** to get stuck in mud; **b.** to involve sb or sth in difficulties
> **tenuous** /ˈtenjuəs/ *adj.* **a.** thin and fine, and therefore easily broken; **b.** weak and unconvincing
> **fragility** /frəˈdʒɪlɪti/ *n.* **a.** quality of being easily damaged or destroyed; **b.** lock of physical strength

In my opinion, freedom is one of the greatest values in life. It is in our very nature and that is the reason every one resents if his/her freedom is encroached upon. The only trouble is that most of us are not even aware of our shackles. We do not even have a faint inkling of the numerous ways our freedom is denied to us. On the surface it appears that modern man has certainly acquired a degree of freedom unimaginable in the past. But it is only a mirage. There exists no freedom at all. There is a subtle and vicious system of slavery which has become all pervading. You need to ask one question only to see through the mist we are all mired in. The question is: can I identify the person, group or element who can take away my freedom?

If you cannot identify a single element, let me congratulate you. You are fortunate in the sense that you are not aware of the tenuousness and fragility of the so called freedom of yours. It means that you have not really had any brush with authorities (in any sense of the word). It is only a matter of time and if you are fortunate enough the time of realization may not come in your life at all and you will depart happily from this world thinking that you lived a free life. If you can identify even one force on this earth which can curtail your freedom in any way, let me congratulate you too. For it means that you can see things if you wish to. Our freedom can maintain its status only as long as someone more powerful than us doesn't see us as a threat to his interests. Step in his way and he will force you to open your eyes. It is not at all difficult to conclude that the so called freedom we have lasts only as long as someone else (who is more powerful than us) allows us.

This article does not intend to discuss our freedom in political or social sense. It can be shown that freedom does not exist in this sense anywhere on this earth. It is easy to see that the moment your interests, however personal, go against some authority you are subdued by the powers whose interests collide with yours. It is almost futile to aspire for freedom at such a level simply because at this level it is "power" which defines freedom. The more the power, the more the freedom. And since ordinary human beings like us, who are not politicians or officials or priests, cannot wield much power, we should not hope for freedom in this sense.

All this relates to the world outside of us. What about freedom at a much deeper and personal level? I want to talk of a certain level where all human beings are equally powerful. Where guns or jails or police do not come into play at all. Where, if you can recognize and earn your freedom, such powers of the world would not matter at all. This is purely at the level of an individual, where there is no one else to take away or grant you some freedom. Where it is only you who can decide whether you want freedom or not.

Just as there are various degrees of freedom, there are various degrees of slavery too. At a certain level, there exists the most vicious form of slavery. It is at the existential level. While political slavery curtails political freedom, existential slavery curtails the most profound form of freedom. Humanity has recognized the superficial levels of freedom but is almost unaware of the ultimate or true freedom. We are not even aware that we are not free at all.

One of my favorite Zen story goes like this:

A Zen Guru was going somewhere with his disciples. They saw a man who was coming towards them with a cow. The cow had a rope tied around its neck and the man was holding the other end of the rope. The Guru asked his disciples, "Who is the slave, the man or the cow?" The disciples said, "The cow is the slave. It is tied with the rope. The man is the master since he is controlling the cow." The Guru smiled and said, "No! You are wrong. If the rope slips from the man's hands and the cow starts running away you will find that the man will run after the cow. The

---

subdue /sʌbˈdjuː/ *v.* **a.** to bring a person or group of people under control using force; **b.** soften sth; **c.** repress or control feelings repress or control feelings

aspire /əˈspaɪə/ *v.* have an ambitious plan or a lofty goal

guru /ˈɡʊruː/ *n.* **a.** a religious leader or teacher in Hinduism and Sikhism; **b.** someone who has a reputation as an expert leader, teacher, or practitioner in a particular field

disciple /dɪˈsaɪp ə l/ *n.* **a.** someone who believes in the ideas of a great teacher or leader, esp. a religious one; **b.** one of the first 12 men to follow Christ

man is also tied down with the cow, only his rope is invisible."

> **vow** /vaʊ/ *v.* to promise or decide solemnly
> **naught** /ˈnɔːt/ *n.* **a.** the number zero; **b.** nothing
> **time and again** time and time again, very often
> **irrespective** /ˌɪrɪˈspektɪv/ *adj.* in spite of everything

We are also tied down with so many invisible ropes. We are not free. We want to be happy but can we? Does it depend on us? No, our Happiness and sorrow depend on someone else. Anyone can make you angry anytime he wishes. You might have vowed many times that you will not get angry, but all your vows come to naught time and again. Anyone can make you unhappy anytime he wishes. You have no control over your own emotions. You have control over other people's emotions and they have control over yours. You are their slave and they are yours. You are not even free to choose your own emotions. It seems that the switches, which control our emotions, are not accessible to us while being fully accessible to others. You can switch on or off any emotion in me and I can do the same to you. But your own emotional switches are out of your reach.

This is the deepest form of slavery. We have become slaves by nature. At least, we should have freedom to choose our own feelings and emotions. If I wish to remain happy, why should someone else be able to take my Happiness away so easily? If one wants to remain peaceful why should he not be able to maintain his peace irrespective of the outside disturbances?

Cultural Notes

1. **Ashok Kumar Gupta**—An Indian engineer by profession, a programmer by hobby, and a thinker by nature. His other major writings include *What is destiny? Is there a free will? Astrology: A Science or Superstition? What is Happiness and How to achieve it? How India lost its Glory?* etc.

2. **Zen**—Buddhist school that developed in China and later in Japan as the result of a fusion between the Mahayana form of Buddhism originating in India and the Chinese philosophy of **Daoism** (Taoism). **Zen (Buddhism)** derives from **Chinese Chan (Buddhism)** and emerged in Japan in the 12th century. **Zen** and **Chan**, respectively, the Japanese and Chinese ways of pronouncing the Sanskrit term **dhyana** which designates a state of mind roughly equivalent to contemplation or meditation. **Dhyana** denotes specifically the state of consciousness of a **Buddha**, one whose mind is free from the assumption that the distinct individuality of oneself and other things is real. **Zen** or **Chan** asserts that enlightenment can come through

meditation and intuition rather than faith. The way of **Zen** or **Chan** is an intriguing one. Its predilection for paradox and intuition—as opposed to reason and logic—challenges our innate assumptions about the world and our own minds. As a major school of Buddhism, **Zen** or **Chan** has a tremendous influence on Chinese philosophy and people's life attitude. Besides, it influences various areas of Chinese culture in a profound way. Down the centuries, the **Zen** or **Chan** way has found unique expression in Chinese architecture, literature, music, painting, gardening, tea ceremonies and so on. The inconceivable value of **Zen Buddhism** enables it to continue playing an active role on the cultural stage of China and even the whole world in the present day.

Comprehension Exercises

I. Answer the following questions based on the text.

1. What is the essence of wars, according to the author?
2. Why is modern autonomy superficial?
3. For how long can one's freedom maintain its status?
4. Why does the author tell a Zen story?
5. What is the deepest form of slavery?

II. Write T for true and F for false in the brackets before each of the following statements.

1. (   ) History is a fight against slavery.
2. (   ) People tend to enslave others.
3. (   ) Some people can enjoy absolute freedom while others can't.
4. (   ) It was quite unusual for people to keep their independence in the past.
5. (   ) In the modern world one can enjoy complete freedom to end his marriage and nothing can prevent him from doing it.
6. (   ) Compared with those in the past, modern people acquire more freedom and also have the initiative to keep the freedom as long as possible.
7. (   ) It is impossible to find political or social freedom on the earth.
8. (   ) Power defines freedom.
9. (   ) People cannot remain happy as they wish because their happiness depends on someone else.
10. (   ) The target readers of this article include politicians, officials, priests and ordinary people.

III. Select the most appropriate word or phrase and use its proper form to complete each of the following sentences.

aspire	autonomy	curtail	collide	defy
disciple	enslave	encroach	futile	fragile
humanity	incessantly	manifestation	mirage	mire
subordinate	subdue	tenuous	vicious	vow

1. To my disappointment, nowadays some people seem to doubt the existence of the goodness in _____.
2. Education makes a people easy to lead, but difficult to drive; easy to govern, but impossible to _____.
3. The exchange and cooperation in the field of culture, education and tourism has been expanding _____.
4. This version exceeds my expectations and is a beautiful _____ of what I originally imagined while crafting this story.
5. Subsequent measurements six months later allowed the researchers to compare growth rates of dominant and _____ females.
6. What really motivates people is the quest for _____, mastery and purpose, not external rewards.
7. Trees _____ gravity. They are the only natural element in perpetual movement toward the sky.
8. By the same token, reduced military budgets would force the government to _____ its foreign involvement.
9. New housing is starting to _____ upon the surrounding fields.
10. A _____ is an optical illusion caused by hot air conditions.
11. He is a wolf in sheep's clothing, outwardly kind but inwardly _____.
12. The lines connecting these disparate findings are still _____, but studies are continuing to bring in new data.
13. The _____ land quickly lost its topsoil and became nothing but sand and dust.
14. Neither riches nor honors can corrupt him; neither poverty nor humbleness can make him swerve from principle; and neither threats nor forces can _____ him.
15. They would have to respond to our call with enough speed so that they would not themselves act as missiles that would _____ with the aircraft.

IV. Paraphrase the underlined words or expressions in each sentence.

1. Today, in the modern world, autonomy seems <u>to be the norm</u>.

2. A <u>behind the scene</u> power struggle is going on every where.

3. You need to ask one question only to see through the mist <u>we are all mired in</u>.

4. <u>Step in his way</u> and he will force you to open your eyes.

5. You might have vowed many times that you will not get angry, but all your vows <u>come to naught</u> time and again.

V. Discuss with your partner about each of the following statements and write an essay in no less than 200 words about your understanding of one of them.

1. The idea of freedom in modern China has broadened.

2. The focuses of Western and Chinese philosophy are radically different.

3. When we have children, they are not ours to own.

VI. List four websites where we can learn more about freedom and provide a brief introduction to each of them.

1.

2.

3. _____
   _____.
4. _____
   _____.

Text B

I'm Too Busy for Me
Dawn Fields

《我忙得没空做自己》在这个高速发展的时代,似乎每个人都在为自己忙碌。但是每个人又都忙得没有时间做自己:在这个生活的悖论中我们如何找到自己,不妨我们细读此文。

Everyone is busy nowadays. It's hard to find time for anything. From the time we wake up in the morning until the time we go to bed, it's hard to find 30 minutes to simply be by yourself. If you are married with children, I know you can relate to what I am saying.

I have a girlfriend who is single and we were having the discussion about how the grass is always greener on the other side. I said I would love to have a few days when I come Home to an empty house with peace and quiet. She said she would love to put the key in the door, knowing that someone is on the other end.

I had to laugh because although that sounds great, once it is a reality there are days when you wish everyone on the other side of the door would simply disappear for about an hour so you can come home and relax without having to start dinner, do Homework, bathe children, iron clothes for the next day or prepare lunch for everyone to take to school and work the following day. I know I sure wish that would happen and I believe that most married women with children can relate to what I am saying.

Don't get me wrong! I love my family with all of my heart and all of my soul. But if they disappeared for an hour or two, I would probably love them even more. If I had just one day when no one was yelling, "Mommy!" or "Honey!" I wouldn't be mad.

In fact, finding time to be by yourself is totally necessary if you wish to live a happy, prosperous and purpose-driven life. If there is noise going on around you 24/7 it's impossible to hear the quiet voice that speaks inside of us—that guides us and gives us direction on which path we should take. If that voice is not used to being heard, eventually, it would quiet itself and that is no good.

I know how hectic life can be. Trust me.

I know what it feels like to wish there were 35 hours each day and be willing to spend only 3 of those hours sleeping so you can get all the other things that you need to get done done.

But the problem is most of the stuff that we need to get done, does nothing towards working towards our personal development.

If you simply let life dictate to you what you do with your life, you will find that there is never time to take simply for yourself. Yes, you can schedule a vacation every now and then and that is great. But, generally, on vacation you still are not spending time by yourself. You have planned an exhausting schedule that takes you here and there and everywhere. You are trying to get in all the sites and events that you can over a 5-to-7-day period. Most of us actually need a vacation after coming back from a vacation with all the activities that we've covered during that time period.

No matter how hectic your life may be IT IS IMPERATIVE THAT YOU SPEND TIME EACH AND EVERY DAY BY YOURSELF TO THINK AND REFLECT ON LIFE AND LISTEN TO THAT INNER VOICE.

The same way each day you make sure that you have enough time to take a shower each morning or the same way you make sure that you eat lunch each day, make it a part of your daily routine to spend time with and by yourself.

hectic /ˈhektɪk/ *adj.* constantly busy and hurried
dictate /dɪkˈteɪt/ *v.* **a.** say out loud for the purpose of recording; **b.** tell someone what to do, give orders **c.** control or influence sth

When I say by yourself—that's exactly

what I mean—by yourself. Go somewhere you won't be disturbed by the children, the spouse, the phone, the television, the radio, or your emails. Go somewhere you can have total peace and quiet.

Pick a time that is convenient for you.

I like the early morning. The reason I pick early morning is because everyone else is asleep. No one calls me early in the morning. There isn't any television or radio on or children or husband calling my name for any reason. I have total peace and quiet.

But it is entirely up to you as to what time works best with your schedule.

Once you find a quiet place and a quiet time try your best to be consistent in both the time and the location. Meaning, try to make sure you have your quiet time the same time and place each and every day.

And simply SIT and BE STILL.

I always start by saying a little prayer to God asking Him for His guidance on whatever it is that I am trying to overcome in my life. Right now, I am asking Him to help me be more like Him. I am asking that I am always mindful of the way that I speak and treat people—especially those that are closest to me.

I don't know about you, but I have the tendency sometimes to be more short-tempered with the people who are closest to me than I am with strangers. I am asking God to help me with this and to help me be more like Him in every way possible.

You can ask for whatever it is that you want to work on in your life.

Then, simply sit and relax. Pay attention to any thoughts that come to you.

These thoughts that we receive during our quiet "meditation" periods, are God's guidance. Our spirits are communicating with us and giving us direction on things to do in our life that will bring us the results that we are seeking.

mindful /ˈmaɪndfəl/ *adj.* bearing in mind; attentive to
short-tempered /ʃɔːtˈtempəd/ easily made angry or impatient
meditation /ˌmedɪˈteɪʃən/ *n.* **a.** the practice of emptying your mind of thoughts and feelings, in order to relax completely or for religious reasons; **b.** the act of thinking deeply and seriously about sth

You can achieve anything that you desire once you take the time to listen to that inner voice, that guiding light inside of you and TRUST it. This is important. You must TRUST that voice and do as it says. Don't second-guess it. There is no need to second-guess because those directions are coming directly to you from God. Just LISTEN, TRUST and ACT.

> **second-guess a.** attempt to anticipate or predict; **b.** to criticize sth after it has already happened

ACTION POINT: For the next 30 days, find 30 minutes each day for quiet time. Whether it is in the morning, afternoon, or evening, doesn't matter. What matters is that you pick a time and be consistent. Find a quiet place. You can decide to go walking each morning in the park; or the bathroom might be the only place you can get peace and quiet, it doesn't matter. Perhaps you can only find time during your lunch break so you decide to spend 30 minutes sitting in your car in the back of the parking lot. Be creative. It doesn't matter where or when you do this, just make sure that you do.

Think of something that you would like to change about yourself, your life or your situation to make it better. And go into your quiet time with the impression on your mind and listen to your inner voice—that guiding voice.

Listen. Trust. Act. It will never steer you wrong.

Cultural Notes

1. **Dawn Fields**—A motivational speaker, life coach and author. She teaches how to discover your life's purpose and incorporate it into a career, in a really, down-to-earth, no nonsense sort of approach. Her other major writings include *Can a Little Faith Move Mountains? What You Sow, So Shall You Reap, Don't Be Afraid-Just Believe, What's Missing In Your Life, Jesus Tells the Secret of How to Get Everything You Desire In Life, A Burning Desire*, etc.

2. **Uppercase Letters and Lowercase Letters**—The shape of lowercase letters (or "small letters") varies roughly in three ways. Some of them ascend (e.g. b, h, d, k, l, etc.) or descend (e.g. g, j, p, q, y, etc.) and the left have no ascenders or descenders (e.g. a, c, e, i, o, m, n, r, s, etc.) at all. Because lower-case letters are characteristic of going up and down and sometimes just staying in the middle, the words or phrases in the small form can be recognized and

understood more easily and quickly. Uppercase letters (or "capital letters"), in contrast, do not have any "shape" for they are of the same height. That's probably why people find it difficult to read the words in capitals. They have to slow down and read the capitalized part very carefully if they intend to figure out the meaning. To focus readers' attention on the essential points, the author, obviously taking advantage of the features of uppercase letters for emphasis, capitalizes all the letters of quite a few words and even a whole long sentence here in this article.

Comprehension Exercises

I. Answer the following questions based on the text.

1. What did the author's girlfriend want to do?
2. Why did the author have a different idea from her girlfriend?
3. How can we make our life happy, prosperous and purpose-driven according to the author?
4. When is the best time for the author to enjoy total peace and quiet?
5. What should we think of in our quiet "meditation" periods?

II. Write T for true and F for false in the brackets before each of the following statements.

1. (   ) The author has at least one child.
2. (   ) The author is sure that all married women with children can understand her words.
3. (   ) The author has got tired of the housework and her family.
4. (   ) It is impossible to enjoy a happy life unless we set aside some time to be by ourselves.
5. (   ) Housework has nothing to do with one's personal development.
6. (   ) Going on vacation is a good way for us to spend time by ourselves.
7. (   ) It is necessary for us to spend some time each day listening to the quiet voice inside of us.
8. (   ) The author is more patient with others than her family.
9. (   ) The inner voice functions as a guiding light.
10. (   ) It's really important we choose a right place at a right time to listen to our inner voice which is actually God's direction.

III. Select the most appropriate word or phrase and use its proper form to complete each of the following sentences.

communicate	consistent	dictate	disturb	eventually
guidance	hectic	iron	imperative	location
mindful	meditation	prosperous	routine	spouse
short-tempered	steer	schedule	tendency	vacation

1. The crisis brought pain, but also healthy changes that cleared the decks for more _____ growth and innovation.
2. He expects to _____ out these difficulties at a special conference next week.
3. But gradually that water freezes too, expanding as it turns to ice and _____ bursting the pipe inside the wall.
4. At any rate, Picasso seems to have come alive and felt a new freedom to comment on the increasingly _____ events of his life.
5. The change would allow universities to _____ how those staff members allocated their time between teaching and other activities
6. If you have a particular number of days' or weeks' _____, you do not have to go to work for that number of days or weeks.
7. It is _____ that people understand and believe the science: rhino horns are not medicine and have no magical power.
8. Kathleen finds that she is helped by having a particular _____ for her first half-hour of the morning.
9. Her father is an ultra-conservative who is still opposed to freedom to choose her _____.
10. The anatomy of the rest of the dinosaur's approximately four-foot-long body is _____ with a unique and varied lifestyle.
11. _____ of the needs of its students, Cardiff has invested heavily in providing new and improved residences.
12. There is a _____ for people to look at puppetry as a metaphor for manipulation, for taking away someone's will or autonomy.
13. They often learn to fight at an early age, sometimes using _____ adults around them as role models.
14. The result is not only a fascinating travelogue, but also a personal _____ on loss and fate.
15. I think you are perfectly correct in trying to _____ your mother towards increased independence.

IV. Paraphrase the underlined words or expressions in each sentence.

1. If you are married with children, I know you can <u>relate to</u> what I am saying.

2. Don't <u>get me wrong</u>!

3. And go into your quiet time with the impression on your mind and listen to your <u>inner voice</u>—that <u>guiding voice</u>.

4. Listen. Trust. Act. It will never <u>steer you wrong</u>.

5. If that voice is not used to being heard, eventually, it would <u>quiet itself</u> and that is no good.

V. Discuss with your partner about each of the following statements and write an essay in no less than 200 words about your understanding of one of them.

1. Our jobs or careers seem to cause constant stress.

2. "I'm too busy" doesn't mean that you are.

3. You should always listen to your body, your mind, and your emotions.

VI. List four websites where we can learn more about meditation and provide a brief introduction to each of them.

1.

2.

3. _____
   _____
   _____.
4. _____
   _____
   _____.

Twenty Minutes' Reading

You are required to read the following sections within 20 minutes.

 **SECTION A**

The word religion is derived from the Latin noun religion, which denotes both earnest observance of ritual obligations and an inward spirit of reverence. In modern usage, religion covers a wide spectrum of meaning that reflects the enormous variety of ways the term can be interpreted. At one extreme, many committed believers recognize only their own tradition as a religion, understanding expressions such as worship and prayer to refer exclusively to the practices of their tradition. Although many believers stop short of claiming an exclusive status for their tradition, they may nevertheless use vague or idealizing terms in defining religion for example, true love of God, or the path of enlightenment. At the other extreme, religion may be equated with ignorance, fanaticism, or wishful thinking.

By defining religion as a sacred engagement with what is taken to be a spiritual reality, it is possible to consider the importance of religion in human life without making claims about what it really is or ought to be. Religion is not an object with a single, fixed meaning, or even a zone with clear boundaries. It is an aspect of human experience that may intersect, incorporate, or transcend other aspects of life and society. Such a definition avoid the drawbacks of limiting the investigation of religion to Western or biblical categories such as monotheism (belief in one god only) or to church structure, which are not universal. For example, in tribal societies, religion unlike the Christian church usually is not a separate institution but pervades the whole of public and private life.

In Buddhism, gods are not as central as the idea of a Buddha. In many traditional cultures, the idea of a sacred cosmic order is the most prominent religious belief. Because of this variety, some scholars prefer to use a general term such as the sacred to designate the common foundation of religious life.

Religion in this understanding includes a complex of activities that cannot be reduced to any single aspect of human experience. It is a part of individual life but also of group dynamics. Religion includes patterns of behavior but also patterns of language and thought. It is sometimes a highly organized institution that sets itself apart from a culture, and it is sometimes an integral part of a culture. Religious experience may be expressed in visual symbols, dance and performance, elaborate philosophical systems, legendary and imaginative stories, formal ceremonies, and detailed rules of ethical conduct and law. Each of these elements assumes innumerable cultural forms. In some ways there are as many forms of religious expression as there are human cultural environments.

1. What is the passage mainly concerned about?
   A. Religion has a variety of interpretation.
   B. Religion is a reflection of ignorance.
   C. Religion is not only confined to the Christian categories.
   D. Religion includes all kinds of activities.
2. What does the word "observance" probably convey in Para.1?
   A. notice
   B. watching
   C. conformity
   D. experience
3. According to the passage what people generally consider religion to be?
   A. Fantastic observance.
   B. Spiritual practice.
   C. Individual observance of tradition.
   D. A complex of activities.
4. Which of the following is not true?
   A. It is believed by some that religion should be what it ought to be.
   B. "The path of enlightenment" is a definition that the author doesn't agree to.
   C. According to the author, the committed believers define religion improperly.
   D. The author doesn't speak in favor of the definition of "the sacred".
5. Which of the following is religion according to the passage?
   A. Performance of human beings.
   B. Buddha, monotheism and some tribal tradition.
   C. Practice separated from culture.
   D. All the above.

SECTION B

In the early days of nuclear power, the United States makes money on it. But today opponents（反对者）have so complicated its development that nonnuclear plants have been ordered or built here in 12 years.

The greatest fear of nuclear power opponents has always been a reactor "meltdown". Today, the chances of a meltdown that would threaten U. S. public health are very little. But to even further reduce the possibility, engineers are testing new reactors that rely not on human judgment to shut them down but on the laws of nature. Now General Electric is already building two advanced reactors in Japan. But don't expect them even on U. S. shores unless things change in Washington.

The procedure for licensing nuclear power plants is a bad dream. Any time during, or even after, construction, an objection by any group or individual can bring everything to a halt while the matter is investigated or taken to court. Meanwhile, the builder must add nice-but-not-necessary improvements, some of which force him to knock down walls and start over. In every case when a plant has been opposed, the Nuclear Regulation Commission has ultimately granted a license to construct or operate. But the victory often costs so much that the utility ends up abandoning the plant anyway.

A case in point is the Shoreham plant on New York's Long Island. Shoreham was a virtual twin to the Millstone plant in Connecticut, both ordered in the mid-60. Millstone, completed for $101 million, has been generating electricity for two decades. Shoreham, however, was singled out by antinuclear activists who, by sending in endless protests, drove the cost over $5 billion and delayed its use for many years.

Shoreham finally won its operation license. But the plant has never produced a watt power. Governor Mario Cuomo, an opponent of a Shoreham start up, used his power to force New York's public-utilities commission to accept the following settlement: the power company could pass the cost of Shoreham along to its consumers only if it agreed not to operate the plant. I'd say, a perfectly good facility, capable of servicing hundreds of thousands of homes, sits rusting.

6. The author's attitude toward the development of nuclear power is _____.
   A. negative
   B. neutral
   C. positive
   D. questioning

7. What has made the procedure for licensing nuclear power plants a bad dream?

   A. The inefficiency of the Nuclear Regulation Commission.

   B. The enormous cost of construction and operation.

   C. The length of time it takes to make investigations.

   D. The objection of the opponents of nuclear power.

8. It can be inferred from Para. 2 that _____.

   A. there are not enough safety measures in the U. S. for running new nuclear power plants

   B. it is not technical difficulties that prevent the building of nuclear power plants in the U. S.

   C. there are already more nuclear power plants than necessary in the U. S.

   D. the American government will not allow Japanese nuclear reactors to be installed in the U. S.

9. Governor Mario Cuomo's chief intention in proposing the settlement was to _____.

   A. stop the Shoreham plant from going into operation

   B. urge the power company to further increase its power supply

   C. permit the Shoreham plant to operate under certain conditions

   D. help the power company to solve its financial problems

10. The phrase "single out" is closest in meaning to _____.

    A. delay

    B. end up

    C. complete

    D. separate

Unit Five

Text A

On Photography I
Susan Sontag

It is a nostalgic time right now, and photographs actively promote nostalgia. Photography is an elegiac art, a twilight art. Most subjects photographed are, just by virtue of being photographed, touched with pathos. An ugly or grotesque subject may be moving because it has been dignified by the attention of the photographer. A beautiful subject can be the object of rueful feelings, because it has aged or decayed or no longer exists. All photographs are memento mori. To take a photograph is to participate in another person's (or thing's) mortality, vulnerability, mutability. Precisely by slicing out this moment and freezing it, all photographs testify to time's relentless melt.

Cameras began duplicating the world at that moment when the human landscape started to undergo a vertiginous rate of change: while an untold number of forms of biological and social life are being destroyed in a brief span of time, a device is available to record what is disappearing. The moody, intricately textured Paris of Atget and Brassai is mostly gone. Like the dead relatives and friends preserved in the family album, whose presence in photographs exorcises some of the anxiety and remorse prompted by their disappearance, so the photographs of neighborhoods now torn down, rural places disfigured and made barren, supply our pocket relation to the past.

A photograph is both a pseudo-presence and a token of absence. Like a wood fire in a room, photographs—especially those of people, of distant landscapes and faraway cities, of the vanished past—are incitements to reverie. The sense of the unattainable that can be evoked by photographs feeds directly into the erotic feelings of those for whom desirability is enhanced by distance. The lover's photograph hidden in a married woman's

> **elegiac** /ˌelɪˈdʒaɪək/ *adj.* **a.** resembling or characteristic of or appropriate to an elegy; **b.** expressing sorrow often for something past
> **rueful** /ˈruːfl/ *adj.* feeling or expressing pain or sorrow for sins or offenses
> **memento mori** a reminder of mortality
> **mutability** /ˌmjuːtəˈbɪlətɪ/ *n.* capability of changing or being changed
> **vertiginous** /vɜːˈtɪdʒɪnəs/ *adj.* causing or suffering from vertigo, especially by being at great height above the ground
> **exorcise** /ˈeksɔːsaɪz/ *v.* **a.** to expel (an evil spirit) by adjuration or to get rid of (something troublesome, menacing, or oppressive); **b.** to free of an evil spirit
> **reverie** /ˈrevəri/ *n.* **a.** (a state of) pleasant thoughts and dreams while awake; **b.** daydream

wallet, the poster photograph of a rock star tacked up over an adolescent's bed, the campaign-button image of a politician's face pinned on a voter's coat, the snapshots of a cabdriver's children clipped to the visor—all such talismanic uses of photographs express a feeling both sentimental and implicitly magical: they are attempts to contact or lay claim to another reality.

> **talismanic** /ˌtælɪzˈmænɪk/ *adj.* (of an object) believed to have magic powers of protection
> **abet** /əˈbet/ *v.* to encourage or give help to (a crime or a criminal)
> **persona** /pəˈsəʊnə/ *n.* (in psychology) the outward character a person takes on in order to persuade other people that he or she is a particular type of person
> **unequivocal** /ˌʌnɪˈkwɪvəkl/ *adj.* **a.** completely clear; **b.** allowing no possibility of doubt
> **consensus** /kənˈsensəs/ *n.* **a.** a general agreement; **b.** the opinion of most of the people in a group
> **nascent** /ˈnæsnt/ *adj.* coming into existence or starting to develop

Photographs can abet desire in the most direct, utilitarian way—as when someone collects photographs of anonymous examples of the desirable as an aid to masturbation. The matter is more complex when photographs are used to stimulate the moral impulse. Desire has no history—at least, it is experienced in each instance as all foreground, immediacy. It is aroused by archetypes and is, in that sense, abstract. But moral feelings are embedded in history, whose personae are concrete, whose situations are always specific. Thus, almost opposite rules hold true for the use of the photograph to awaken desire and to awaken conscience. The images that mobilize conscience are always linked to a given historical situation. The more general they are, the less likely they are to be effective.

A photograph that brings news of some unsuspected zone of misery cannot make a dent in public opinion unless there is an appropriate context of feeling and attitude. The photographs Mathew Brady and his colleagues took of the horrors of the battlefields did not make people any less keen to go on with the Civil War. The photographs of ill-clad, skeletal prisoners held at Andersonville inflamed Northern public opinion—against the South. (The effect of the Andersonville photographs must have been partly due to the very novelty, at that time, of seeing photographs.) The political understanding that many Americans came to in the 1960s would allow them, looking at the photographs Dorothea Lange took of Nisei on the West Coast being transported to internment camps in 1942, to recognize their subject for what it was—a crime committed by the government against a large group of American citizens. Few people who saw those photographs in the 1940s could have had so unequivocal a reaction; the grounds for such a judgment were covered over by the pro-war consensus. Photographs cannot create a moral position, but they can reinforce one—and can help build a nascent one.

Photographs may be more memorable than moving images, because they are a neat slice of time, not a flow. Television is a stream of underselected images, each of which cancels its predecessor. Each still photograph is a privileged moment, turned into a slim object that one can keep and look at again. Photographs like the one that made the front page of most newspapers in the world in 1972—a naked South Vietnamese child just sprayed by American napalm, running down a highway toward the camera, her arms open, screaming with pain—probably did more to increase the public revulsion against the war than a hundred hours of televised barbarities.

One would like to imagine that the American public would not have been so unanimous in its acquiescence to the Korean War if it had been confronted with photographic evidence of the devastation of Korea, an ecocide and genocide in some respects even more thorough than those inflicted on Vietnam a decade later. But the supposition is trivial. The public did not see such photographs because there was, ideologically, no space for them. No one brought back photographs of daily life in Pyongyang, to show that the enemy had a human face, as Felix Greene and Marc Riboud brought back photographs of Hanoi. Americans did have access to photographs of the suffering of the Vietnamese (many of which came from military sources and were taken with quite a different use in mind) because journalists felt backed in their efforts to obtain those photographs, the event having been defined by a significant number of people as a savage colonialist war. The Korean War was understood differently—as part of the just struggle of the Free World against the Soviet Union and China—and, given that characterization, photographs of the cruelty of unlimited American firepower would have been irrelevant.

Though an event has come to mean, precisely, something worth photographing, it is still ideology (in the broadest sense) that determines what constitutes an event. There can be no evidence, photographic or otherwise, of an event until the event itself has been named and characterized. And it is never photographic evidence which can construct—more properly, identify—events; the contribution of photography always follows the naming of the event. What determines the possibility of being affected morally by photographs is the existence of a relevant political consciousness. Without a politics, photographs of the slaughter-bench of history will most likely be experienced as, simply, unreal or as a

revulsion /rɪˈvʌlʃn/ *n.* feeling of being deeply shocked and revolted
unanimous /juˈnænɪməs/ *adj.* (of people) all agreeing completely
devastate /ˈdevəsteɪt/ *v.* to destroy completely (a city, area of land etc.) so that nothing useful or valuable remains
trivial /ˈtrɪvɪəl/ *n.* **a.** of little worth or importance; **b.** insignificant

demoralizing emotional blow.

The quality of feeling, including moral outrage, that people can muster in response to photographs of the oppressed, the exploited, the starving, and the massacred also depends on the degree of their familiarity with these images. Don McCullin's photographs of emaciated Biafrans in the early 1970s had less impact for some people than Werner Bischof's photographs of Indian famine victims in the early 1950s because those images had become banal, and the photographs of Tuareg families dying of starvation in the sub-Sahara that appeared in magazines everywhere in 1973 must have seemed to many like an unbearable replay of a now familiar atrocity exhibition.

> **outrage** /ˈaʊtreɪdʒ/ *n.* **a.** a very wrong or cruel act; **b.** anger caused by such an act
> **muster** /ˈmʌstə(r)/ *v.* to gather or collect
> **emaciated** /ɪˈmeɪʃieɪtɪd/ *adj.* extremely thin from hunger or illness
> **banal** /bəˈnɑːl/ *adj.* **a.** uninteresting because very common; **b.** lacking new or original ideas
> **atrocity** /əˈtrɒsəti/ *n.* **a.** (an act of) great evil, especially cruelty; **b.** something that is very unpleasant or ugly
> **proliferation** /prəˌlɪfəˈreɪʃn/ *n.* a rapid increase or spreading
> **instantaneous** /ˌɪnstənˈteɪniəs/ *adj.* happening at once
> **transfix** /trænsˈfɪks/ *v.* **a.** to force a hole through (as if) with a sharp pointed weapon; **b.** to cause to be unable to move or think because of terror, shock etc.
> **anesthetize** /əˈnesθətaɪz/ *v.* to make unable to feel pain by giving an anesthetic, especially in order to perform an operation

Photographs shock insofar as they show something novel. Unfortunately, the ante keeps getting raised—partly through the very proliferation of such images of horror. One's first encounter with the photographic inventory of ultimate horror is a kind of revelation, the prototypically modern revelation: a negative epiphany. For me, it was photographs of Bergen-Belsen and Dachau which I came across by chance in a bookstore in Santa Monica in July 1945. Nothing I have seen—in photographs or in real life—ever cut me as sharply, deeply, instantaneously. Indeed, it seems plausible to me to divide my life into two parts, before I saw those photographs (I was twelve) and after, though it was several years before I understood fully what they were about. What good was served by seeing them? They were only photographs—of an event I had scarcely heard of and could do nothing to affect, of suffering I could hardly imagine and could do nothing to relieve. When I looked at those photographs, something broke. Some limit had been reached, and not only that of horror; I felt irrevocably grieved, wounded, but a part of my feelings started to tighten; something went dead; something is still crying.

To suffer is one thing; another thing is living with the photographed images of suffering, which does not necessarily strengthen conscience and the ability to be compassionate. It can also corrupt them. Once one has seen such images, one has started down the road of seeing more—and more. Images transfix. Images anesthetize. An event known through photographs certainly becomes more real than it would have been if one had never seen the photographs—think of the Vietnam War. (For a counter-example, think of the Gulag Archipelago, of which we have no photographs.) But after repeated exposure to images it also becomes less real.

（To be continued on Text B）

Cultural Notes

1. **Mathew Brady** (1822—1896)—He was one of the most celebrated 19th century American photographers, best known for his portraits of celebrities and his documentation of the American Civil War. He is credited with being the father of photojournalism.

2. **Dorothea Lange** (1895—1965)—She was an influential American documentary photographer and photojournalist, best known for her Depression-era work for the Farm Security Administration (FSA). Lange's photographs humanized the consequences of the Great Depression and influenced the development of documentary photography.

3. **Felix Greene** (1909—1985)—He was a British-American journalist who chronicled several Communist countries in the 1960s. Some of his material has been reproduced for A-Level history, within the Vietnam War topic. Born in England, Greene first visited China for the BBC in 1957. He later produced documentary films, including *One Man's China, Tibet, Cuba va!, Vietnam! And Inside North Viet Nam.* These films have been accused of giving a very rosy and one-sided view of the communist society. Some have argued that Greene purposely hid negative information about the extent of starvation in China.

4. **Marc Riboud**—He was born on 24 June 1923 in Lyon, France, is a French photographer, best known for his extensive reports on the East: *The Three Banners of China, Face of North Vietnam, Vision of China, and In China.*

5. **Donald McCullin**—He was born on 9 October 1935, Finsbury Park, London, England, is an internationally known British photojournalist, particularly recognized for his was photography and images of urban strife. His career, which began in 1959, has specialized in examining the underside of society, and his photographs have depicted the unemployed, downtrodden and the impoverished.

6. **Werner Bischof** (1916—1954)—He was a Swiss photographer and photojournalist.

7. **Bergen-Belsen and Dachau**—It was a Nazi concentration camp in what is

today Lower Saxony in northern Germany, southwest of the town of Bergen near Celle. Originally established as a prisoner of war camp, in 1943, parts of it became a concentration camp.

8. **Gulag Archipelago**—It is a book by Aleksandr Solzhenitsyn about the Soviet forced labor camp system. The three-volume book is a narrative relying on eyewitness testimony and primary research material, as well as the author's own experiences as a prisoner in a gulag labor camp.

Comprehension Exercises

I. Answer the following questions based on the text.

1. What is the function of a lover's photograph in a person's wallet?
2. Which may be more memorable, according to the author, photographs or television?
3. In the author's opinion, what constitutes an event?
4. Does photograph help an event be real or less real?
5. How does photography help build up people's understanding of war?

II. Write T for true and F for false in the brackets before each of the following statements.

1. (　　) Photographs were taken as protection from evil things by some people.
2. (　　) Abstract images are likely to awaken conscience.
3. (　　) Photographs may be less memorable than television.
4. (　　) Korean War was understood by American people as a just struggle against the Soviet Union and China.
5. (　　) Photographs determine what constitutes an event.

III. Select the most appropriate word or phrase and use its proper form to complete each of the following sentences.

abet	ante	anesthetize	compassionate	corrupt
duplicate	erotic	implicit	inventory	intricate
massacre	nostalgic	proliferation	plausible	revulsion
transfix	testify	unequivocal	utilitarian	unanimous

1. Instructors need to get with the program and stop waxing _____ for a past era.
2. Grant wanted to _____ at the corruption trial of his secretary, but was talked out of it by his cabinet.

3. The team set out to _____ the chemistry within interstellar clouds in the laboratory.
4. They had arrived from another valley and were attempting an _____ series of crossings.
5. Under their stagnant respectability are whirlpools of evil and _____ passion.
6. Whether or not a guarantee of quality is a contractual obligation, it's_____ in the project itself.
7. The government needs to make clear that it will no longer _____ or condone this behavior.
8. Carvers and stone sculptors have left _____ objects and artworks of surprising aesthetic quality.
9. What really bothers me about your post is the _____ way you present your conjectures as facts.
10. Her announcement was met with doubt by the scientific community and with _____ by many ethicists.
11. Reviewers were almost _____ in their ridicule of the concert and its composer.
12. His oration upon the _____ of the fifth of March, is distinguished for its patriotic sentiments, as well as elegance of style.
13. The _____ of cross-purposes and strange bedfellows makes for pernicious and complicated arbitrating.
14. The idea of making market forces work to bring down health-care and health-insurance costs is _____.
15. When both parties are restrained and _____ about each other's needs, they are mutually reinforcing.

IV. Paraphrase the underlined words or expressions in each sentence.

1. Like the dead relatives and friends preserved in the family album, whose presence in photographs <u>exorcises</u> some of the anxiety and remorse prompted by their disappearance, so the photographs of neighborhoods now torn down, rural places <u>disfigured</u> and made barren, <u>supply our pocket relation to the past</u>.

2. A photograph that brings news of some unsuspected zone of misery cannot <u>make a dent</u> in public opinion unless there is an appropriate context of feeling and attitude.

3. A photograph is both a pseudo-presence and a token absence.

4. Photographs cannot create a moral position, but they can reinforce one—and can help build a nascent one.

5. Photographs shock insofar as they show something novel. Unfortunately, the ante keeps getting raised—partly through the very proliferation of such images of horror.

V. Discuss with your partner about each of the following statements and write an essay in no less than 200 words about your understanding of one of them.

1. To take a photograph is to participate in another person's (or thing's) mortality, vulnerability, mutability.

2. Thus, almost opposite rules hold true for the use of the photograph to awaken desire and to awaken conscience.

3. Though an event has come to mean, precisely, something worth photographing, it is still ideology (in the broadest sense) that determines what constitutes an event.

VI. List four websites where we can learn more about philosophical discussion on photography and provide a brief introduction to each of them.

1.

2.

3. _____
   _____.

4. _____
   _____.

Text B

On Photography Ⅱ
Susan Sontag

The ethical content of photographs is fragile. With the possible exception of photographs of those horrors, like the Nazi camps, that have gained the status of ethical reference points, most photographs do not keep their emotional charge. A photograph of 1900 that was affecting then because of its subject would, today, be more likely to move us because it is a photograph taken in 1900. The particular qualities and intentions of photographs tend to be swallowed up in the generalized pathos of time past. Aesthetic distance seems built into the very experience of looking at photographs, if not right away, then certainly with the passage of time. Time eventually positions most photographs, even the most amateurish, at the level of art.

The industrialization of photography permitted its rapid absorption into rational—that is, bureaucratic—ways of running society. No longer toy images, photographs became part of the general furniture of the environment—touchstones and confirmations of that reductive approach to reality which is considered realistic. Photographs were enrolled in the service of important institutions of control, notably the family and the police, as symbolic objects and as pieces of information. Thus, in the bureaucratic cataloguing of the world, many important documents are not valid unless they have, affixed to them, a photograph-token of the citizen's face.

The "realistic" view of the world compatible with bureaucracy redefines knowledge—as techniques and information. Photographs are valued because they give information. They tell one what there is; they make an inventory. To spies,

absorption /əbˈsɔːpʃn/ *n.* **a.** the process of absorbing or of being absorbed; **b.** entire occupation of the mind
bureaucratic /ˌbjʊərəˈkrætɪk/ *adj.* using or connected with many complicated rules and ways of doing things
affix /əˈfɪks/ *v.* to attach in any way

meteorologists, coroners, archaeologists, and other information professionals, their value is inestimable. But in the situations in which most people use photographs, their value as information is of the same order as fiction. The information that photographs can give starts to seem very important at that moment in cultural history when everyone is thought to have a right to something called news. Photo-graphs were seen as a way of giving information to people who do not take easily to reading. *The Daily News* still calls itself "New York's Picture Newspaper", its bid for populist identity. At the opposite end of the scale, Le Monde, a newspaper designed for skilled, well-informed readers, runs no photographs at all. The presumption is that, for such readers, a photograph could only illustrate the analysis contained in an article.

A new sense of the notion of information has been constructed around the photographic image. The photograph is a thin slice of space as well as time. In a world ruled by photographic images, all borders ("framing") seem arbitrary. Anything can be separated, can be made discontinuous, from anything else: all that is necessary is to frame the subject differently. (Conversely, anything can be made adjacent to anything else.) Photography reinforces a nominalist view of social reality as consisting of small units of an apparently infinite number—as the number of photographs that could be taken of anything is unlimited. Through photographs, the world becomes a series of unrelated, freestanding particles; and history, past and present, a set of anecdotes and faits divers. The camera makes reality atomic, manage-able, and opaque. It is a view of the world which denies interconnectedness, continuity, but which confers on each moment the character of a mystery. Any photograph has multiple meanings; indeed, to see something in the form of a photograph is to encounter a potential object of fascination. The ultimate wisdom of the photographic image is to say: "There is the surface. Now think—or rather feel, intuit— what is beyond it, what the reality must be like if it looks this way." Photographs, which cannot themselves explain anything, are inexhaustible invitations to deduction, speculation, and fantasy.

meteorology /ˌmiːtɪəˈrɒlədʒɪ/ *n.* the science that deals with the atmosphere and with weather
coroner /ˈkɒrənə(r)/ *n.* a public official whose job is to find out the cause of death when people die in ways that are violent, sudden, etc.
archaeology /ˌɑːkɪˈɒlədʒɪ/ *n.* the scientific study of material remains (as fossil relics, artifacts, and monuments) of past human life and activities
arbitrary /ˈɑːbɪtrərɪ/ *adj.* **a.** depending on individual discretion and not fixed by law; **b.** not restrained or limited in the exercise of power
adjacent /əˈdʒeɪsnt/ *adj.* not distant
anecdote /ˈænɪkdəʊt/ *n.* a short story about an interesting or funny event or occurrence
opaque /əʊˈpeɪk/ *adj.* **a.** not letting light through; **b.** not transparent; **c.** difficult to understand or explain.
intuit /ɪnˈtjuːɪt/ *v.* **a.** to know or understand (something) because of what you feel or sense rather than because of evidence; **b.** to know or understand through intuition

Photography implies that we know about the world if we accept it as the camera records it. But this is the opposite of understanding, which starts from not accepting the world as it looks. All possibility of understanding is rooted in the ability to say no. Strictly speaking, one never understands anything from a photograph. Of course, photographs fill in blanks in our mental pictures of the present and the past: for example, Jacob Riis's images of New York squalor in the 1880s are sharply instructive to those unaware that urban poverty in late-nineteenth-century America was really that Dickensian. Nevertheless, the camera's rendering of reality must always hide more than it discloses. As Brecht points out, a photograph of the Krupp works reveals virtually nothing about that organization. In contrast to the amorous relation, which is based on how something looks, understanding is based on how it functions. And functioning takes place in time, and must be explained in time. Only that which narrates can make us understand.

The limit of photographic knowledge of the world is that, while it can goad conscience, it can, finally, never be ethical or political knowledge. The knowledge gained through still photographs will always be some kind of sentimentalism, whether cynical or humanist. It will be a knowledge at bargain prices—a semblance of knowledge, a semblance of wisdom; as the act of taking pictures is a semblance of appropriation, a semblance of rape. The very muteness of what is, hypothetically, comprehensible in photographs is what constitutes their attraction and provocativeness. The omnipresence of photographs has an incalculable effect on our ethical sensibility. By furnishing this already crowded world with a duplicate one of images, photography makes us feel that the world is more available than it really is.

Needing to have reality confirmed and experience enhanced by photographs is an aesthetic consumerism to which everyone is now addicted. Industrial societies turn their citizens into image-junkies; it is the most irresistible form of mental pollution. Poignant longings for beauty, for an end to probing below the surface, for a redemption and celebration of the body of the world—all these elements of erotic feeling are affirmed in the pleasure we take in photographs. But other, less liberating feelings are expressed as well. It would not be

squalor /ˈskwɒlə(r)/ *n.* very bad and dirty conditions
amorous /ˈæmərəs/ *adj.* having or showing strong feelings of sexual attraction or love
goad /ɡəʊd/ *n.* **a.** a pointed rod used to make an animal move forward; **b.** someone or something that urges or forces someone to do something
semblance /ˈsembləns/ *n.* the state of being somewhat like something but not truly or fully the same thing
provocative /prəˈvɒkətɪv/ *adj.* **a.** causing discussion, thought, argument, ect.; **b.** causing sexual feelings or excitement.
poignant /ˈpɔɪnjənt/ *adj.* causing a strong feeling of sadness
erotic /ɪˈrɒtɪk/ *adj.* **a.** relating to sex; **b.** causing sexual feelings

compulsion /kəmˈpʌlʃn/ n. a. a very strong desire to do something; b. the act of using force or pressure to make someone do something; c. the state of being forced to do something

wrong to speak of people having a compulsion to photograph: to turn experience itself into a way of seeing. Ultimately, having an experience becomes identical with taking a photograph of it, and participating in a public event comes more and more to be equivalent to looking at it in photographed form. That most logical of nineteenth-century aesthetes, Mallarmé, said that everything in the world exists in order to end in a book. Today everything exists to end in a photograph.

Cultural Notes

1. **Le Monde**—It is a French daily evening newspaper founded by Hubert Beuve-Mery and continuously published in Paris since its first edition on 19 December 1944. It is one of two French newspapers of record along with *Le Figaro*, and the main publication of La Vie-Le Monde Group. It reports an average circulation of 323,039 copies per issue in 2009, about 40,000 of which are sold abroad. It has been available on the Internet since 19 December 1995, and is often the only French newspaper easily obtainable in non-French-speaking countries. It should not be confused with the monthly publication *Le Monde Diplomatique*, of which *Le Monde* has 51% ownership, but which is editorially independent.

2. **Jacob August Riis** (1849—1914)—He was a Danish American social reformer, "muckraking" journalist and social documentary photographer. He is known for using his photographic and journalistic talents to help the impoverished in New York City; those impoverished New Yorkers were the subject of most of his prolific writings and photography. He endorsed the implementation of "model tenements" in New York with the help of humanitarian Lawrence Veiller. Additionally, as one of the most famous proponents of the newly practicable casual photography, he is considered one of the fathers of photography due to his very early adoption of flash in photography.

Comprehension Exercises

I. Answer the following questions based on the text.

1. Why is the ethical content of photographs fragile?
2. What is the bureaucratic use of photography?

3. Which one helps understanding? Photographs or narrates?
4. What is the limit of photographic knowledge of the world?
5. What kind of desire is satisfied in photography?

II. Write T for true and F for false in the brackets before each of the following statements.

1. (   ) Amateurish photographs could also become art with the passage of time.
2. (   ) Knowledge is information.
3. (   ) To most common people, photographs are not valued for their information.
4. (   ) Photographs can never explain anything.
5. (   ) Photography makes people feel that the world is less available than it really is.

III. Select the most appropriate word or phrase and use its proper form to complete each of the following sentences.

adjacent	amateurish	atomic	arbitrary	amorous
compatible	compulsion	confer	cynical	erotic
ethical	inexhaustible	instructive	inestimable	nominalist
populist	provocative	poignant	rational	semblance

1. In fact, they were so enamored of their _____ designs that they valued them as highly as origami made by experts.
2. Well thank goodness the fossil fuel industry is based on sound economics and _____ politics.
3. Using plastic rather than silicon is also more _____ with manufacturing processes that use other plastics.
4. Two years' experience convinces the writer of the _____ value to consumptives of the open-air treatment.
5. Special attention was paid to the _____ metaphors and debates over silver and gold.
6. This _____ and nonsensical technique is characteristic of the entire book.
7. We live in two _____ suburbs, close enough to cover each other for child minding needs but we do not wish to be closer.
8. It's a terrific show for the same reason, rewarding our attention with a blizzard of _____ ideas.
9. Much of his early work centered on _____ energy, and he opposed both nuclear and coal-fired plants.
10. All college teachers require a dedicated corner where they can _____ with their students.

11. Eternal and _____ gravity power is the future path for us in my opinion.
12. It is _____ to see how quickly evolutionists were to jump on a fossil finding that they believe proves their theory.
13. Music does a pretty good job of expressing affection, _____ intention, and other feelings that can be screwed up by mere words.
14. He seems to mean that he is in favor of ignoring general moral and _____ principles because they are meaningless.
15. The quote is commonly recited for its wry pragmatism and seeming _____ irreverence.

IV. Paraphrase the underlined words or expressions in each sentence.

1. It is a view of the world which <u>denies interconnectedness</u>, continuity, but which <u>confers</u> on each moment the character of a mystery.

2. Nevertheless, the camera's <u>rendering of reality</u> must always hide more than it <u>discloses</u>.

3. Only that which <u>narrates</u> can make us understand.

4. The <u>omnipresence of photographs</u> has an <u>incalculable effect</u> on our ethical sensibility.

5. <u>Poignant longings for beauty</u>, for an end to probing below the surface, for a redemption and celebration of the body of the world—all these elements of erotic feeling are affirmed in the pleasure we take in photographs.

V. Discuss with your partner about each of the following statements and write an essay in no less than 200 words about your understanding of one of them.

1. Time eventually positions most photographs, even the most amateurish, at the level of art.

2. Photographs were seen as a way of giving information to people who do not take easily to reading.

3. Strictly speaking, one never understands anything from a photograph.

VI. List four websites where we can learn more about journalistic photography and provide a brief introduction to each of them.

1.

2.

3.

4.

Twenty Minutes' Reading

You are required to read the following sections within 20 minutes.

SECTION A

You stare at waterfall for a minute or two, and then shift your gaze to its surroundings. What you now see appears to drift upward.

These optical illusions occur because the brain is constantly matching its model of reality to signals from the body's sensors and interpreting what must be happening—that your brain must have moved, not the other; that downward motions is now normal, so a change from it must now be perceived as upward motion.

The sensors that make this magic are of two kinds. Each eye contains about 120 million rods, which provide somewhat blurry black and white vision. These are the windows of night vision; once adapted to the dark, they can detect a candle burning ten miles away.

Color vision in each eye comes from six to seven million structures called cones. Under ideal conditions, every cone can "see" the entire rainbow spectrum of visible colors, but one type of cone is most sensitive to red, another to green, a third to blue.

Rods and cones send their messages pulsing an average 20 to 25 times per second along the optic nerve. We see an image for a fraction of a second longer than it actually appears. In movies, reels of still photographs are projected onto screens at 24 frames per second, tricking our eyes into seeing a continuous moving picture.

Like apparent motion, color vision is also subject to unusual effects. When day gives way to night, twilight brings what the poet T.S. Eliot called "the violet hour". A light levels fall, the rods become progressively less responsive. Rods are most sensitive to the shorter wavelengths of blue and green, and they impart a strange vividness to the garden's blue flowers.

However, look at a white shirt during the reddish light of sunset, and you'll still see it in its "true" color—white, not red. Our eyes are constantly comparing an object against its surroundings. They therefore observe the effect of a shift in the color of illuminating on both, and adjust accordingly.

The eyes can distinguish several million graduations of light and shade of color. Each waking second they flash tens of millions of pieces of information to the brain, which weaves them incessantly into a picture of the world around us.

Yet all this is done at the back of each eye by a fabric of sensors, called the retina, about as wide and as thick as a postage stamp. As the Renaissance inventor and artist Leonardo da Vinci wrote in wonder, "Who would believe that so small a space could contain the images of all the universe?"

1. Visual illusions often take place when the image of reality is _____.
    A. matched to six to seven million structures called cones
    B. confused in the body's sensors of both rods and cones
    C. interpreted in the brain as what must be the case
    D. signaled by about 120 million rods in the eye
2. The visual sensor that is capable of distinguishing shades of color is called _____.
    A. cones
    B. color vision
    C. rod
    D. spectrum
3. The retina send pulses to the brain _____.
    A. in short wavelengths

B. as color pictures
  C. by a ganglion cell
  D. along the optic nerve
4. Twenty-four still photographs are made into a continuous moving picture just because _____.
  A. the image we see usually stays longer than it actually appears
  B. we see an object in comparison with its surroundings
  C. the eyes catch million pieces of information continuously
  D. rods and cones send messages 20 to 25 times a second
5. The author's purpose in writing the passage lies in _____.
  A. showing that we sometimes are deceived by our own eyes
  B. informing us about the different functions of the eye organs
  C. regretting that we are too slow in the study of eyes
  D. marveling at the great work done by the retina

SECTION B

Art is considered by many people to be little more than a decorative means of giving pleasure. This is not always the case, however; at times, art may be seen to have a purely functional side as well. Such could be said of the sandpaintings of the Navaho Indians of the American Southwest; these have a medicinal as well as an artistic purpose.

According to Navaho traditions, one who suffers from either a mental or a physical illness has in some way disturbed or come in contact with the supernatural—perhaps a certain animal, a ghost, or the dead. To counteract this evil contact, the ill person or one of his relatives will employ a medicine man called a "singer" to perform a healing ceremony which will attract a powerful supernatural being.

During the ceremony, which may last from 2 to 9 days, the "singer" will produce a sandpainting on the floor of the Navaho hogan. On the last day of the ceremony, the patient will sit on this sandpainting and the "singer" will rub the ailing parts of the patient's body with sand from a specific figure in the sandpainting. In this way the patient absorbs the power of that particular supernatural being and becomes strong like it. After the ceremony, the sandpainting is then destroyed and disposed of so its power will not harm anyone.

The art of sandpainting is handed down from old "singer" to their students. The material used are easily found in the areas the Navaho inhabit; brown, red, yellow, and white sandstone, which is pulverized by being crushed between 2 stones much as corns is ground into flour. The "singer" holds a small amount of this sand in his hand and lets it flow between his thumb and fore-finger onto a clean, flat surface on the floor. With a steady hand and great patience, he is thus able to create designs of stylized people, snakes and other creatures that have power in the Navaho belief system. The traditional Navaho does not allow reproduction of sandpaintings, since he believes the supernatural powers that taught him the craft have forbidden this; however, such reproductions can in fact be purchased today in tourist shops in Arizona and New Mexico. These are done by either Navaho Indians or by other people who wish to preserve this craft.

6. The purpose of the passage is to _____.
   A. discuss the medical uses of sandpaintings in medieval Europe
   B. study the ways Navaho Indians handed down their painting art
   C. consider how Navaho "singer" treat their ailments with sandpaintings
   D. tell how Navaho Indians apply sandpainting for medical purposes

7. The purpose of a healing ceremony lies in _____.
   A. pleasing the ghosts
   B. attracting supernatural powers
   C. attracting the ghosts
   D. creating a sandpainting

8. The "singer" rubs sand on the patient because _____.
   A. the patient receives strength from the sand
   B. it has pharmaceutical value
   C. it decorates the patient
   D. none of the above

9. What is used to produce a sandpainting?
   A. Paint.
   B. Beach sand.
   C. Crushed sandstone.
   D. Flour.

10. Which of the following titles will be best suit the passage?
    A. A New Direction for Medical Research
    B. The Navaho Indians' Sandpainting
    C. The Process of Sandpainting Creation
    D. The Navaho Indians' Medical History

Unit Six

Text A

The Bridges of Madison County
Robert James Waller

The Beginning

《廊桥遗梦》是一个著名的爱情故事,古老的廊桥,孤独的远游者,两颗中年人的心渐渐贴近,撞出火花,寻觅已久的灵魂找到了永恒的归宿。这段不了情缘,应该有一个美丽的缘起。让我们顺着作者的笔触,缓缓回溯……

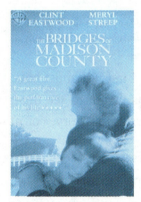

There are songs that come free from the blue-eyed grass, from the dust of a thousand country roads. This is one of them. In late afternoon, in the autumn of 1989, I'm at my desk, looking at a blinking cursor on the computer screen before me, and the telephone rings.

On the other end of the wire is a former Iowan named Michael Johnson. He lives in Florida now. A friend from Iowa has sent him one of my books. Michael Johnson has read it; his sister, Carolyn, has read it; and they have a story in which they think I might be interested. He is circumspect, refusing to say anything about the story, except that he and Carolyn are willing to travel to Iowa to talk with me about it.

That they are prepared to make such an effort intrigues me, in spite of my skepticism a bout such offers. So I agree to meet with them in Des Moines the following week. At a Holiday Inn near the airport, the introductions are made, awkwardness gradually declines, and the two of them sit across from me, evening coming down outside, light snow falling.

blue-eyed grass a substantial group of flowering plants of the iris family, all native to the America. The flowers are relatively simple and often grow in clusters. In addition to blue, flower colors also include white, yellow, purple, etc.
cursor /ˈkɜːsə/ *n.* a moving marker on a computer screen that marks the point at which keyed characters will appear or be deleted
circumspect /ˈsɜːkəmspekt/ *adj.* cautious and careful not to take risks
intrigue /ɪnˈtriːg/ *v.* **a.** to make interested or curious; **b.** to plot secretly or dishonestly
skepticism /ˈskeptɪsɪzəm/ *n.* an attitude of doubting that claims or statements are true or that sth will happen

They extract a promise: If I decide not to write the story, I must agree never to disclose what transpired in Madison County, Iowa, in 1965 or other related events that followed over the next twenty-four years. All right, that's reasonable. After all, it's their story, not mine.

So I listen. I listen hard, and I ask hard questions. And they talk. On and on they talk. Carolyn cries openly at times, Michael struggles not to. They show me documents and magazine clippings and a set of journals written by their mother, Francesca.

> **extract** /ɪksˈtrækt/ **a.** *v.* to pull out or uproot by force; **b.** to remove from a container; **c.** to derive (pleasure, information, etc.) from some source; **d.** to obtain information, money, etc., often by taking it from sb who is unwilling to give it
> **transpire** /trænsˈpaɪə/ *v.* **a.** to happen; **b.** give off (water) through the skin; **c.** come to light, become known
> **clipping** /ˈklɪpɪŋ/ *n.* **a.** a piece that has been cut off sth; **b.** an article cut from a newspaper
> **tangentially** /tænˈdʒenʃəli/ *adj.* (*formal*) having only a slight or indirect connection with sth
> **tawdry** /ˈtɔːdri/ *adj.* **a.** intended to be bright and attractive but cheap and of low quality; **b.** involving low moral standards, extremely unpleasant or offensive
> **gossip** /ˈgɒsɪp/ *n.* **a.** idle talk, usu. about other people's private lives, esp. of a disapproving or malicious nature; **b.** an informal conversation, esp. about other people's private lives; **c.** a person who habitually talks about other people, usually maliciously
> **debasement** /dɪˈbeɪsmənt/ *n.* reduce of the quality or value of sth
> **commitment** /kəˈmɪtmənt/ *n.* **a.** an obligation, responsibility, or promise that restricts freedom of action; **b.** dedication to a cause or principle
> **shatter** /ˈʃætə/ *v.* **a.** to break suddenly into many small pieces; **b.** to damage badly or destroy; **c.** to upset (someone) greatly

Room service comes and goes. Extra coffee is ordered. As they talk, I begin to see the images. First you must have the images, then come the words. And I begin to hear the words, begin to see them on pages of writing. Sometime just after midnight, I agree to write the story—or at least attempt it.

Their decision to make this information public was a difficult one for them. The circumstances are delicate, involving their mother and, more tangentially, their father. Michael and Carolyn recognized that coming forth with the story might result in tawdry gossip and unkind debasement of whatever memories people have of Richard and Francesca Johnson.

Yet in a world where personal commitment in all of its forms seems to be shattering and love has become a matter of convenience, they both felt this remarkable tale was worth the telling. I believed then, and I believe even more strongly now, they were correct in their assessment.

In the course of my research and writing, I asked to meet with Michael and Carolyn three more times. On each occasion, and without complaint, they traveled to Iowa. Such was their eagerness to make sure the story was told accurately. Sometimes we merely talked; sometimes we slowly drove the roads of Madison

County while they pointed out places having a significant role in the story.

In addition to the help provided by Michael anal Carolyn, the story as I tell it here is based on information contained in the journals of Francesca Johnson; research conducted in the northwestern United States, particularly Seattle and Bellingham, Washington; research carried out quietly in Madison County, Iowa; information gleaned from the photographic essays of Robert Kincaid; assistance provided by magazine editors; detail supplied by manufacturers of photographic films and equipment; and long discussions with several wonderful elderly people in the county home at Barnesville, Ohio, who remembered Kincaid from his boyhood days.

> **essence** /ˈesəns/ *n.* **a.** the most important and distinctive feature of sth, which determines its identity; **b.** a liquid taken from a plant, etc. that contains its smell and taste in a very strong form
> **elusive** /ɪˈluːsɪv/ *adj.* difficult to find, define, or achieve
> **ethereal** /ɪˈθɪəriəl/ *adj.* **a.** extremely delicate or refined; **b.** seeming to belong to another, more spiritual, world
> **spectral** /ˈspektrəl/ *adj.* **a.** connected with a spectrum; **b.** (liter) like a ghost, connected with a ghost
> **consummate** /ˈkɒnsəmɪt/ *adj.* (*formal*) extremely skilled
> **obsolete** /ˈɒbsəliːt/ *adj.* no longer used, out of date
> **wail** /weɪl/ *n.* a prolonged high-pitched cry of pain or sorrow
> **haunt** /hɔːnt/ *v.* **a.** to visit (a person or place) in the form of a ghost; **b.** to remain in the memory or thoughts of; **c.** to visit (a place) frequently

In spite of the investigative effort, gaps remain. I have added a little of my own imagination in those instances, but only when I could make reasoned judgments flowing from the intimate familiarity with Francesca Johnson and Robert Kincaid I gained through my research. I am confident that I have come very close to what actually happened.

One major gap involves the exact details of a trip made across the northern United States by Kincaid. We knew he made this journey, based on a number of photographs that subsequently were published, a brief mention of it by Francesca Johnson in her journals, and handwritten notes he left with a magazine editor. Using these sources as my guide, I retraced what I believe was the path he took from Bellingham to Madison County in August of 1965. Driving toward Madison County at the end of my travels, I felt I had, in many ways, become Robert Kincaid.

Still, attempting to capture the essence of Kincaid was the most challenging part of my research and writing. He is an elusive figure. At times he seems rather ordinary. At other times ethereal, perhaps even spectral. In his work he was a consummate professional. Yet he saw himself as a peculiar kind of male animal becoming obsolete in a world given over to increasing amounts of organization. He once talked about the "merciless wail" of time in his head, and Francesca Johnson characterized him as living "in strange, haunted places, far back along the stems of

Darwin's logic".

Two other intriguing questions are still unanswered. First, we have been unable to determine what became of Kincaid's photographic files. Given the nature of his work, there must have been thousands, probably hundreds of thousands, of photographs. These never have been recovered. Our best guess—and this would be consistent with the way he saw himself and his place in the world—is that he destroyed them prior to his death.

The second question deals with his life from 1975 to 1982. Very little information is available. We know he earned a sparse living as a portrait photographer in Seattle for several years and continued to photograph the Puget Sound area. Other than that, we have nothing. One interesting note is that all letters mailed to him by the Social Security Administration and Veterans Administration were marked "Return to Sender" in his handwriting and s e n t back.

Preparing and writing this book has altered my world view, transformed the way I think, and, most of all, reduced my level of cynicism about what is possible in the arena of human relationships. Coming to know Francesca Johnson and Robert Kincaid as I have through my research, I find the boundaries of such relationships can be extended farther than I previously thought. Perhaps you will have the same experience in reading this story.

That will not be easy. In an increasingly callous world, we all exist with our own carapaces of scabbed-over sensibilities. Where great passion leaves off and mawkishness begins, I'm not sure. But our tendency to scoff at the possibility of the former and to label genuine and profound feelings as maudlin makes it difficult to enter the realm of gentleness required to understand the story of Francesca Johnson and Robert Kincaid. I know I had to overcome that tendency initially

---

prior to before
sparse /spɑːs/ *adj.* small in amount and spread out widely
cynicism /ˈsɪnɪsɪzəm/ *n.* the beliefs or philosophy of the ancient Greek Cynics. cf. **cynic a.** a person who believes that people only do things to help themselves, rather than for good or sincere reasons **b.** a person who does not believe that sth good will happen or that sth is important
arena /əˈriːnə/ *n.* **a.** a seated enclosure where sports events take place; **b.** a sphere of intense activity; **c.** the area of an ancient Roman amphitheatre where gladiators fought
callous /ˈkæləs/ *adj.* showing no concern for other people's feelings
carapace /ˈkærəpeɪs/ *n.* the hard shell on the back of some animals such as crabs and tortoises, that protects them
scabbed-over a coined word by the writer, which means "having scabs all over sth" in the context. cf. **scab** crust over healing wound
mawkish /ˈmɔːkɪʃ/ *adj.* foolishly or embarrassingly sentimental
scoff /skɒf/ v. **a.** (at) to speak in a scornful and mocking way about (sth); **b.** (*infml*) to eat (food) fast and greedily
maudlin /ˈmɔːdlɪn/ overly or tearfully sentimental, esp. because affected by alcohol

before I could begin writing.

If, however, you approach what follows with a willing suspension of disbelief, as Coleridge put it, I am confident you will experience what I have experienced. In the indifferent spaces of your heart, you may even find, as Francesca Johnson did, room to dance again.

Summer 1991

Cultural Notes

1. **The *Bridges of Madison County*** — A best-selling novel by Robert James Waller. The novel is presented as a novelization of a true story, but it is in fact completely fiction. The famous compelling story tells about an Italian woman, Francesca, who lived on a farm in Iowa with her husband and children, once met a National Geographic photographer, Robert, and they fell in love with each other and found the promise of perfect personal happiness. They understood, with sadness, that the most important things in life were not always about making yourself happy, though. The most moving part of the story for the reader may be to see how they struggled to decide not to spend the rest of their lives together in the end. The novel was successfully made into a film of the same name in 1995, directed by Clint Eastwood. The film stars are Eastwood and Meryl Streep.

2. **Robert James Waller** (1939—   ) — American author, photographer and musician. He was born in Rockford, Iowa and currently resides in Texas. Waller received his Ph D in business in 1968 and later taught at the University of Northern Iowa. Several of his books have been on the *New York Times* bestseller list including 1992's *The Bridges of Madison County* which was the top best-seller in 1993. Both that novel and his 1995 novel, *Puerto Vallarta Squeeze*, have been made into motion pictures.

3. **Madison County** — A county in the state of Iowa, which is located in the Midwest of the U S Madison County is famous for being the birthplace of John Wayne, a former American film star, and for a number of covered bridges (or "roofed bridge", a bridge with a roof and walls that protect it against the weather).

4. **Coleridge** (1772—1834) — Samuel Taylor Coleridge was an English poet, critic, and philosopher, who was one of the founders of the Romantic Movement in England and one of the Lake Poets. His best-known poems are perhaps *The Rime of the Ancient Mariner and Kubla Khan*. His major prose

work is *Biographia Literaria*.

5. **Puget Sound**—A deep inlet of the Pacific Ocean, in northwestern Washington.

Comprehension Exercises

I. Answer the following questions based on the text.

1. Where did the author get the story?
2. How did Michael and Carolyn know their mother's story?
3. Who was Robert Kincaid and what did he do for a living?
4. What else did the author exert to accomplish the story except his investigative effort?
5. According to the author, what made Francesca's story extraordinary and impressive?

II. Write T for true and F for false in the brackets before each of the following statements.

1. (   ) Both Michael and Carolyn cried as they told their mother's story to the writer.
2. (   ) The author didn't decide whether or not to write Francesca's story until the next day.
3. (   ) Michael and Carolyn had to travel to Iowa from northern America to meet the writer.
4. (   ) Michael and Carolyn were worried that their mother's story was not remarkable, which might result in people's bad comments on their parents.
5. (   ) The author is under the impression that modern people don't take personal responsibility seriously.
6. (   ) The author met Michael and Carolyn five times altogether before completing the novel.
7. (   ) Seattle lies in the southwestern United States.
8. (   ) Robert Kincaid grew up in Ohio.
9. (   ) Penetrating Francesca was the most difficult part for the author to write.
10. (   ) Robert Kincaid lived in Bellingham ten years after he left Madison County.

III. **Select the most appropriate word or phrase and use its proper form to complete each of the following sentences.**

arena	circumspect	consummate	commitment	callous
disclose	debasement	essence	elusive	ethereal
extract	glean	intrigue	obsolete	spectral
scoff	skepticism	transpire	tangentially	tawdry

1. We must not expect a lively young man to be always so guarded and _____.
2. The discovery is sure to _____ not only researchers, but poachers.
3. But researchers who study the rare dolphin have expressed deep _____ that such a dramatic turnaround could have occurred.
4. They used torture to _____ information about their families.
5. This law would allow journalists to refuse to _____ their confidential sources without facing the threat of fines or jail time.
6. It surely knows that all eyes are upon it this year to see what might _____.
7. The circumstances are delicate, involving their mother and, more _____, their father.
8. She slopped about her room, unkempt and disheveled, in her _____ dressing-gown.
9. It is pretty obvious that the _____ of the human mind caused by a constant flow of fraudulent advertising is no trivial thing. There is more than one way to conquer a country.
10. However, an intelligent reader will _____ the important information from this possibly-biased article.
11. We try to make a book accessible by capturing the _____ of the romance, rather than faithfully depicting the book's contents.
12. The formula for creative thinking is pretty _____, but scientists have a few evidence-based clues.
13. The setting sun sheds an _____ light on the scene of temples, pavilions, and terraces.
14. The camera surveys the ice surface, searching for any clumps of matter and reading their _____ signatures.
15. Hammerhead sharks are _____ predators that use their oddly shaped heads to improve their ability to find prey.

IV. **Paraphrase the underlined words or expressions in each sentence.**

1. First you must <u>have the images</u>, then <u>come the words</u>.

_____

_____

2. Yet in a world where <u>personal commitment</u> in all of its forms seems to be shattering and love has become <u>a matter of convenience</u>, they both felt this remarkable tale was worth the telling.

3. In spite of the <u>investigative effort</u>, <u>gaps remain</u>.

4. Our <u>best guess</u>—and this would <u>be consistent with</u> the way he saw himself and his place in the world—is that he destroyed them prior to his death.

5. In an increasingly <u>callous</u> world, we all exist <u>with our own carapaces of scabbed-over sensibilities</u>.

V. Discuss with your partner about each of the following statements and write an essay in no less than 200 words about your understanding of one of them.

1. The most important things in life are not always about making yourself happy.

2. Chinese and American people have shared plenty of similar family values, but differences still exist in various forms.

3. Only do you understand what marriage entails and clarify your expectations, you can finally enjoy a happy life after marriage.

VI. List four websites where we can learn more about the novel and the movie and provide a brief introduction to each of them.

1.

2. _____
_____.
3. _____
_____.
4. _____
_____.

Text B

Letter in the Wallet
Anonymous

《钱包里的信》爱情总是能够打动我们,这是一种永恒的,使人心灵净化的感情。但是苦苦期盼的爱情较之那些从最初就很顺利的爱情更令我们感动,因为这种等待里有一种切实的纯粹。

It was a freezing day, a few years ago, when I stumbled on a wallet in the street. There was no identification inside. Just three dollars, and a crumpled letter that looked as if it had been carried around for years. The only thing legible on the torn envelope was the return address. I opened the letter and saw that it had been written in 1924-almost 60 years ago. I read it carefully, hoping to find some clue to the identity of the wallet's owner.

It was a "Dear John" letter. The writer, in a delicate script, told the recipient, whose name was Michael, that her mother forbade her to see him again. Nevertheless, she would always love him. It was signed Hannah.

It was a beautiful letter. But there was no way, beyond the name Michael, to identify the owner. Perhaps if I called information the operator could find the phone number for the address shown on the envelope.

stumble /ˈstʌmbəl/ *v.* **a.** to walk unsteadily; **b.** to miss a step and fall or nearly fall; **c.** to encounter by chance; **d.** to make a mistake

crumple /ˈkrʌmpəl/ *v.* **a.** to crease and wrinkle; **b.** to collapse; **c.** look upset or disappointed

legible /ˈledʒəbəl/ *adj.* (of written or printed words) clear enough to read

script /skrɪpt/ *n.* **a.** a written text of a play, film/movie, broadcast, talk, etc; **b.** writing done by hand; **c.** a set of letters in which a language is written; **d.** series of commands in computer program

recipient /rɪˈsɪpiənt/ *n.* (*formal*) a person who receives sth

"Operator, this is an unusual request. I'm trying to find the owner of a wallet I found. Is there any way you could tell me the phone number for an address that was on a letter in the wallet?"

> **party** /ˈpɑːti/ *n.* **a.** a person or group participating in an action or affair; **b.** a group of people sharing a common political aim; **c.** a social gathering for pleasure; **d.** a particular individual
>
> **take a chance** take a risk in the hope of a favorable outcome

The operator gave me her supervisor, who said there was a phone listed at the address, but that she could not give me the number. However, she would call and explain the situation. Then, if the party wanted to talk, she would connect me. I waited a minute and she came back on the line. "I have a woman who will speak with you."

I asked the woman if she knew a Hannah.

"Oh, of course! We bought this house from Hannah's family thirty years ago." "Would you know where they could be located now?" I asked.

"Hannah had to place her mother in a nursing home years ago. Maybe the home could help you track down the daughter."

The woman gave me the name of the nursing home. I called and found out that Hannah's mother had died. The woman I spoke with gave me an address where she thought Hannah could be reached.

I phoned. The woman who answered explained that Hannah herself was now living in a nursing home. She gave me the number. I called and was told, "Yes, Hannah is with us."

I asked if I could stop by to see her. It was almost 10 p.m. The director said Hannah might be asleep. "But if you want to take a chance, maybe she's in the day room watching television."

The director and a guard greeted me at the door of the nursing home. We went up to the third floor and saw the nurse, who told us that Hannah was indeed watching TV. We entered the day room.

Hannah was a sweet, silver-haired old-timer with a warm smile and friendly eyes. I told her about finding the wallet and showed her the letter. The second she saw it, she took a deep breath. "Young man," she said, "This letter was the last contact I had with Michael." She looked away for a moment, then said pensively, "I loved him very much. But I was only sixteen and my mother felt I was too young. He was so handsome. You know, like Sean Connery, the actor."

We both laughed. The director then left us alone. "Yes, Michael Goldstein was his name. If you find him, tell him I still think of him often. I never did marry," she said, smiling through tears that welled up in her eyes. "I guess no one ever matched up to Michael…"

I thanked Hannah, said good-bye and took the elevator to the first floor. As I stood at the door, the guard asked, "Was the old lady able to help you?"

I told him she had given me a lead. At least I have a last name. But I probably won't pursue it further for a while. I explained that I had spent almost the whole day trying to find the wallet's owner.

While we talked, I pulled out the brown-leather case with its red-lanyard lacing and showed it to the guard. He looked at it closely and said, "Hey, I'd know that anywhere. That's Mr. Goldstein's. He's always losing it. I found it in the hall at least three times."

"Who's Mr. Goldstein?" I asked. "He's one of the old-timers on the eighth floor. That's Mike Goldstein's wallet, for sure. He goes out for a walk quite often."

I thanked the guard and ran back to the director's office to tell him what the guard had said. He accompanied me to the eighth floor. I prayed that Mr. Goldstein would be up.

"I think he's still in the day room," the nurse said. "He likes to read at night…a darling old man."

---

old-timer a. someone who has been or worked in a place for a long time; **b.** an old or elderly person

pensive /ˈpensɪv/ *adj.* thinking deeply about sth, esp. in a sad or serious manner

well up a. (of a liquid) to rise to the surface of sth and start to flow; **b.** (*lit.*) (of an emotion) to become stronger

match up to (usu. used in negative sentences) to be as good, interesting, successful as sb/sth

give (sb) a lead a. encourage others by doing first; **b.** provide a hint towards the solution of a problem

lanyard /ˈlænjəd/ *n.* **a.** a cord worn round the neck to hold a whistle or knife; **b.** a short rope or cord used to hold or fasten sth on a ship

lacing /ˈleɪsɪŋ/ *n.* **a.** lace that fastens; **b.** a small amount of alcohol or a drug added to a drink or to food

accompany /əˈkʌmpəni/ *v.* **a.** to travel or go somewhere with someone; **b.** to happen or appear with sth else; **c.** to play a musical instrument, esp. a piano, while someone else sings or plays the main tune

We went to the only room that had lights on, and there was a man reading a book. The director asked him if he had lost his wallet. Michael Goldstein looked up, felt his back pocket and then said, "Goodness, it is missing."

elevator /ˈelɪveɪtə/ n. a machine that carries people or goods up and down to different levels in a building or a mine. cf. escalator (moving stairs that carry people between different floors of a large building)

"This kind gentleman found a wallet. Could it be yours?"

The second he saw it, he smiled with relief. "Yes," he said, "that's it. Must have dropped it this afternoon. I want to give you a reward."

"Oh, no, thank you," I said. "But I have to tell you something. I read the letter in the hope of finding out who owned the wallet."

The smile on his face disappeared. "You read that letter?"

"Not only did I read it, I think I know where Hannah is."

He grew pale. "Hannah? You know where she is? How is she? Is she still as pretty as she was?"

I hesitated.

"Please tell me!" Michael urged.

"She's fine, and just as pretty as when you knew her."

"Could you tell me where she is? I want to call her tomorrow."

He grabbed my hand and said, "You know something? When that letter came, my life ended. I never married. I guess I've always loved her."

"Michael," I said. "Come with me." The three of us took the elevator to the third floor. We walked toward the day room where Hannah was sitting, still watching TV. The director went over to her.

"Hannah," he said softly. "Do you know this man?" Michael and I stood waiting in the doorway.

She adjusted her glasses, looked for a moment, but didn't say a word.

"Hannah, it's Michael. Michael Goldstein. Do you remember?"

"Michael? Michael? It's you!"

He walked slowly to her side. She stood and they embraced. Then the two of them sat on a couch, held hands and started to talk. The director and I walked out, both of us crying.

> **embrace** /ɪmˈbreɪs/ v. **a.** to clasp (someone) with one's arms as an expression of affection or a greeting; **b.** to accept eagerly; **c.** to include or be made up of
>
> **break away a.** leave or get away; **b.** to escape suddenly from sb who is keeping you prisoner; **c.** to change or depart from established customs or procedures
>
> **tie the knot** (*infml*) to get married
>
> **beige** /beɪʒ/ *adj.* light yellowish-brown in color

"See how the good Lord works," I said philosophically. "If it's meant to be, it will be." Three weeks later, I got a call from the director who asked. "Can you break away on Sunday to attend a wedding?" He didn't wait for an answer. "Yup (= yes), Michael and Hannah are going to tie the knot!"

It was a lovely wedding, with all the people at the nursing home joining in the celebration. Hannah wore a beige dress and looked beautiful. Michael wore a dark blue suit and stood tall. The home gave them their own room, and if you ever wanted to see a 76- year-old bride and a 78-year old groom acting like two teen-agers, you had to see this couple.

A perfect ending for a love affair that had lasted nearly 60 years.

Cultural Notes

1. **"Dear John" letter**—The term "Dear John letter" refers to a letter written by a woman to her husband or boyfriend to inform him their relationship is over, usually because she has found another man. While the exact origins of the phrase are unknown, it is commonly believed to have been coined by Americans during World War II. Large numbers of American troops were stationed overseas for many months or years, and as time passed many of their wives or girlfriends decided to begin a relationship with a new man rather than wait for their old one to return. As letters to servicemen from wives or girlfriends back home would typically contain affectionate language, a serviceman receiving a note beginning with a curt "Dear John" (as opposed to the expected "Dear Johnny", "My dearest John", or simply "Darling", for example) would instantly be aware of the letter's purpose. In

more recent times, women have come to be subjected to such impersonal break-up letters as well. These are referred to as "Dear Jane" letters.

2. **Nursing home**—Skilled nursing facility (SNF), or skilled nursing unit (SNU), also known as a rest home. It's a place of residence for people who require constant nursing care and have significant deficiencies with activities of daily living. Residents include the elderly and younger adults with physical disabilities. Adults 18 or older can stay in a skilled nursing facility to receive physical, occupational, and other rehabilitative therapies following an accident or illness. In the United States, nursing homes are required to have a licensed nurse on duty 24 hours a day, and during at least one shift each day, one of those nurses must be a Registered Nurse.

3. **Sean Connery** (1930—)—British movie superstar. Sir Thomas Sean Connery is a Scottish actor and producer who is perhaps best known as the first actor to portray James Bond in cinema, starring in seven Bond films. In 1987 he won the Academy Award for Best Supporting Actor for his role in *The Untouchables*. His other successful films include *The Name of the Rose* (1986), *The Hunt for Red October* (1990), *The Russia House* (1990), *The Rock* (1996), *Entrapment* (1999), etc. Connery has repeatedly been named as one of the most attractive men alive by various magazines, though he is older than most sex symbols. Sir Sean Connery was knighted by Queen Elizabeth II in July 2000.

Comprehension Exercises

I. Answer the following questions based on the text.

1. What happened to the author on a freezing day?
2. Who was Hannah?
3. Where did the author find Hannah and Michael?
4. Who finally helped the author find the owner of the wallet and why?
5. How did the story about Hannah and Michael go after the author helped them meet again 60 years later?

II. Write T for true and F for false in the brackets before each of the following statements.

1. (   ) The author read the letter in the wallet because he was curious about it.
2. (   ) The author called the operator to find the address of the owner of the wallet.

3. (　　) The operator helped the author find the phone number of the address.
4. (　　) Hannah didn't marry Michael because her mother didn't like him.
5. (　　) Michael was around eighteen years old when he fell in love with Hannah.
6. (　　) Young Michael was so handsome that no one could match up to him.
7. (　　) It took the author two days to find the owner of the wallet.
8. (　　) The guard knew the wallet very well because he had found it several times before.
9. (　　) Mr. Goldstein always put his wallet in his coat pocket.
10. (　　) Hannah and Michael continued to live in the nursing room after getting married.

III. Select the most appropriate word or phrase and use its proper form to complete each of the following sentences.

accompany	crumple	delicate	embrace	greet
identify	knot	legible	operator	pensively
pursue	pray	recipient	relief	reward
stumble	script	party	lacing	elevator

1. Occasionally, researchers _____ across something extraordinary in a system that has been studied for decades.
2. The extra weight was built in to take care of the air bags, _____ zones and other safety requirements of modern cars.
3. Although the handwriting may require some deciphering, ink on paper remains _____ for centuries.
4. People traditionally needed to _____ alarm sounds quickly, but sounds of play were relatively unimportant.
5. The producer said there was no noticeable reaction from the audience, who may have thought the incident was part of the _____.
6. The postman spent almost a whole day looking for the _____ of the letter.
7. Under these reflections I continued very _____ and sad for near a month.
8. In my junior year of high school, my guidance counselor did his best to encourage me to _____ a career in art education.
9. A group of young pioneers always _____ the disabled girl to the school.
10. He took rosary beads from his pocket and began to _____ silently.
11. How unpleasant writing a grant can be is brought into _____ by the sheer amount of effort required to succeed.
12. The big ship creaked and groaned as she descended, her steel hull actually being compressed by the sea's _____.

13. If part of your face or your muscles _____, they become tense, usually because you are worried or angry.
14. A bonus of up to 5 per cent can be added to a pupil's final exam marks as a _____ for good spelling, punctuation and grammar.
15. This sensitive book tackles the _____ issue of adoption with care and simplicity.

IV. Paraphrase the underlined words or expressions in each sentence.

1. The operator <u>gave me her supervisor</u>, who said there was a phone listed at the address, but that she could not give me the number.

2. Then, <u>if the party</u> wanted to talk, she would connect me.

3. "See <u>how the good Lord works</u>," I said philosophically. "If <u>it's meant to be, it will be</u>."

4. I told him she had <u>given me a lead</u>.

5. I prayed that Mr. Goldstein would <u>be up</u>.

V. Discuss with your partner about each of the following statements and write an essay in no less than 200 words about your understanding of one of them.

1. The heart that loves is always young.

2. True love is immortal.

3. Love is the attachment that results from deeply appreciating another's goodness.

VI. List four websites where we can learn more about love and provide a brief introduction to each of them.

1. _____
   _____ .

2. _____
   _____ .

3. _____
   _____ .

4. _____
   _____ .

Twenty Minutes' Reading

You are required to read the following sections within 20 minutes.

SECTION A

Merchant and passenger ships are generally required to have a life preserver for every person aboard and, in many cases, a certain percentage of smaller sizes for children. According to United States Coast Guard requirements, life preservers must be simple in design, reversible, capable of being quickly adjusted to fit the uninitiated individual, and must be so designed as to support the wearer in the water in an upright or slightly backward position.

Sufficient buoyancy (浮力) to support the wearer should be retained by the life preserver after 48 hour in the water, and it should be reliable even after long period of storage. Thus it should be made of materials resistant to sunlight, gasoline, and oils, and it should not be easily set on fire.

The position in which the life preserver will support a person who jumps or falls into the water is most important, as is its tendency to turn the wearer in the water from a face-down position to an upright or slightly backward position, with his face clear of the water, even when the wearer is exhausted or unconscious.

The method of adjustment to the body should be simple, and self-evident to uninitiated persons even in the dark under the confused conditions which follow a disaster. Thus, the life preserver should be reversible, so that it is nearly impossible to set it on wrong. Catches, straps, and ties should be kept to a minimum. In addition, the life preserver must be adjustable to the wide variety of shapes and sizes of wearers, since this greatly affects the position of floating and the self-righting qualities. A suitable life preserver should also be comfortable to wear at all times, in and out of the water, not so heavy as to encourage to take it off on shipboard while the ship is in danger, nor so burdensome that it hinders a person in the water while trying to swim.

1. The passage is mainly about _____.
   A. the uses of life preservers
   B. the design of life preservers
   C. the materials for life preservers
   D. the buoyancy of life preservers

2. According to the passage, a life preserver should be first of all, _____.
   A. adjustable
   B. comfortable
   C. self-evident
   D. self-righting

3. United States Coast Guard does NOT require the life preserver to be made ____.
   A. with as few strings as possible
   B. capable of being worn on both sides
   C. according to each wearer's size
   D. comfortable and light to wear

4. By "the uninitiated individual" (Line 6, Para. 1) the author refers to be person _____.
   A. who has not been instructed how to use a life preserver
   B. who has a little experience in using a life preserver
   C. who uses a life preserver without permission
   D. who becomes nervous before a disaster

5. What would happen if a person were supported by the life preserver in a wrong position?
   A. The waves would move him backwards.
   B. The water would choke him.
   C. He would immediately sink to the bottom.
   D. He would be exhausted or unconscious.

SECTION B

Which is safer—staying at home, traveling to work on public transport, or working in the office? Surprisingly, each of these carries the same risk, which is very low. However, what about flying compared to working in the chemical industry? Unfortunately, the former is 65 times riskier than the latter! In fact, the accident rate of workers in the chemical industry is less than that of almost any of human activity, and almost as safe as staying at home.

The trouble with the chemical industry is that when things go wrong they often cause death to those living nearby. It is this which makes chemical accidents so newsworthy. Fortunately, they are extremely rare. The most famous ones happened at Texas City (1947), Flixborough (1974), Seveso (1976), Pemex (1984) and Bhopal (1984).

Some of these are always in the minds of the people even though the loss of life was small. No one died at Seveso, and only 28 workers at Flixborough. The worst accident of all was Bhopal, where up to 3,000 were killed. The Texas City explosion of fertilizer killed 552. The Pemex fire at a storage plant for natural gas in the suburbs of Mexico City took 542 lives, just a month before the unfortunate event at Bhopal.

Some experts have discussed these accidents and used each accident to illustrate a particular danger. Thus the Texas City explosion was caused by tons of ammonium nitrate（硝酸铵）, which is safe unless stored in great quantity. The Flixborough fireball was the fault of management, which took risks to keep production going during essential repairs. The Seveso accident shows what happens if the local authorities lack knowledge of the danger on their doorstep. When the poisonous gas drifted over the town, local leaders were incapable of taking effective action. The Pemex fire was made worse by an overloaded site in an overcrowded suburb. The fire set off a chain reaction as exploding storage tanks. Yet, by a miracle, the two largest tanks did not explode. Had these caught fire, then 3,000 strong rescue team and fire fighters would all have died.

6. Which of the following statements is true?
   A. Working at the office is safer than staying at home.
   B. Travelling to work on public transport is safer than working at the office.
   C. Staying at home is safer than working in the chemical industry.
   D. Working in the chemical industry is safer than traveling by air.

7. Chemical accidents are usually important enough to be reported as news because _____.

   A. they are very rare

   B. they often cause loss of life

   C. they always occur in big cities

   D. they arouse the interest of all the readers

8. According to passage, the chemical accident that caused by the fault of management happened at _____.

   A. Texas city   B. Flixborough   C. Seveso   D. Mexico City

9. From the passage we know that ammonium nitrate is a kind of _____.

   A. natural gas, which can easily catch fire

   B. fertilizer, which can't be stored in a great quantity

   C. poisonous substance, which can't be used in overcrowded areas

   D. fuel, which is stored in large tanks

10. From the discussion among some experts we may conclude that _____.

    A. to avoid any accidents we should not repair the facilities in chemical industry

    B. the local authorities should not be concerned with the production of the chemical industry

    C. all these accidents could have been avoided or controlled if effective measure had been taken

    D. natural gas stored in very large tanks is always safe

Unit Seven

The Dream-work

Sigmund Freud

Every attempt that has hitherto been made to solve the problem of dreams has dealt directly with their manifest content as it is presented in our memory. All such attempts have endeavored to arrive at an interpretation of dreams from their manifest content or (if no interpretation was attempted) to form a judgment as to their nature on the basis of that same manifest content. We are alone in taking something else into account .We have introduced a new class of psychical material between the manifest content of dreams and the conclusions of our enquiry: namely, their latent content, or (as we say) the "dream-thoughts", arrived at by means of our procedure . It is from these dream—thoughts and not from a dream's manifest content that we disentangle its meaning. We are thus presented with a new task which had no previous existence: the task, that is, of investigating the relations between the manifest content of dreams and the latent dream-thoughts, and of tracing out the processes by which the latter have been changed into the former.

The dream-thoughts and the dream-content are presented to us like two versions of the same like a transcript of the dream-thoughts into another mode of expression, whose characters and syntactic laws it is our business to discover by comparing the original and the translation. The dream-thoughts are immediately comprehensible, as soon as we have learnt them. The dream-content, on the other hand, is expressed as it were in a pictographic script, the characters of which have to be transposed individually into the language of the dream-thoughts. If we attempted to read these

---

manifest /ˈmænɪfest/ *adj.* **a.** able to be seen; **b.** clearly shown or visible; **c.** easy to understand or recognize

psychical /ˈsaɪkɪkl/ *adj.* used to describe strange mental powers and abilities (such as the ability to predict the future, to know what other people are thinking, or to receive messages from dead people) that cannot be explained by natural laws

enquiry /ɪnˈkwaɪəri/ *n.* a request for information

latent /ˈleɪtnt/ *adj.* used to describe something (such as disease) that exists but is not active or cannot be seen

disentangle /ˌdɪsɪnˈtæŋgl/ *v.* **a.** to separate (things that are twisted together or caught on one another); **b.** to remove the twists or knots in (something)

transcript /ˈtrænskrɪpt/ *n.* **a.** a written, printed, or typed copy of words that have been spoken; **b.** an official record of a student's grades

syntactic /sɪnˈtæktɪk/ *adj.* of or relating to or conforming to the rules of syntax

pictographic /ˌpɪktəˈgræfɪk/ *adj.* consisting of or characterized by the use of a graphic character in picture writing

transpose /trænˈspəʊz/ *v.* **a.** to change the position or order of (two things); **b.** to change (something) by giving it a different form, using it in a different place or situation

characters according to their pictorial value instead of according to their symbolic relation, we should clearly be led into error. Suppose I have a picture-puzzle, a rebus, in front of me. It depicts a house with a boat on its roof, a single letter of the alphabet, the figure of a running man whose head has been conjured away, and so on. Now I might be misled into raising objections and declaring that the picture as a whole and its component parts are nonsensical. A boat has no business to be on the roof of a house, and a headless man cannot run. Moreover, the man is bigger than the house; and if the whole picture is intended to represent a landscape, letters of the alphabet are out of place in it since objects do not occur in nature. But obviously we can only form a proper judgement of the rebus if we put aside criticisms such as these of the whole composition and its parts and if, instead, we try to replace each separate element by a syllable or word that can be represented by that element in some way or other. The words which are put together in this way are no longer nonsensical but may form a poetical phrase of the greatest beauty and significance. A dream is a picture-puzzle of this sort and our predecessors in the field of dream-interpretation have made the mistake of treating the rebus as a pictorial composition: and as such it has seemed to them nonsensical and worthless.

rebus /ˈriːbəs/ *n.* a riddle or puzzle made up of letters, pictures, or symbols whose names sound like the parts or syllables of a word or phrase

predecessor /ˈpriːdɪsesə(r)/ *n.* **a.** a person who had a job or position before someone else; **b.** something that comes before something else

condensation /ˌkɒndenˈseɪʃn/ *n.* **a.** small drops of water that form on a cold surface; **b.** the act or process of making something shorter; **c.** the act or process of condensing something

meager /ˈmiːgə/ *adj.* **a.** very small or too small in amount; **b.** not having enough of something (such as money or food) for comfort or happiness

laconic /ləˈkɒnɪk/ *adj.* using few words in speech or writing

conceal /kənˈsiːl/ *v.* **a.** to hide (something or someone) from sight; **b.** to keep (something) secret

The work of condensation

The first thing that becomes clear to anyone who compares the dream-content with the dream-thoughts is that a work of condensation on a large scale has been carried out. Dreams are brief, meager and laconic in comparison with the range and wealth of the dream-thoughts. If a dream is written out it may perhaps fill half a page. The analysis setting out the dream-thoughts underlying it may occupy six, eight or a dozen times as much space. This relation varies with different dreams; but so far as my experience goes its direction never varies. As a rule one underestimates the amount of compression that has taken place, since one is inclined to regard the dream-thoughts that have been brought to light as the complete material, whereas if the work of interpretation is carried further it may reveal still more thoughts concealed behind the dream. I have already had occasion to point out that it is in fact never possible to be sure that a dream has been completely interpreted. Even if the solution seems satisfactory and without gaps, the possibility always remains that the dream may have yet another meaning. Strictly speaking, then, it is impossible to determine the amount of condensation.

There is an answer, which at first sight seems most plausible, to the argument that the great lack of proportion between the dream-content and the dream-thoughts implies that the psychical material has undergone an extensive process of condensation in the course of the formation of the dream. We very often have an impression that we have dreamt a great deal all through the night and have since forgotten most of what we dreamt. On this view, the dream which we remember when we wake up would only be a fragmentary remnant of the total dream-work; and this, if we could recollect it in its entirety, might well be as extensive as the dream-thoughts, there is undoubtedly some truth in this: there can be no question that dreams can be reproduced most accurately if we try to recall them as soon as we wake up and that our memory of them becomes more and more incomplete towards evening. But on the other hand it can be shown that the impression that we have dreamt a great deal more than we can reproduce is very often based on an illusion, the origin of which I shall discuss later. Moreover the hypothesis that condensation occurs during the dream-work is not affected by the possibility of dreams being forgotten, since this hypothesis is proved to be correct by the quantities of ideas which are related to each individual piece of the dream which has been retained. Even supposing that a large piece of the dream has escaped recollection, this may merely have prevented our having access to another group of dream-thoughts. There is no justification for supposing that the lost pieces of the dream would have related to the same thoughts which we have already reached from the pieces of the dream that have survived.

In view of the very great number of associations produced in analysis to each individual element of the content of a dream, some readers may be led to doubt whether, as a matter of principle, we are justified in regarding as part of the dream-thoughts all the associations that occur to us during the subsequent analysis whether we are justified, that is, in supposing that all these thoughts were already active during the state of sleep and played a part in the formation of the dream. Is it not more probable that new trains of thought have

plausible /ˈplɔːzəbl/ *adj.* **a.** possibly true; **b.** believable or realistic
fragmentary /ˈfrægməntri/ *adj.* **a.** made up of parts or pieces; **b.** made up of fragments
remnant /ˈremnənt/ *n.* **a.** the part of something that is left when the other parts are gone; **b.** a small piece of cloth that is left after the rest of the cloth has been sold
justification /ˌdʒʌstɪfɪˈkeɪʃn/ *n.* **a.** an acceptable reason for doing something; **b.** something that justifies an action

arisen in the course of the analysis which had no share in forming the dream? I can only give limited assent to this argument. It is no doubt true that some trains of thought arise for the first time during the analysis. But one can convince oneself in all such cases that these new connections are only set up between thoughts which were already linked in some other way in the dream-thoughts. The new connections are, as it were, loop-lines or short-circuits, made possible by the existence of other and deeper-lying connecting paths. It must be allowed that the great bulk of the thoughts which are revealed in analysis were already active during the process of forming the dream; for, after working through a string of thoughts which seem to have no connection with the formation of a dream, one suddenly comes upon one which is represented in its content and is indispensable for its interpretation, but which could not have been reached except by this particular kind of approach. I may here recall the dream of the botanical monograph, which strikes one as the product of an astonishing amount of condensation, even though I have not reported its analysis in full.

> **assent** /əˈsent/ *v.* to agree to or approve of something (such as an idea or suggestion) especially after carefully thinking about it
> **botanical** /bəˈtænɪkl/ *adj.* of or relating to plants or the study of plants
> **purposive** /ˈpɜːpəsɪv/ *adj.* **a.** having or showing or acting with a purpose or design; **b.** having a purpose
> **ideational** /ˌaɪdiˈeɪʃənəl/ *adj.* being (or being of the nature of) a notion or concept;
> **provisional** /prəˈvɪʒənl/ *adj.* existing or accepted for the present time but likely to be changed

How, then, are we to picture psychical conditions during the period of sleep which precedes dreams? Are all the dream-thoughts present alongside one another? Or do they occur in sequence? Or do a number of trains of thought start out simultaneously from different centers and afterwards unite? There is no need for the present, in my opinion, to form any plastic idea of psychical conditions during the formation of dreams. It must not be forgotten, however, that we are dealing with an unconscious process of thought, which may easily be different from what we perceive during purposive reflection accompanied by consciousness.

The unquestionable fact remains, however, that the formation of dreams is based on a process of condensation. How is that condensation brought about?

When we reflect that only a small minority of all the dream-thoughts revealed are represented in the dream by one of their ideational elements, we might conclude that condensation is brought about by omission: that is, that the dream is not a faithful translation or a point-for-point projection of the dream-thoughts, but a highly incomplete and fragmentary version of them. This view, as we shall soon discover, is a most inadequate one. But we may take it as a provisional starting-point and go on to a further question. If only a few elements from the dream-thoughts find their way into the dream-content, what are the conditions which determine their selection?

In order to get some light on this question we must turn our attention to those elements of the dream-content which must have fulfilled these conditions. And the most favorable material for such an investigation will be a dream to the construction of which a particularly intense process of condensation has contributed. I shall accordingly begin by choosing for the purpose the dream which I have already recorded.

Cultural Notes

Sigmund Freud—Sigmund Freud was born in Freiberg, in Moravia, on 6th of May 1856. He was an Austrian neurologist who became known as the founding father of psychoanalysis. Freud's redefinition of sexuality to include its infantile forms led him to formulate the Oedipus complex as the central tenet of psychoanalytical theory. His analysis of dreams as wish-fulfillments provided him with models for the clinical analysis of symptom formation and the mechanisms of repression as well as for elaboration of his theory of the unconscious as an agency disruptive of conscious states of mind. Freud postulated the existence of libido, an energy with which mental processes and structures are invested and which generates erotic attachments, and a death drive, the source of repetition, hate, aggression and neurotic guilt. In his later work Freud developed a wide-ranging interpretation and critique of religion and culture.

Comprehension Exercises

I. Answer the following questions based on the text.
1. What's the relationship between dream-thoughts and dream-content?
2. What's the new task presented to us?
3. How does Freud compare dreams to a picture-puzzle?
4. Why is it impossible to determine the amount of condensation?
5. Is condensation affected by the dreams being forgotten?

II. Write T for true and F for false in the brackets before each of the following statements.

1. (   ) We disentangle the meaning of dreams from its manifest content.
2. (   ) The dream-content is easily understandable.
3. (   ) We should try to understand our dreams through their symbolic relations.
4. (   ) The impression that we have dreamt more than we can reproduce is often based on an illusion.
5. (   ) It is possible to determine the amount of condensation.

III. Select the most appropriate word or phrase and use its proper form to complete each of the following sentences.

assent	botanical	conceal	condensation	disentangle
enquiry	entirety	fragmentary	ideational	justification
laconic	latent	manifest	meager	plausible
perceive	purposive	provisional	transcript	transpose

1. There may be unrecognized cases of _____ injustice of which we are unaware.
2. The _____ should end with a review of the discussion findings and confirmation by the participants to ensure accuracy.
3. Advertisements attempt to project a _____ meaning behind an overt message.
4. He learned to mentally _____ the effects of meteor impacts to see the underlying rock types.
5. The entire show is fascinating background listening, but there's also a _____ if you want to skim the interview.
6. Taking the _____ of both sides does not change the left-hand side of the equation.
7. The term _____ is now firmly entrenched in the literature of polymer science.
8. Grandmothers have often been through hard times and know how to make a meal from _____ ingredients.
9. The war experience helped to give the New Frontier generations casual and _____ tone.
10. In response to the furor, artists began to avoid forbidden images or _____ them under dotting, stippling and cross-hatches.
11. He cast about in his mind for some _____ excuse for not turning up at the meeting.

12. American writers have been able to stand outside society in this way partly because society itself was too _____, too much in the flux of becoming, to lay close hold upon them.
13. Though Eleanor gave no verbal _____ to this, she did not express dissent.
14. You see the good as normal and _____ the bad as a minor aberration.
15. In much of the popular commentary, this conclusion was stated in highly _____ terms.

IV. Paraphrase the underlined words or expressions in each sentence.

1. If we attempted to read these characters according to their <u>pictorial value</u> instead of according to their symbolic relation, we should clearly <u>be led into error</u>.

2. On this view, the dream which we remember when we wake up would only be a <u>fragmentary remnant</u> of the total dream-work; and this, if we could recollect it <u>in its entirety</u>, might well be as extensive as the dream-thoughts, there is undoubtedly some truth in this.

3. I can only <u>give limited assent to</u> this argument.

4. Or do a number of trains of thought start out <u>simultaneously</u> from different centers and afterwards <u>unite</u>?

5. But we may take it as a <u>provisional starting-point</u> and go on to a further question.

V. Discuss with your partner about each of the following statements and write an essay in no less than 200 words about your understanding of one of them.

1. Dreams are brief, meager and laconic in comparison with the range and wealth of the dream-thoughts.

2. Even if the solution seems satisfactory and without gaps, the possibility always remains that the dream may have yet another meaning.

3. When we reflect that only a small minority of all the dream-thoughts revealed are represented in the dream by one of their ideational elements, we might conclude that condensation is brought about by omission: that is , that the dream is not a faithful translation or a point-for-point projection of the dream-thoughts, but a highly incomplete and fragmentary version of them.

VI. List four websites where we can learn more about the author Sigmund Freud and his works and provide a brief introduction to each of them.

1.
2.
3.
4.

Text B

Group Psychology and the Analysis of the Ego
Sigmund Freud

Identification is known to psycho-analysis as the earliest expression of an emotional tie with another person. It plays a part in the early history of the Oedipus complex. A little boy will exhibit a special interest in his father; he would like to grow like him and be like him, and take his place everywhere, we may say simply that he takes his father as his ideal. This behavior has nothing to do with a passive or feminine attitude towards his father (and towards males in general); it is on the contrary typically masculine. It fits in very well with the Oedipus complex, for which it helps to prepare the way.

At the same time as this identification with his father, or a little later, the boy has begun to develop a true object-cathexis towards his mother according to the attachment [anaclitic] type. He then exhibits, therefore, two psychologically distinct ties: straightforward sexual object- cathexis towards his mother and an identification with his father which takes him model. The two subsist side by side for a time without any mutual influence or interference. In consequence of the irresistible advance towards a unification of mental life, they come together at last; and the normal Oedipus complex originates from their confluence. The little boy notices that his father stands in his way with his mother. His identification with his father then takes on a hostile coloring and becomes identical with the wish to replace his father in regard to his mother as well. Identification, in fact, is ambivalent from the very first; it can turn into an expression of tenderness as easily as into a wish for someone's removal. It behaves like a derivative of the first, oral phase of the organization of the libido, in which the object that we long for and prize is assimilated by eating and is in that way annihilated as such. The cannibal, as we know, has remained at this standpoint; he has a devouring affection for his enemies and only devours people of whom he is fond.

The subsequent history of this identification with the father may easily be lost sight of. It may happen that the Oedipus complex becomes inverted, and that the father is taken as the object of a feminine attitude, an object from which the directly sexual instincts look for satisfaction; in that event the identification with the father has become the precursor of an object-tie with the father. The same holds good, with the necessary substitutions, of the baby daughter as well.

It is easy to state in a formula the distinction between an identification with the father and the choice of the father as an object. In the first case one's father is what one would like to be, and in the second he is what one would like to have. The distinction, that is, depends upon whether the tie attaches to the subject or to the object

cathexis /kəˈθeksɪs/ *n.* (psychoanalysis) the libidinal energy invested in some idea or person or object
anaclitic /ˌɑːnəkˈlɪtɪk/ *adj.* of or related to relationships that are characterized by the strong dependence of one person on another
subsist /səbˈsɪst/ *v.* to exist or continue to exist
confluence /ˈkɒnfluəns/ *n.* a situation in which two things come together or happen at the same time
ambivalent /æmˈbɪvələnt/ *adj.* having or showing very different feelings (such as love and hate) about someone or something at the same time
removal /rɪˈmuːvl/ *n.* the act of moving or taking something away from a place
derivative /dɪˈrɪvətɪv/ *n.* something that comes from something else
annihilate /əˈnaɪəleɪt/ *v.* **a.** to destroy (something or someone) completely; **b.** to defeat (someone) completely
cannibal /ˈkænɪbl/ *n.* a person who eats the flesh of human beings or an animal that eats its own kind
precursor /priːˈkɜːsə(r)/ *n.* something that comes before something else and that often leads to or influences its development

of the ego. The former kind of tie is therefore already possible before any sexual object-choice has been made. It is much more difficult to give a clear meta-psychological representation of the distinction. We can only see that identification endeavors to mold a person's own ego the fashion of the one that has been taken as a model.

Let us disentangle identification as it occurs in the structure of a neurotic symptom from its rather complicated connections. Supposing that a little girl (and we will keep to her for the present) develops the same painful symptom as her mother—for instance, the same tormenting cough. This may come about in various ways. The identification may come from the Oedipus complex; in that case it signifies a hostile desire on the girl's part to take her mother's place, and the symptom expresses her object—love towards her father, and brings about a realization, under the influence of a sense of guilt, of her desire to take her mother's place: "You wanted to be your mother, and now you are—anyhow so far as your sufferings are concerned." This is the complete mechanism of the structure of a hysterical symptom. Or, on the other hand, the symptom may be the same as that of the person who is loved; so, for instance, Dora imitated her father's cough. In that case we can only describe the state of things by saying that identification has appeared instead of object-choice, and that object-choice has regressed to identification. We have heard that identification is the earliest and original form of emotional tie; it often happens that under the conditions in which symptoms are constructed, that is, where there is repression and where the mechanisms of the unconscious are dominant, object-choice is turned back into identification—the ego assumes the characteristics of the object. It is noticeable that in these identifications the ego sometimes copies the person who is not loved and sometimes the one who is loved. It must also strike us that in both cases the identification is a partial and extremely limited one and only borrows a single trait from the person who is its object.

There is a third particularly frequent and important case of symptom formation, in which the identification leaves entirely out of account any object-relation to the person who is being copied. Supposing, for instance, that one of the girls in a boarding school has had a letter from someone with whom she is secretly in love which arouses

mold /məʊld/ *v.* **a.** to form or press (something, such as wax, plastic, clay, or dough) into a particular shape; **b.** to create, influence, or affect the character of (someone or something)

neurotic /njʊəˈrɒtɪk/ *adj.* **a.** having or suggesting neurosis; **b.** often or always fearful or worried about something; **c.** tending to worry in a way that is not healthy or reasonable

hysterical /hɪˈsterɪkl/ *adj.* **a.** feeling or showing extreme and uncontrolled emotion; **b.** very funny

regress /rɪˈgres/ *v.* to return to an earlier and usually worse or less developed condition or state

her jealousy, and that she reacts to it with a fit of hysterics; then some of her friends who know about it will catch the fit, as we say, by mental infection. The mechanism is that of identification based upon the possibility or desire of putting oneself in the same situation.

pathogenic /ˈpæθəˈdʒenɪk/ *n.* something (such as a type of bacteria or virus) that causes disease
libidinal /lɪˈbɪdənl/ *adj.* belonging to the libido (a person's desire to have sex)
introjection /ˌɪntrəˈdʒekʃən/ *n.* **a.** the internalization of the parent figures and their values; **b.** leads to the formation of the superego

The other girls would like to have a secret love affair too, and under the influence of a sense of guilt they also accept the suffering involved in it. It would be wrong to suppose that they take on the symptom out of sympathy. On the contrary, the sympathy only arises out of the identification, and this is proved by the fact that infection or imitation of this kind takes place in circumstances where even less pre-existing sympathy is to be assumed than usually exists between friends in a girls' school. One ego has perceived a significant analogy with another upon one point—in our example upon openness to a similar emotion; an identification is thereupon constructed on this point, and, under the influence of the pathogenic situation, is displaced on to the symptom which the one ego has produced. The identification by means of the symptom has thus become the mark of a point of coincidence between the two egos which has to be kept repressed.

What we have learned from these three sources may be summarized as follows. First, identification is the original form of emotional tie with an object; secondly, in a regressive way it becomes a substitute for a libidinal object-tie, as it were by means of introjection of the object into the ego; and thirdly, it may arise with any new perception of a common quality shared with some other person who is not an object of the sexual instinct. The more important this common quality is, the more successful may this partial identification become, and it may thus represent the beginning of a new tie.

Cultural Notes

Ego—According to Freud, the ego is part of personality that mediates the demands of the id, the superego and reality. The ego prevents us from acting on our basic urges (created by the id), but also works to achieve a balance with our moral and idealistic standards (created by the superego). While the ego operates in both the preconscious and conscious, it's strong ties to the id means that it also operates in the unconscious.

Comprehension Exercises

I. Answer the following questions based on the text.

1. What is the expression of an emotional tie with another person?
2. What is Oedipus complex?
3. Where does Oedipus complex originate from?
4. What's the difference between an identification with the father and the choice of the father as an object?
5. What are the three things that the author concluded?

II. Write T for true and F for false in the brackets before each of the following statements.

1. (   ) When a little boy identified with his father, he might want to replace his father.
2. (   ) Oedipus complex is different for the relationship between daughters and their fathers.
3. (   ) Identification with the father means that one wants to have the father.
4. (   ) Identification helps the make one be like his father.
5. (   ) Usually, sympathy comes from identification.

III. Select the most appropriate word or phrase and use its proper form to complete each of the following sentences.

ambivalent	assimilate	annihilate	cannibal	complex
confluence	devour	derivative	hysterics	hysterical
identification	irresistible	mold	mutual	neurotic
precursor	removal	regress	subsist	unification

1. A machine-readable _____ card for identifying an operator at a computer terminal.
2. Had he not struck a bargain with the doctor, he and his mutineers, deserted by the ship, must have been driven to _____ on clear water and the proceeds of their hunting.
3. Design works best when there is a relationship of _____ trust and respect among Design, Business, and Engineering.
4. By an _____ association of ideas, he went beyond logic and reason.
5. The search for generality and _____ is one of the distinctive features of twentieth century mathematics.

128

6. A _____ of social trends has elevated young Koreans to their newfound status as consumer trendsetters, observers say.
7. She had been _____ about their Jewish friends and his relatives, though outwardly she seemed not a prejudiced person.
8. Strains require special treatments for _____ such as spotting with organic solvents.
9. The name Cambridge is a _____ of the name of the River "Cam".
10. Awed by the dimensionless task, students struggle with uneven success to _____ and survive.
11. Such terror of the unseen is so far above mere sensual cowardice that it will _____ that cowardice.
12. The ants cultivate the fungus, turning it into a sooty _____ that acts as living cement, reinforcing the structure of their traps.
13. In some way he depended upon the excitement he could arouse in her _____ nature.
14. As we _____ back toward epochs when the universe was younger, we come to the stage when the primordial radiation originated.
15. She seems to be pushing for as many _____ as she can get in every scene.

IV. Paraphrase the underlined words or expressions in each sentence.

1. The two <u>subsist side by side</u> for a time without any <u>mutual influence</u> or interference.

2. <u>The cannibal</u>, as we know, has remained at this standpoint; he has a <u>devouring affection</u> for his enemies and only devours people of whom he is fond.

3. <u>The same holds good</u>, with <u>the necessary substitutions</u>, of the baby daughter as well.

4. We can only see that identification <u>endeavors to mold a person's own ego the fashion of the one that has been taken as a model</u>.

5. Supposing, for instance, that one of the girls in a boarding school has had a letter from someone with whom she is secretly in love which arouses her

jealousy, and that she reacts to it with a fit of hysterics; then some of her friends who know about it will catch the fit, as we say, by mental infection.

V. Discuss with your partner about each of the following statements and write an essay in no less than 200 words about your understanding of one of them.

1. On the contrary, the sympathy only arises out of the identification, and this is proved by the fact that infection or imitation of this kind takes place in circumstances where even less pre-existing sympathy is to be assumed than usually exists between friends in a girls' school.

2. The cannibal, as we know, has remained at this standpoint; he has a devouring affection for his enemies and only devours people of whom he is fond.

3. The identification by means of the symptom has thus become the mark of a point of coincidence between the two egos which has to be kept repressed.

VI. List four websites where we can learn more about ego and other related concepts and provide a brief introduction to each of them.

1.
2.
3.
4.

Twenty Minutes' Reading

You are required to read the following sections within 20 minutes.

SECTION A

It is a curious paradox that we think of the physical sciences as "hard", the social sciences as "soft", and the biological sciences as somewhere in between. This is interpreted to mean that our knowledge of physical system is more certain than our knowledge of biological systems, and these in turn are more certain than our knowledge of social systems. In terms of our capacity of sample the relevant universes, however, and the probability that our images of these universes are at least approximately correct, one suspects that a reverse order is more reasonable. We are able to sample earth's social systems with some degree of confidence that we have a reasonable sample of the total universe being investigated. Our knowledge of social systems, therefore, while it is in many ways extremely inaccurate, is not likely to be seriously overturned by new discoveries. Even the folk knowledge in social systems on which ordinary life is based in earning, spending, organizing, marrying, taking part in political activities, fighting and so on, is not very dissimilar from the more sophisticated images of the social system derived from the social sciences, even though it is built upon the very imperfect samples of personal experience.

In contrast, our image of the astronomical universe, or even if earth's geological history, can easily be subject to revolutionary changes as new data come in and new theories are worked out. If we define the "security" of our image of various parts of the total system as the probability of their suffering significant changes, then we would reverse the order for hardness and as the most secure, the physical sciences as the least secure, and again the biological sciences as somewhere in between. Our image of the astronomical universe is the least secure of all simply because we observe such a fantastically small sample of it and its record-keeping is trivial records of biological systems. Records of the astronomical universe, despite the fact that we learnt things as they were long age, are limited in the extreme.

Even in regard to such a close neighbor as the moon, which we have actually visited, theories about its origin and history are extremely different, contradictory, and hard to choose among. Our knowledge of physical evolution is incomplete and insecure.

1. The word "paradox" (Line 1, Para. 1) means "_____".
   A. implication   B. contradiction   C. interpretation   D. confusion
2. According to the author, we should reverse our classification of the physical sciences as "hard" and the social sciences as "soft" because _____.
   A. a reverse ordering will help promote the development of the physical sciences
   B. our knowledge of physical systems is more reliable than that of social systems
   C. our understanding of the social systems is approximately correct
   D. we are better able to investigate social phenomena than physical phenomena
3. The author believes that our knowledge of social systems is more secure than that of physical systems because _____.
   A. it is not based on personal experience
   B. new discoveries are less likely to occur in social sciences
   C. it is based on a fairly representative quantity of data
   D. the records of social systems are more reliable
4. The chances of the physical sciences being subject to great changes are the biggest because _____.
   A. contradictory theories keep emerging all the time
   B. new information is constantly coming in
   C. the direction of their development is difficult to predict
   D. our knowledge of the physical world is inaccurate
5. We know less about the astronomical universe than we do about any social system because _____.
   A. theories of its origin and history are varied
   B. our knowledge of it is highly insecure
   C. only a very small sample of it has been observed
   D. few scientists are involved in the study of astronomy

SECTION B

It is not only possible but even easy to predict which ten-year-old boys are at greatest risk of growing up to be persistent offenders, what are we doing with the information? Just about the last thing that we should do is to wait until their troubles have escalated in adolescence and then attack them with the provisions of the new Criminal Justice Bill.

If this bill becomes law, magistrates will have the power to impose residential care orders. More young people will be drawn into institutional life when all the evidence shows that this worsens rather than improves their prospects. The introduction of short sharp shocks in detention centers will simply give more young people a taste of something else they don't need; the whole regime of detention centers is one of toughening delinquents, and if you want to train someone to be anti-establishment, "I can't think of a better way to do it," says the writer of this report.

The Cambridge Institute of Criminology comes up with five key factors that are likely to make for delinquency: a low income family a large family, parents deemed by social workers to be bad at raising children, parents who themselves have a criminal record, and low intelligence in the child. Not surprisingly, the factors tend to overlap. Of the 63 boys in the sample who had at least three of them when they were ten, half became juvenile delinquents—compared with only a fifth of the sample as a whole.

Three more factors make the prediction more accurate: being judged troublesome by teachers at the age of ten, having a father with at least two criminal convictions and having another member of the family with a criminal record. Of the 35 men who had at least two of these factors in their background 18 became persistent delinquents and 8 more were in trouble with the law.

Among those key factors, far and away the most important was having a parent with a criminal record, even if that had been acquired in the distant past, even though very few parents did other than condemn delinquent behavior in their children.

The role of the schools emerges as extremely important. The most reliable prediction of all on the futures of boys came from teachers' ratings of how troublesome they were at the age of ten. If the information is there in the classroom there must be a response that brings more attention to those troublesome children: a search for things to give them credit for other than academic achievement, a refusal to allow them to go on playing truant, and a fostering of ambition and opportunity which should start early in their school careers.

6. According to the author, delinquency should be tackled _____.
   A. before adolescence
   B. during institutional treatment
   C. during adolescence
   D. when the problem becomes acute

7. The number of young offenders could be reduced by the way of _____.
   A. new legal measures
   B. better residential care
   C. brief periods of harsh punishment
   D. examination of their backgrounds

8. What is the outcome result of putting young offenders into detention centers?
   A. They become more violent.
   B. They receive useful training.
   C. They become used to institutions.
   D. They turn against society.
9. Ten-year-old children likely to become offenders are usually _____.
   A. spoilt children from small families
   B. bright children in a poor family
   C. dull children with many brothers and sisters
   D. children whose parents have acquired wealth dishonestly
10. The writer concludes that potential offenders could be helped by _____.
    A. spending more time at school
    B. more encouragement at school
    C. more activities outside school
    D. stricter treatment from teachers

Unit Eight

Text A

The Oval Portrait
Edgar Allen Poe

《椭圆画像》艾德加·艾伦·坡的小说一直以怪异荒诞驰名,本文通过死者还魂的故事,展现了这一特点。该主题是坡的小说中一个反复出现的主题。

THE CHATEAU into which my valet had ventured to make forcible entrance, rather than permit me, in my desperately wounded condition, to pass a night in the open air, was one of those piles of commingled gloom and grandeur which have so long frowned among the Appennines, not less in fact than in the fancy of Mrs. Radcliffe. To all appearance it had been temporarily and very lately abandoned. We established ourselves in one of the smallest and least sumptuously furnished apartments. It lay in a remote turret of the building. Its decorations were rich, yet tattered and antique. Its walls were hung with tapestry and bedecked with manifold and multiform armorial trophies, together with an unusually great number of very spirited modern paintings in frames of rich golden arabesque. In these paintings, which depended from the walls not only in their main surfaces, but in very many nooks which the bizarre architecture of the chateau rendered necessary—in these paintings my incipient delirium, perhaps, had caused me to take deep interest; so that I bade Pedro to close the heavy shutters of the room-since it

commingle /kəˈmɪŋɡəl/ *v.* **a.** to blend thoroughly into a harmonious whole; **b.** to combine (funds or properties) into a common fund or stock.
sumptuous /ˈsʌmptjuəs/ *adj.* extremely costly, rich, luxurious, or magnificent
turret /ˈtʌrɪt/ *n.* a little tower; specifically an ornamental structure at an angle of a larger structure
tattered /ˈtætəd/ *adj.* **a.** worn to shreds; or wearing torn or ragged clothing; **b.** ruined or disrupted
bedeck /bɪˈdek/ *v.* decorate
arabesque /ˌærəˈbesk/ *n.* **a.** an ornament or style that employs flower, foliage, or fruit and sometimes animal and figural outlines to produce an intricate pattern of interlaced lines; **b.** a posture (as in ballet) in which the body is bent forward from the hip on one leg with one arm extended forward and the other arm and leg backward; **c.** an elaborate or intricate pattern
incipient /ɪnˈsɪpiənt/ *adj.* only partly in existence; imperfectly formed
delirium /dɪˈlɪriəm/ *n.* **a.** state of violent mental agitation; **b.** a usually brief state of excitement and mental confusion often accompanied by hallucinations

was already night-to light the tongues of a tall candelabrum which stood by the head of my bed—and to throw open far and wide the fringed curtains of black velvet which enveloped the bed itself. I wished all this done that I might resign myself, if not to sleep, at least alternately to the contemplation of these pictures, and the perusal of a small volume which had been found upon the pillow, and which purported to criticise and describe them.

Long—long I read—and devoutly, devotedly I gazed. Rapidly and gloriously the hours flew by and the deep midnight came. The position of the candelabrum displeased me, and outreaching my hand with difficulty, rather than disturb my slumbering valet, I placed it so as to throw its rays more fully upon the book.

candelabrum /ˌkændiˈlɑːbrəm/ *n.* branched ornamental candlestick having several lights
fringe /frɪndʒ/ *n.* an ornamental border consisting of short straight or twisted threads or strips hanging from cut or raveled edges or from a separate band
peruse /pəˈruːz/ *v.* **a.** to examine or consider with attention and in detail, study; **b.** to look over or through in a casual or cursory manner; **c.** read; esp. to read over in an attentive or leisurely manner. **perusal** *n.*
purport /pɜːˈpɔːt/ *v.* **a.** to have the often specious appearance of being, intending, or claiming (sth implied or inferred); claim; **b.** intend, purpose
devout /dɪˈvaʊt/ *adj.* **a.** expressing devotion or piety; **b.** devoted to a pursuit, belief, or mode of behavior, earnest; **c.** warmly sincere
niche /nɪtʃ/ *n.* **a.** a recess in a wall esp. for a statue; **b.** sth that resembles a niche
hitherto /ˌhɪðəˈtuː/ *adv.* used to describe a situation that has existed up to this point or up to the present time
aright /əˈraɪt/ *adv.* in a correct manner
dissipate /ˈdɪsɪpeɪt/ *v.* **a.** to break up and drive off (as a crowd); **b.** to cause to spread thin or scatter and gradually vanish; **c.** to spend or use up wastefully or foolishly
stupor /ˈstjuːpə/ *n.* **a.** the feeling of distress and disbelief that you have when sth bad happens accidentally; **b.** marginal consciousness

But the action produced an effect altogether unanticipated. The rays of the numerous candles (for there were many) now fell within a niche of the room which had hitherto been thrown into deep shade by one of the bed-posts. I thus saw in vivid light a picture all unnoticed before. It was the portrait of a young girl just ripening into womanhood. I glanced at the painting hurriedly, and then closed my eyes. Why I did this was not at first apparent even to my own perception. But while my lids remained thus shut, I ran over in my mind my reason for so shutting them. It was an impulsive movement to gain time for thought—to make sure that my vision had not deceived me—to calm and subdue my fancy for a more sober and more certain gaze. In a very few moments I again looked fixedly at the painting.

That I now saw aright I could not and would not doubt; for the first flashing of the candles upon that canvas had seemed to dissipate the dreamy stupor which was stealing over my senses, and to startle me at once into waking life.

The portrait, I have already said, was that of a young girl. It was a mere head and shoulders, done in what is technically termed a vignette manner; much in the style of the favorite heads of Sully. The arms, the bosom, and even the ends of the radiant hair melted imperceptibly into the vague yet deep shadow which formed the back-ground of the whole. The frame was oval, richly gilded and filigreed in Moresque. As a thing of art nothing could be more admirable than the painting itself. But it could have been neither the execution of the work, nor the immortal beauty of the countenance, which had so suddenly and so vehemently moved me. Least of all, could it have been that my fancy, shaken from its half slumber, had mistaken the head for that of a living person. I saw at once that the peculiarities of the design, of the vignetting, and of the frame, must have instantly dispelled such idea—must have prevented even its momentary entertainment. Thinking earnestly upon these points, I remained, for an hour perhaps, half sitting, half reclining, with my vision riveted upon the portrait. At length, satisfied with the true secret of its effect, I fell back within the bed. I had found the spell of the picture in an absolute life-likeliness of expression, which, at first startling, finally confounded, subdued, and appalled me. With deep and reverent awe I replaced the candelabrum in its former position. The cause of my deep agitation being thus shut from view, I sought eagerly the volume which discussed the paintings and their histories. Turning to the number which designated the oval portrait, I there read the vague and quaint words which follow:

"She was a maiden of rarest beauty, and not more lovely than full of glee. And evil was the hour when she saw, and loved, and wedded the painter. He, passionate, studious, austere, and having already a bride in his Art; she a maiden of rarest beauty, and not more lovely than full of glee; all light and smiles, and frolicsome as the young fawn; loving and cherishing all things; hating only the Art which was her rival; dreading only the pallet and brushes and other untoward instruments which deprived her of the countenance of her lover. It was thus a terrible thing for this lady to hear the painter speak of his desire to portray even his young bride. But she was humble and obedient, and sat meekly for many weeks in the dark, high turret-chamber where the light dripped upon the pale canvas only

filigree /ˈfɪlɪgriː/ *n.* delicate and intricate ornamentation (usually in gold or silver or other fine twisted wire)

countenance /ˈkaʊntɪnəns/ *n.* **a.** the appearance conveyed by a person's face; **b.** the human face

confound /kənˈfaʊnd/ *v.* to throw (a person) into confusion or perplexity

subdue /sʌbˈdjuː/ *v.* **a.** put down by force or intimidation; **b.** hold within limits and control; **c.** get on top of; deal with successfully

appall /əˈpɔːl/ *v.* to overcome with shock or dismay

quaint /kweɪnt/ *adj.* **a.** unusual or different in character or appearance, odd; **b.** pleasingly or strikingly old-fashioned or unfamiliar

glee /gliː/ *n.* exultant high-spirited joy

austere /ɔːˈstɪə/ *adj.* **a.** stern and cold in appearance or manner; **b.** somber, grave

frolicsome /ˈfrɒlɪksəm/ *adj.* full of gaiety, playful

pallet /ˈpælɪt/ *n.* board that provides a flat surface on which artists mix paints and the range of colors used

untoward /ʌntəˈwɔːd/ *adj.* difficult to guide, manage, or work with

from overhead. But he, the painter, took glory in his work, which went on from hour to hour, and from day to day. And he was a passionate, and wild, and moody man, who became lost in reveries; so that he would not

surpassing /sə'pɑːsɪŋ/ *adj.* greatly exceeding others, of a very high degree
surpassingly *adv.*
pallid /'pælɪd/ *adj.* **a.** deficient in color, wan; **b.** lacking sparkle or liveliness, dull
aghast /ə'gɑːst/ *adj.* struck with terror, amazement, or horror, shocked

see that the light which fell so ghastly in that lone turret withered the health and the spirits of his bride, who pined visibly to all but him. Yet she smiled on and still on, uncomplainingly, because she saw that the painter (who had high renown) took a fervid and burning pleasure in his task, and wrought day and night to depict her who so loved him, yet who grew daily more dispirited and weak. And in sooth some who beheld the portrait spoke of its resemblance in low words, as of a mighty marvel, and a proof not less of the power of the painter than of his deep love for her whom he depicted so surpassingly well. But at length, as the labor drew nearer to its conclusion, there were admitted none into the turret; for the painter had grown wild with the ardor of his work, and turned his eyes from canvas merely, even to regard the countenance of his wife. And he would not see that the tints which he spread upon the canvas were drawn from the cheeks of her who sat beside him. And when many weeks had passed, and but little remained to do, save one brush upon the mouth and one tint upon the eye, the spirit of the lady again flickered up as the flame within the socket of the lamp. And then the brush was given, and then the tint was placed; and, for one moment, the painter stood entranced before the work which he had wrought; but in the next, while he yet gazed, he grew tremulous and very pallid, and aghast, and crying with a loud voice, 'This is indeed life itself!' turned suddenly to regard his beloved:—She was dead!"

Cultural Notes

1. **Edgar Allen Poe** (1809—1849)—Born on 19 January 1809 in Boston, Massachusetts, the son of actors Elizabeth Arnold Hopkins (1787—1811) and David Poe (1784—1810). He had a brother named William Henry (1807—1831) and sister Rosalie (1811—1874). After the death of his parents Edgar was taken in by John Allan, a wealthy merchant in Richmond, Virginia. Young Edgar traveled with the Allans to England in 1815 and attended school in Chelsea. In 1820 he was back in Richmond where he attended the University of Virginia and studied Latin and poetry and also loved to swim and act. While in school he became estranged from his foster

father after accumulating gambling debts. Unable to pay them or support himself, Poe left school and enlisted in the United States Army where he served for two years. He had been writing poetry for some time and in 1827 *Dreams* first appeared in the Baltimore North American, the same year his first book *Tamerlane and Other Poems* was published, at his own expense. Poe enlisted in the West Point Military Academy but was dismissed a year later. In 1829 his second book *Al Aaraaf, Tamerlane and Minor Poems* was published. The same year *Poems* (1831) was published Poe moved to Baltimore to live with his aunt Maria Clemm, mother of Virginia Eliza Clemm (1822—1847) who would become his wife at the age of thirteen. His brother Henry was also living in the Clemm household but he died of tuberculosis soon after Edgar moved in. In 1833, *the Baltimore Saturday Visiter* published some of his poems and he won a contest in it for his story *MS found in a Bottle*. In 1835 he became editor and contributor of *the Southern Literary Messenger*. Though not without his detractors and troubles with employers, it was the start of his career as respected critic and essayist. Other publications which he contributed to were Burton's *Gentleman's Magazine* (1839—1840), Graham's *Magazine* (1841—1842), *Evening Mirror,* and Godey's *Lady's Book*. As an important American poet, critic, short story writer, and author of such macabre works as *The Fall of the House of Usher* (1840), Edgar Poe contributes greatly to the genres of horror and science fiction and is now considered the father of the modern detective story. He is especially highly lauded as a poet. Poe's psychologically thrilling tales examining the depths of the human psyche earned him much fame during his lifetime and after his death. His own life was marred by tragedy at an early age (his parents died before he was three years old) and in his oft-quoted works we can see his darkly passionate sensibilities—a tormented and sometimes neurotic obsession with death and violence and overall appreciation for the beautiful yet tragic mysteries of life. Poe's literary criticisms of poetry and the art of short story writing include *The Poetic Principal* and *The Philosophy of Composition*. There have been numerous collections of his works published and many of them have been inspiration for popular television and film adaptations including *The Tell-Tale Heart, The Black Cat*, and *The Raven*. He has been the subject of numerous biographers and has significantly influenced many other authors even into the 21st Century.

2. **Mrs. Radcliffe** (1764—1823)—Ann Radcliffe, English novelist, born in London. The daughter of a successful tradesman, she married William

Radcliffe, a law student who later became editor of the English Chronicle. Her best works, *The Romance of the Forest* (1791), *The Mysteries of Udolpho* (1794), and *The Italian* (1797), give her a prominent place in the tradition of the Gothic romance. Her works were extremely popular among the upper class and the growing middle class, especially among young women. Stylistically, Radcliffe was noted for her vivid descriptions of exotic locales, though in reality the author had rarely or never visited the actual locations. In her tales, scenes of terror and suspense are infused with an aura of romantic sensibility. Her excellent use of landscape to create mood and her sense of mystery and suspense had an enormous influence on later writers and produced many imitators.

3. **vignette**—A photographic portrait which is clear in the center, and fades off into the surrounding color at the edges. It's a visual effect of darkened corners used to help frame an image or soften the frame outline. Graphically the term refers to a kind of decorative design usually in books, used both to separate sections or chapters and to decorate borders; these were often based on vine—leaves. It's also used for short descriptive literature focusing on a particular moment or person.

4. **Sully**—Thomas Sully, born in Horncastle in Lincolnshire, England, on June 8 (some sources say June 19), 1783, to actors Sarah Chester and Matthew Sully. Thomas Sully emigrated to America with his parents and eight siblings at age nine and lived in Charleston, South Carolina. He received coaching from school friend Charles Fraser, who became Charleston's most famous miniaturist, and from an elder brother, Lawrence Sully, who also painted miniatures. Thomas Sully was best known as a portrait artist who reflected the manners and demeanor of great people of his day. A naturalized American citizen, he preserved for posterity the nation's politicians, military heroes, inventors, actors, and aristocrats as well as European nobles and the queen of England. In the decades preceding the invention of photography, his prolific output of portraits and historic scenes became a storehouse of details from the past. A year after his death on November 5, 1872, in Philadelphia, his heirs published posthumously *Hints to Young Painters and the Process of Portrait-Painting as Practiced by the Late Thomas Sully* (1873). Its explanation of artistic works from the colonial and federal periods retained for history the inside information on color selection, lighting, and technique. His likenesses of 500 historic figures, including Daniel Boone, Benjamin Franklin, and US presidents Thomas Jefferson, James Monroe, and Andrew Jackson, are national treasures.

5. **Moresque**—Moors were the Muslim peoples of mixed Arab race who conquered Spain and held power there in the years from 711 to 1492. The term Moresque means an ornament or a decoration in Moorish style or having all the usual qualities of the Moorish style of art or architecture.

Comprehension Exercises

I. Answer the following questions based on the text.
1. Can you infer what kind of chateau they had entered?
2. Why did the speaker shut his eyes upon the portrait for a few moments?
3. What was so special about the painting that it had absorbed the speaker entirely?
4. Did the painter love his young bride much more than his Art?
5. How do you understand the death of the young lady on the completion of the work by the painter?

II. Write T for true and F for false in the brackets before each of the following statements.
1. (　) Many paintings hung from the main walls of the chateau, but nothing in the corners.
2. (　) He didn't notice the oval portrait at first because it was in the shadow.
3. (　) He asked his valet to move the position of the candelabrum so as to read the book better.
4. (　) The speaker took no interest in the pictures because he was wounded and wanted to have a good sleep.
5. (　) He fixed his eyes on the painting of the young girl once he found it there.
6. (　) It was the immortal beauty of the countenance that moved him profoundly.
7. (　) Unable to fall asleep, he eagerly turned to the paged in the book for a detailed explanation of the portrait.
8. (　) The young lady didn't lead a happy life after wedding the painter.
9. (　) The bride was happy to act as the model of her husband because she wanted to have more time together with him.
10. (　) The painter himself was overwhelmed by the power of life in his work.

III. Select the most appropriate word or phrase and use its proper form to complete each of the following sentences.

austere	antique	bedeck	bizarre	confound
contemplation	dissipate	devoutly	dispel	execution
frolicsome	glee	glide	hitherto	impulsive
immortal	purport	resign	subdue	startle

1. The image is made literal in the flowers that are grown to _____ the corpses and end up in the flames of cremation.
2. As this cluster of gerberas shows, the technique results in colors and textures that exude an _____ romance.
3. In a _____ profession anything which belongs to an everyday routine gains great values.
4. A man has been forced to _____ as a result of being pilloried by some of the press.
5. The sensation produced by music is that evoked by _____ of the interplay of architectural forms.
6. The closing letters do not _____ to be an exhaustive list of all possible problem areas since the audits are limited in scope.
7. Bertha was _____ grateful to Miss Ley for her opportune return on Gerald's last night.
8. She discovered a world of parties and pleasure she had _____ only known by hearsay.
9. Something about the dizzying lights mixed with being broke among successful entrepreneurs made us feel mischievous and _____.
10. Motivated by individual greed, they turn on one another until they unite to _____ a stranger prone to violence.
11. Merely closing the bathroom door and opening a window will _____ excess water vapor resulting from tub bathing or showering.
12. He who would gather immortal palms must not be _____ by the name of goodness, but must explore if it be goodness.
13. Veterinarians and servicemen can and should help _____ this apprehension by maintaining high ethical standards
14. No error is more common than to _____ democracy as an element in national character with democracy as a form of government.
15. He rubbed his hands in _____ as he thought of all the money he would make.

IV. Paraphrase the underlined words or expressions in each sentence.

1. <u>To all appearance</u> it had been temporarily and very lately abandoned.

2. ...in these paintings my <u>incipient delirium</u>, perhaps, had caused me to take deep interest.

3. ...for the first flashing of the candles upon that canvas had seemed to dissipate the dreamy stupor <u>which was stealing over my senses</u>.

4. I had found <u>the spell</u> of the picture in an <u>absolute life-likeliness of expression</u>, which, at first startling, finally confounded, subdued, and appalled me.

5. The cause of my deep agitation <u>being thus shut from view</u>, I sought eagerly the volume which discussed the paintings and their histories.

V. Discuss with your partner about each of the following statements and write an essay in no less than 200 words about your understanding of one of them.

1. The eye is the painter and the ear the singer.

2. Death is just a part of life, something we're all destined to do.

3. Good painting is like good cooking; it can be tasted but not explained.

VI. List four websites where we can learn more about Edgar Allen Poe and provide a brief introduction to each of them.

1. _____

2. _____
   _____ .
3. _____
   _____ .
4. _____
   _____
   _____ .

Text B

A Diagnosis of Death
Ambrose Bierce

在这个故事中,一个人向他的医生讲述他如何开始相信幽灵。这是一个灵异而有趣的话题。

"I am not so superstitious as some of your physicians—men of science, as you are pleased to be called," said Hawver, replying to an accusation that had not been made. "Some of you—only a few, I confess—believe in the immortality of the soul, and in apparitions which you have not the honesty to call ghosts. I go no further than a conviction that the living are sometimes seen where they are not, but have been-where they have lived so long, perhaps so intensely, as to have left their impress on everything about them. I know, indeed, that one's environment may be so affected by one's personality as to yield, long afterward, an image of one's self to

diagnosis /daɪəɡˈnəʊsɪs/ *n.* **a.** the art or act of identifying a disease from its signs and symptoms; **b.** the decision reached by diagnosis; **c.** investigation or analysis of the cause or nature of a condition, situation, or problem; **d.** a statement or conclusion from such an analysis

superstition /suːpəˈstɪʃən/ *n.* **a.** a belief or practice resulting from ignorance, fear of the unknown, trust in magic or chance, or a false conception of causation; **b.** an irrational abject attitude of mind toward the supernatural, nature, or God resulting from superstition.

superstitious *adj.* of, relating to, or swayed by superstition

physician /fɪˈzɪʃən/ *n.* a person skilled in the art of healing; specifically one educated, clinically experienced, and licensed to practice medicine as usually distinguished from surgery

confess /kənˈfes/ *v.* **a.** to tell or make known (as sth wrong or damaging to oneself), admit; **b.** to acknowledge (sin) to God or to a priest

apparition /æpəˈrɪʃən/ *n.* the spirit of a dead person moving in bodily form

conviction /kənˈvɪkʃən/ *n.* **a.** a strong persuasion or belief; **b.** the state of being convinced

the eyes of another. Doubtless the impressing personality has to be the right kind of personality as the perceiving eyes have to be the right kind of eyes—mine, for example."

"Yes, the right kind of eyes, conveying sensations to the wrong kind of brains," said Dr. Frayley, smiling.

"Thank you; one likes to have an expectation gratified; that is about the reply that I supposed you would have the civility to make."

"Pardon me. But you say that you know. That is a good deal to say, don't you think? Perhaps you will not mind the trouble of saying how you learned."

"You will call it a hallucination," Hawver said, "but that does not matter." And he told the story.

"Last summer I went, as you know, to pass the hot weather term in the town of Meridian. The relative at whose house I had intended to stay was ill, so I sought other quarters. After some difficulty I succeeded in renting a vacant dwelling that had been occupied by an eccentric doctor of the name of Mannering, who had gone away years before, no one knew where, not even his agent. He had built the house himself and had lived in it with an old servant for about ten years. His practice, never very extensive, had after a few years been given up entirely. Not only so, but he had withdrawn himself almost altogether from social life and become a recluse. I was told by the village doctor, about the only person with whom he held any relations, that during his retirement he had devoted himself to a single line of study, the result of which he had expounded in a book that did not commend itself to the approval of his professional brethren, who, indeed, considered him not entirely sane. I have not seen the book and cannot now recall the title of it, but I am told that it expounded a rather

perceive /pə'siːv/ *v.* to have or come to have knowledge of (sth) through one of the senses (esp. sight) or through the mind; see
convey /kən'veɪ/ *v.* **a.** to bear from one place to another; esp. to move in a continuous stream or mass; **b.** to impart or communicate by statement, suggestion, gesture, or appearance
gratify /'grætɪfaɪ/ *v.* **a.** to give pleasure and satisfaction to; **b.** to satisfy (a desire)
hallucination /həˌluːsɪ'neɪʃən/ *n.* **a.** perception of objects with no reality usually arising from disorder of the nervous system or in response to drugs (as LSD); **b.** the object so perceived
vacant /'veɪkənt/ *adj.* **a.** not lived in; **b.** not put to use; **c.** devoid of thought, reflection, or expression
eccentric /ɪk'sentrɪk/ *adj.* **a.** deviating from an established or usual pattern or style; **b.** deviating from conventional or accepted usage or conduct esp. in odd or whimsical ways
recluse /rɪ'kluːs/ *n.* a person who leads a secluded or solitary life
expound /ɪks'paʊnd/ *v.* **a.** to explain by setting forth in careful and often elaborate detail; **b.** to defend with argument
commend /kə'mend/ *v.* **a.** to officially recognize (someone or sth) as being worthy of praise, notice, etc.; speak favourably of (someone or sth); **b.** to put (someone or sth, esp. oneself) into the care or charge of someone else
sane /seɪn/ *adj.* **a.** proceeding from a sound mind, rational; **b.** mentally sound; esp. able to anticipate and appraise the effect of one's actions; **c.** healthy in body

startling theory. He held that it was possible in the case of many a person in good health to forecast his death with precision, several months in advance of the event. The limit, I think, was eighteen months. There were local tales of his having exerted his powers of prognosis, or perhaps you would say diagnosis; and it was said that in every instance the person whose friends he had warned had died suddenly at the appointed time, and from no assignable cause. All this, however, has nothing to do with what I have to tell; I thought it might amuse a physician."

> **forecast** /ˈfɔːkɑːst/ v. **a.** to calculate or predict (some future event or condition) usu as a result of study and analysis of available pertinent data; especially to predict (weather conditions) on the basis of correlated meteorological observations; **b.** to indicate as likely to occur
> **prognosis** /prɒgˈnəʊsɪs/ n. **a.** a doctor's opinion, based on medical experience, of what course a disease will probably take; **b.** a description of the future, judgment concerning the course and result of a set of events already begun
> **melancholy** /ˈmelənkəli/ n. **a.** an abnormal state attributed to an excess of black bile and characterized by irascibility or depression; **b.** depression of spirits
> **disposition** /ˌdɪspəˈzɪʃən/ n. **a.** prevailing tendency, mood, or inclination; **b.** temperamental makeup; **c.** the tendency of sth to act in a certain manner under given circumstances
> **addict** /əˈdɪkt/ v. to devote or surrender (oneself) to sth habitually or obsessively
> **dejection** /dɪˈdʒekʃən/ n. lowness of spirits, sadness
> **impending** /ɪmˈpendɪŋ/ adj. (usually of sth unpleasant) about to happen
> **haunt** /hɔːnt/ v. **a.** to have a disquieting or harmful effect on, trouble; **b.** to recur constantly and spontaneously to; **c.** to reappear continually in; **d.** to visit or inhabit as a ghost
> **uncanny** /ʌnˈkæni/ adj. **a.** seeming to have a supernatural character or origin, eerie, mysterious; **b.** being beyond what is normal or expected, suggesting superhuman or supernatural powers

"The house was furnished, just as he had lived in it. It was a rather gloomy dwelling for one who was neither a recluse nor a student, and I think it gave something of its character to me—perhaps some of its former occupant's character; for always I felt in it a certain melancholy that was not in my natural disposition, nor, I think, due to loneliness. I had no servants that slept in the house, but I have always been, as you know, rather fond of my own society, being much addicted to reading, though little to study. Whatever was the cause, the effect was dejection and a sense of impending evil; this was especially so in Dr. Mannering's study, although that room was the lightest and most airy in the house. The doctor's life-size portrait in oil hung in that room, and seemed completely to dominate it. There was nothing unusual in the picture; the man was evidently rather good looking, about fifty years old, with iron-grey hair, a smooth-shaven face and dark, serious eyes. Something in the picture always drew and held my attention. The man's appearance became familiar to me, and rather 'haunted' me."

"One evening I was passing through this room to my bedroom, with a lamp—there is no gas in Meridian. I stopped as usual before the portrait, which seemed in the lamplight to have a new expression, not easily named, but distinctly uncanny. It interested but did not disturb me. I moved the lamp from one side to the other and observed the effects of the altered light. While so engaged I felt an impulse to turn round. As I did so I saw a man moving across the room directly toward me! As soon as he came near enough for the lamplight to illuminate the face I saw that it was Dr. Mannering himself; it was as if the portrait were walking!"

"I beg your pardon," I said, somewhat coldly, "but if you knocked I did not hear."

"He passed me, within an arm's length, lifted his right forefinger, as in warning, and without a word went on out of the room, though I observed his exit no more than I had observed his entrance."

"Of course, I need not tell you that this was what you will call a hallucination and I call an apparition. That room had only two doors, of which one was locked; the other led into a bedroom, from which there was no exit. My feeling on realizing this is not an important part of the incident."

"Doubtless this seems to you a very commonplace "ghost story"—one constructed on the regular lines laid down by the old masters of the art. If that were so I should not have related it, even if it were true. The man was not dead; I met him to-day in Union Street. He passed me in a crowd."

Hawver had finished his story and both men were silent. Dr. Frayley absently drummed on the table with his fingers.

"Did he say anything to-day?" he asked, "anything from which you inferred that he was not dead?"

Hawver stared and did not reply.
"Perhaps," continued Frayley, "he made a sign, a gesture—lifted a finger, as in warning. It's a trick he had—a habit when saying something serious—announcing the result of a diagnosis, for example."

"Yes, he did—just as his apparition had done. But, good God! Did you ever know him?"

Hawver was apparently growing nervous.

"I knew him. I have read his book, as will every physician some

impulse /'ɪmpʌls/ *n.* **a.** a sudden spontaneous inclination or incitement to some usually unpremeditated action; **b.** a propensity or natural tendency usually other than rational
illuminate /ɪ'lu:mɪneɪt/ *v.* **a.** to supply or brighten with light; **b.** to make clear; **c.** to bring to the fore, highlight
commonplace /'kɒmənpleɪs/ *adj.* commonly found or seen, ordinary, unremarkable

day. It is one of the most striking and important of the century's contributions to medical science. Yes, I knew him; I attended him in an illness three years ago. He died."

> **manifest** /ˈmænɪfest/ *adj*. plain to see or clear to the mind. **manifestly** *adv*.
> **disturbed** /dɪsˈtɜːbd/ *adj*. having or showing signs of an illness of the mind or the feelings

Hawver sprang from his chair, manifestly disturbed. He strode forward and back across the room; then approached his friend, and in a voice not altogether steady, said, "Doctor, have you anything to say to me—as a physician?"

"No, Hawver; you are the healthiest man I ever knew. As a friend I advise you to go to your room. You play the violin like an angel. Play it; play something light and lively. Get this cursed bad Business off your mind."

The next day Hawver was found dead in his room, the violin at his neck, the bow upon the string, his music open before him at Chopin's Funeral March.

Cultural Notes

Ambrose Bierce (1842—1914)—Bierce was born in a log cabin in Ohio. His family, though strongly religious, provided him with no formal education and he left home in his teens for a military academy in Kentucky. At the outbreak of civil war, he enlisted in the Union Army in which he served with distinction—rising quickly from private to major. At the end of the war, Bierce settled in San Francisco where he began contributing articles to a number of journals. He married in 1971 before heading off to England where he completed three collections of stories. Returning to San Francisco, he worked for several papers, most notably William Randolph Hearst's *San Francisco Examiner* where his cynical but popular columns earned him a reputation as the 'literary dictator of the Pacific Coast'. It was also during this period that he completed the two short story collections *Tales of Soldiers and Civilians* and *Can Such Things Be*. Although a harsh critic of many of the conventions of his day—stating his disapproval of 'human institutions in general, including all forms of government, most laws and customs, and all contemporary literature' — Ambrose Bierce was perhaps most deeply affected by his belief in the waste and futility of war. In 1896 he was set to work on another of Hearst's papers in Washington and the entire capital reportedly 'ran for cover'. But his divorce in 1904 and the deaths of his two sons from suicide and acute alcoholism took their toll. In 1913, at the age of 71, Bierce settled his affairs and headed off to Mexico—the scene of a bloody civil war; he was said to have exclaimed: 'To be a Gringo in Mexico—ah, that is euthanasia'. The exact circumstances of his death remain unknown. His most notable work is *The Devil's Dictionary*.

Comprehension Exercises

I. Answer the following questions based on the text.
1. How did the author relate the ghost story to us?
2. Did Hawver believe in the startling theory held by the eccentric doctor?
3. How did Hawver feel in the house of Dr. Mannering?
4. How did Hawver react when Dr. Frayley told him he knew Dr. Mannering and confirmed his death to him?
5. What is the diagnosis of death in this story?

II. Write T for true and F for false in the brackets before each of the following statements.
1. (   ) Hawver was blamed by other physicians for being superstitious.
2. (   ) Hawver only believed that the image of a person may appear again in a place after he has not bee there for a long time.
3. (   ) Last summer Hawver went to Meridian to see one of his relatives who was ill.
4. (   ) The house where Hawver stayed for the summer had been rented by an eccentric doctor with the name of Mannering before.
5. (   ) Dr. Mannering expounded an appalling theory in his book after years of study.
6. (   ) As a recluse, Hawver enjoyed his own society in a room with a lot of books to read.
7. (   ) Hawver hung the doctor's portrait in his bedroom because he was deeply attracted by it.
8. (   ) Hawver was frightened when he saw the apparition of Dr. Mannering walking silently across the room.
9. (   ) Dr. Mannering had the habit of lifting one of his forefingers when announcing his diagnosis to someone.
10. (   ) Dr. Frayley tried to reassure his friend about his health and suggested him to play the violin.

III. Select the most appropriate word or phrase and use its proper form to complete each of the following sentences.

accusation	addict	amuse	civility	confess
convey	commend	disturb	eccentric	gratify
hallucination	impending	illuminate	infer	manifestly
recluse	sane	superstitious	uncanny	vacant

1. In the countryside as a young doctor she encountered ancient _____ beliefs and prejudices.
2. He was about to _____ to the waitress that he didn't have any money when a stranger approached him.
3. New evidence has emerged which supports the _____ against her.
4. We distributed thousands of leaflets to _____ the message that taking a dip could never ever wash away one's sins.
5. Similarly, a balanced home-made ration could satisfy the specific requirements of old dogs and _____ their owners.
6. The uncertainty about what is _____ and what is real exemplifies the world of the psychotic.
7. It memorializes the meeting of two remarkable _____ minds at a particular moment in intellectual history.
8. His wife became a virtual _____ for the remainder of her life.
9. His ideas are not likely to _____ themselves to most voters.
10. He tried to _____ her by calling her the affectionate nicknames "Dark Sweetie" and "Miss Chocolate."
11. He was not known to be a drug _____, but did use marijuana and alcohol.
12. When you are in the business of putting a bold face on _____ disaster, you have to put up with a lot of unpleasantness.
13. Ninety percent of the energy used to _____ a regular bulb is spent on heat rather than light.
14. He can logically _____ that if the battery is dead then the horn will not sound.
15. The advisers seemed incapable of extricating themselves from policies that were _____ not working.

IV. Paraphrase the underlined words or expressions in each sentence.

1. I know, indeed, that one's environment may be so affected by one's personality as to <u>yield</u>, long afterward, an image of one's self to the eyes of another.

2. One likes to have an expectation gratified; that is about the reply that I supposed you would have the civility to make.

_____
_____

3. During his retirement he had devoted himself to a single line of study, the result of which he had expounded in a book that did not commend itself to the approval of his professional brethren, who, indeed, considered him not entirely sane.

_____
_____

4. I felt in it a certain melancholy that was not in my natural disposition, nor, I think, due to loneliness.

_____
_____

5. If you have searched within and cannot seem to find the right reasons, use those "wrong" reasons to catapult you into action toward fulfilling your life's purpose.

_____
_____

V. Discuss with your partner about each of the following statements and write an essay in no less than 200 words about your understanding of one of them.

1. It is possible in the case of many a person in good health to forecast his death with precision.

_____
_____

2. The environment where one has lived may lend some character of its former occupant to others.

_____
_____

3. Something that always holds your attention may haunt you in a particular period of time.

_____
_____

VI. List four websites where we can learn more about ghost stories and provide a brief introduction to each of them.

1. _____
   _____.
2. _____
   _____.
3. _____
   _____.
4. _____
   _____.

Twenty Minutes' Reading

You are required to read the following sections within 20 minutes.

SECTION A

A hundred years ago it was assumed and scientifically "proved" by economists that the laws of society made it necessary to have a vast army of poor and jobless people in order to keep the economy going. Today, hardly anybody would dare to voice this principle. It is generally accepted that nobody should be excluded from the wealth Western industrialized countries, a system of insurance has been introduced which guarantees everyone a minimum of subsistence (生活维持费) in case of unemployment, sickness and old age. I would go one step further and argue that, even if these conditions are not present, everyone has the right to receive the means to subsist (维持生活), in other words, he can claim this subsistence minimum without having to have any "reason". I would suggest, however, that it should be limited to a definite period of time, let's say two years, so as to avoid the encouraging of an abnormal attitude which refused any kind of social obligation.

This may sound like a fantastic proposal, but so, I think; our insurance system would have sounded to people a hundred years ago. The main objection to such a scheme would be that if each person were entitled to receive minimum support, people would not work. This assumption rests on the fallacy of the inherent laziness in human nature, actually, aside from abnormally lazy people, there would be very few who would not want to earn more than the minimum, and who would prefer to do nothing rather than work.

However, the suspicions against a system of guaranteed subsistence minimum are not groundless, from the standpoint of those who want to use ownership of capital for the purpose of forcing others to accept the work conditions they offer. If nobody were forced to accept work in order not to starve, work would have to be sufficiently interesting and attractive to induce one to accept it. Freedom of contract is possible only if both parties are free to accept and reject it; in the present capitalist system this is not the case.

But such a system would not only be the beginning of real freedom of contract between employers and employees, its principal advantage would be the improvement of freedom in inter-personal relationships in every sphere of daily life.

1. People used to think that poverty and unemployment were due to _____.
   A. the slow development of the economy
   B. the poor and jobless people's own faults
   C. the lack of responsibility on the part of society
   D. the large number of people who were not well-educated
2. Now it is widely accepted that _____.
   A. the present system of social insurance should be improved
   B. everybody should be granted a minimum of subsistence without any "reason"
   C. everybody has the right to share in the wealth of the country
   D. people have to change their attitude towards the poor
3. The writer argues that a system of social insurance should _____.
   A. provide benefits for the sick, old and unemployed
   B. encourage people to take on more social obligations
   C. guarantee everyone the right to be employed
   D. provide everyone with the right to a minimum subsistence for a certain period
4. The word "fallacy" (Line 6, Para. 2) means _____.
   A. doubt
   B. fact
   C. strong argument
   D. wrong belief
5. According to the writer, a system of guaranteed subsistence minimum _____.
   A. demands too much from society
   B. makes freedom of contract impossible
   C. helps people take interest in their work
   D. helps bring about changes in the relationship among people

SECTION B

I live in the land of Disney, Hollywood and year-round sun. You may think people in such a glamorous, fun-filled place are happier than others. If so, you have some mistaken ideas about the nature of happiness.

Many intelligent people still equate happiness with fun. The truth is that fun and happiness have little or nothing in common. Fun is what we experience during an act. Happiness is what we experience after an act. It is a deeper, more abiding emotion.

Going to an amusement park or ball game, watching a movie or television, are fun activities that help us relax, temporarily forget our problems and maybe even laugh. But they do not bring happiness, because their positive effects end when the fun ends.

I have often thought that if Hollywood stars have a role to play, it is to teach us that happiness has nothing to do with fun. These rich, beautiful individuals have constant access to glamorous parties, fancy cars, expensive homes, everything that spells "happiness". But in memoir after memoir, celebrities reveal the unhappiness hidden beneath all their fun: depression, alcoholism, drug addiction, broken marriages, troubled children and profound loneliness.

Ask a bachelor why he resists marriage even though he finds dating to be less and less satisfying. If he's honest, he will tell you that he is afraid of making a commitment. For commitment is in fact quite painful. The single life is filled with fun, adventure and excitement. Marriage has such moments, but they are not its most distinguishing features.

Similarly, couples that choose not to have children are deciding in favor of painless fun over painful happiness. They can dine out ever they want and sleep as late as they want. Couples with infant children are lucky to get a whole night's sleep or a three-day vacation. I don't know any parent who would choose the word fun to describe raising children.

Understanding and accepting that true happiness has nothing to do with fun is one of the most liberating realizations we can ever come to. It liberates time: now we can devote more hours to activities that can genuinely increase our happiness. It liberates money: buying that new car or those fancy clothes that will do nothing to increase our happiness now seems pointless. And it liberates us from envy: we now understand that all those rich and glamorous people we were so sure are happy because they are always having so much fun actually may not be happy at all.

6. Which of the following is true?
    A. Fun creates long-lasting satisfaction.
    B. Fun provides enjoyment while pain leads to happiness.
    C. Happiness is enduring whereas fun is short-lived.
    D. Fun that is long-standing may lead to happiness.
7. To the author, Hollywood stars all have an important role to play that is to _____.
    A. rite memoir after memoir about their happiness
    B. tell the public that happiness has nothing to do with fun
    C. teach people how to enjoy their lives
    D. bring happiness to the public instead of going to glamorous parties
8. In the author's opinion, marriage _____.
    A. affords greater fun
    B. leads to raising children
    C. indicates commitment
    D. ends in pain
9. Couples having infant children _____.
    A. are lucky since they can have a whole night's sleep
    B. find fun in tucking them into bed at night
    C. find more time to play and joke with them
    D. derive happiness from their endeavor
10. If one get the meaning of the true sense of happiness, he will _____.
    A. stop playing games and joking with others
    B. make the best use of his time increasing happiness
    C. give a free hand to money
    D. keep himself with his family

Unit Nine

Text A

The Allegory of the Cave
Plato, translated by Francis M. Cornford

Next, said I, here is a parable to illustrate the degrees in which our nature may be enlightened or unenlightened. Imagine the condition of men living in a sort of cavernous chamber underground, with an entrance open to the light and a long passage all down the cave. Here they have been from childhood, chained by the leg and also by the neck, so that they cannot move and can see only what is in front of them, because the chains will not let them turn their heads. At some distance higher up is the light of a fire burning behind them; and between the prisoners and the fire is a track with a parapet built along it, like the screen at a puppet show which hides the performers while they show their puppets over the top.

I see, said he.

Now behind this parapet imagine persons carrying along various artificial objects, including figures of men and animals in wood or stone or other materials, which project above the parapet. Naturally, some of these persons will be talking, others silent.

It is a strange picture, he said, and a strange sort of prisoners.

Like ourselves, I replied; for in the first place prisoners so confined would have seen nothing of themselves or of one another, except the shadows thrown by the fire-light on the wall of the Cave facing them, would they?

Not if all their lives they had been prevented from moving their heads.

And they would have seen as little of the objects carried past.

parable /ˈpærəbl/ *n.* a short story that teaches a moral or spiritual lesson
cavernous /ˈkævənəs/ *adj.* resembling a large cave; very large
parapet /ˈpærəpɪt/ *n.* a low wall at the edge of a platform, roof, or bridge
puppet /ˈpʌpɪt/ *n.* **a.** a doll that is moved by putting your hand inside it or by pulling strings or wires that are attached to it; **b.** a person or an organization that is controlled by another person or organization
artificial /ˌɑːtɪˈfɪʃl/ *adj.* **a.** not natural or real; **b.** made, produced, or done to seem like something natural

Of course.

perplex /pəˈpleks/ v. to confuse (someone) very much

Now, if they could talk to one another, would they not suppose that their words referred only to those passing shadows which they saw?

Necessarily.

And suppose their prison had an echo from the wall facing them? When one of the people crossing behind them spoke, they could only suppose that the sound came from the shadow passing before their eyes.

No doubt.

In every way, then, such prisoners would recognize as reality nothing but the shadows of those artificial objects.

Inevitably.

Now consider what would happen if their release from the chains and the healing of their unwisdom should come about in this way. Suppose one of them set free and forced suddenly to stand up, turn his head, and walked with eyes lifted to the light; all these movements would be painful, and he would be too dazzled to make out the objects whose shadows he had been used to seeing. What do you think he would say if someone told him that what he had formerly seen was meaningless illusion, but now, being somewhat nearer to reality and turned towards more real objects, he was getting a truer view? Suppose further that he were shown the various objects being carried by and were made to say, in reply to questions, what each of them was. Would he not be perplexed and believe the objects now shown him to be not so real as what he formerly saw?

Yes, not nearly so real.

And if he were forced to look at the fire-light itself, would not his eyes ache, so that he would try to escape and turn back to the things which he could see distinctly, convinced that they really were clearer that these other objects now being shown to him?

Yes.

And suppose someone were to drag him away forcibly up the steep and rugged ascent and not let him go until he hauled him out into the sunlight, would he not suffer pain and vexation at such treatment and when he had come out into the light, find his eyes so full of its radiance that he could not see a glimpse one of the things that he was now told were real?

Certainly he would not see them all at once.

He would need, then, to grow accustomed before he could see things in that upper world. At first it would be easiest to make out shadows, and then the images of men and things reflected in water, and later on the things themselves. After that, it would be easier to watch the heavenly bodies and the sky itself by night, looking at the light of the moon and stars rather than the Sun and the Sun's light in the daytime.

Yes, surely.

Last of all, he would be able to look at the Sun and contemplate its nature, not as it appears when reflected in water or any alien medium, but as it is in itself in its own domain.

No doubt.

And now he would begin to draw the conclusion that it is the Sun that produces the seasons and the course of the year and controls everything in the visible world, and moreover is in a way the cause of all that he and his companions used to see.

Clearly he would come at last to that conclusion.

Then if he called to mind his fellow prisoners and what passed for wisdom in his former dwelling place, he would surely think himself happy in the change and be sorry for them. They may have had a practice of honoring and commending one another, with prizes for the man who had the keenest eye for

forcibly /ˈfɔːsəbli/ *adv.* made or done by physical force or violence
steep /stiːp/ *adj.* **a.** almost straight up and down; **b.** rising or falling very sharply; **c.** going up or down very quickly
rugged /ˈrʌɡɪd/ *adj.* having a rough, uneven surface
ascent /əˈsent/ *n.* the act or process of rising, moving, or climbing up
haul /hɔːl/ *v.* **a.** vto pull or drag (something) with effort; **b.** to force (someone) to go or come to a place
vexation /vekˈseɪʃn/ *n.* **a.** the state of being worried or annoyed; **b.** irritation or annoyance
radiance /ˈreɪdiəns/ *n.* **a.** a quality of brightness and happiness that can be seen on a person's face; **b.** a warm, soft light that shines from something
contemplate /ˈkɒntəmpleɪt/ *v.* **a.** to think deeply or carefully about (something); **b.** to look carefully at (something)
domain /dəˈmeɪn/ *n.* **a.** the land that a ruler or a government controls; **b.** an area of knowledge or activity

the passing shadows and the best memory for the order in which they followed or accompanied one another, so that he could make a good guess as to which was going to come next. Would our released prisoner

covet /ˈkʌvət/ v. to want (something that you do not have) very much
exalt /ɪɡˈzɔːlt/ v. a. to raise (someone or something) to a higher level; b. to praise (someone or something) highly
surmise /səˈmaɪz/ v. to form an opinion about something without definitely knowing the truth

be likely to covet those prizes or to envy the men exalted to honor and power in the Cave? Would he not feel like Homer's Achilles, that he would far sooner "be on earth as a hired servant in the house of a landless man" or endure anything rather than go back to his old beliefs and live in the old way?

Yes, he would prefer any fate to such a life.

Now imagine what would happen if he went down again to take his former seat in the Cave. Coming suddenly out of the sunlight, his eyes would be filled with darkness. He might be required once more to deliver his opinion on those shadows, in competition with the prisoners who had never been released, while his eyesight was still dim and unsteady; and it might take some time to become used to the darkness. They would laugh at him and say that he had gone up only to come back with his sight ruined; it was worth no one's time even to attempt the ascent. If they could lay hands on the man who was trying to set them free and lead them up, they would kill him.

Yes, they would.

Every feature in this parable, my dear Glaucon, is meant to fit our earlier analysis. The prison dwelling corresponds to the region revealed to us through the sense of sight, and fire-light within it to the power of the Sun. The ascent to see the things in the upper world you may take as standing for the upward journey of the soul into the region of the intelligible; then you will be in possession of what I surmise, since that is what you wish to be told. Heaven knows whether it is true; but this, at any rate, is how it appears to me. In the world of knowledge, the last thing to be perceived, the conclusion must follow that, for all things, this is the cause of whatever is right and good; in the visible world it gives birth to light and to the lord of light, while it is itself sovereign in the intelligible world and the parent of intelligence and truth. Without having had a vision of this Form no one can act with wisdom, either in his own life or in matters of state.

So far as I can understand, I share your belief.

You will see, then, Glaucon, that there will be no real injustice in compelling our philosophers to watch over and care for the other citizens. We can fairly tell them that their compeers in other states may quite reasonably refuse to collaborate: there they have sprung up, like a self-sown plant, in

compeer /kɒmˈpɪə/ *n.* a person who is of equal standing with another in a group
collaborate /kəˈlæbəreɪt/ *v.* **a.** to work with another person or group in order to achieve or do something; **b.** to give help to an enemy who has invaded your country during a war
dissension /dɪˈsenʃn/ *n.* disagreement that causes the people in a group to argue about something that is important to them
desirous /dɪˈzaɪərəs/ *adj.* **a.** wanting or wishing for something very much; **b.** feeling desire for something

despite of their country's institutions; no one has fostered their growth, and they cannot be expected to show gratitude for a care they have never received. "But," we shall say, "it is not so with you. We have brought you into existence for your country's sake as well as for your own, to be like leaders and king-bees in a hive; you have been better and more thoroughly educated than those others and hence you are more capable of playing your part both as men of thought and as men of action. You must go down, then, each in his turn, to live with the rest and let your eyes grow accustomed to the darkness. You will then see a thousand times better than those who live there always; you will recognize every image for what it is and know what it represents, because you have seen justice, beauty, and goodness in their reality; and so you and we shall find life in our commonwealth no mere dream, as it is in most existing states, where men live fighting one another about shadows and quarreling for power, as if that were a great prize; whereas in truth government can be at its best and free from dissension only where the destined rulers are least desirous of holding office."

Quite true.

Then will our pupils refuse to listen and to take their turns at sharing in the work of the community, though they may live together for most of their time in a purer air?

No; it is a fair demand, and they are fair-minded men. No doubt, unlike any ruler of the present day, they will think of holding power as an unavoidable necessity.

Yes, my friend; for the truth is that you can have a well-governed society only if you can discover for your future rulers a better way of life than being in office; then only will power be in the hands of men who are rich, not in gold, but in the wealth that brings happiness, a good and wise life. All goes wrong when, starved for

snatch /snætʃ/ v. **a.** to take (something) quickly or eagerly; **b.** to take (something or someone) suddenly from a person or place by using force

internecine /ˌɪntəˈniːsaɪn/ adj. occurring between members of the same country, group, or organization

lack of anything good in their own lives, men turn to public affairs hoping to <u>snatch</u> from thence the happiness they hunger for. They set about fighting for power, and this <u>internecine</u> conflict ruins them and their country. The life of true philosophy is the only one that looks down upon offices of state; and access to power must be confined to men who are not in love with it; otherwise rivals will start fighting. So whom else can you compel to undertake the guardianship of the commonwealth, if not those who, besides understanding best the principles of government, enjoy a nobler life than the politician's and look for rewards of a different kind?

There is indeed no other choice.

Cultural Notes

1. **Plato** (428/427BCE—348/347 BCE)—He was an ancient Greek philosopher, student of Socrates, teacher of Aristotle, and founder of the Academy, best known as the author of philosophical works of unparalleled influence.
2. **Homer's Achilles**—Homer was a Greek poet, one of the greatest and most influential writers of all time. Though almost nothing is known of his life, tradition holds that he was blind. Modern scholars generally agree that he composed (but probably did not literally write) *The Iliad*, most likely relying on oral traditions, and at least inspired the composition of *The Odyssey*. *The Iliad*, set during the Trojan War, tells the story of the wrath of Achilles, who killed Hector and was killed when Paris wounded him in the heel, his one vulnerable spot, with an arrow.

Comprehension Exercises

I. Answer the following questions based on the text.
1. What idea is the allegory intended to tell us?
2. What could the prisoners in the cave see?
3. What did the prisoners recognize as reality?
4. What would happen if the prisoners were set free?
5. What would the released prisoner draw as a conclusion after he saw the real world?

II. Write T for true and F for false in the brackets before each of the following statements.

1. (   ) The prisoners had a lot to talk about except the passing shadows they saw.
2. (   ) It would be painful for the prisoner to be set free and exposed to real light at first.
3. (   ) The released prisoner would realize that it's the Sun that produced shadows he saw before.
4. (   ) The released prisoner would prefer to go back and live in the old way.
5. (   ) Other prisoners would be happy to be set free after they talked with the released prisoner.

III. Select the most appropriate word or phrase and use its proper form to complete each of the following sentences.

alien	ascent	artificial	confine	collaborate
contemplate	desirous	dissension	echo	forcibly
heal	haul	intelligible	inevitably	illusion
perplex	puppet	steep	sovereign	snatch

1. We watched a performance which included a _____ show and acrobatics.
2. The government's plan for the _____ scenery spots is wholly misconceived.
3. Students are limiting their opportunities if they _____ themselves to their specific degrees.
4. We shouted in the valley, and in an instant the _____ came from the hillside with great distinctness.
5. Industrialization _____ led to the expansion of the urban working class.
6. A sweet balm was poured into the wound which she had thought nothing but death could _____.
7. Individual concrete pads create the _____ that they're hovering lightly above the desert floor.
8. We're dismal enough without conjuring up ghosts and visions to _____ us.
9. If you want me to put your case _____, you must brief me thoroughly beforehand.
10. Where the land doesn't sheer away beneath you, it rises in _____ needle points.
11. The climbers roped up and began the _____ of the cliff face.
12. She knows that becoming world champion is going to be a long _____.

13. They can get back into places fast and don't have the luxury of time that a skier does to _____ where they're going.
14. The sensory system may also undergo long-term adaptation in _____ environments.
15. To make a country's history _____, the historian naturally seeks for some point of unity.

IV. Paraphrase the underlined words or expressions in each sentence.

1. Would our released prisoner be likely to <u>covet those prizes</u> or to <u>envy the men exalted to honor and power</u> in the Cave?

2. He might be required once more to deliver his opinion on those shadows, <u>in competition with the prisoners</u> who had never been released, while his eyesight was still <u>dim and unsteady</u>; and it might take some time to become used to the darkness.

3. They would laugh at him and say that he had gone up only to come back <u>with his sight ruined</u>; it was worth no one's while even to <u>attempt the ascent</u>.

4. The ascent to see the things in the upper world you may take as standing for the upward journey of <u>the soul into the region of the intelligible</u>; then you will be <u>in possession of</u> what I surmise, since that is what you wish to be told.

5. <u>All goes wrong</u> when, starved for lack of anything good in their own lives, men turn to public affairs hoping to <u>snatch from thence</u> the happiness they hunger for.

V. Discuss with your partner about each of the following statements and write an essay in no less than 200 words about your understanding of one of them.

1. If they could lay hands on the man who was trying to set them free and lead them up, they would kill him.

2. Yes, my friend; for the truth is that you can have a well-governed society only if you can discover for your future rulers a better way of life than being in office; then only will power be in the hands of men who are rich, not in gold, but in the wealth that brings happiness, a good and wise life.

3. The life of true philosophy is the only one that looks down upon offices of state; and access to power must be confined to men who are not in love with it; otherwise rivals will start fighting.

VI. List four websites where we can learn more about Plato and his philosophy and provide a brief introduction to each of them.

1. _____
2. _____
3. _____
4. _____

Utopia
Sir Thomas More

Agriculture is that which is so universally understood among them that no person, either man or woman, is ignorant of it; they are instructed in it from their childhood, partly by what they learn at school, and partly by practice, they being led out often into the fields about the town, where they not only see others at work but are likewise exercised in it themselves. Besides agriculture, which is so common to them all, every man has some peculiar trade to which he applies himself; such as the manufacture of wool or flax, masonry, smith's work, or carpenter's work; for there is no sort of trade that is in great esteem among them. Throughout the island they wear the same sort of clothes, without any other distinction except what is necessary to distinguish the two sexes and the married and unmarried. The fashion never alters, and as it is neither disagreeable nor uneasy, so it is suited to the climate, and calculated both for their summers and winters. Every family makes their own clothes; but all among them, women as well as men, learn one or other of the trades formerly mentioned. Women, for the most part, deal in wool and flax, which suit best with their weakness, leaving the ruder trades to the men. The same trade generally passes down from father to son, inclinations often following descent: but if any man's genius lies another way he is, by adoption, translated into a family that deals in the trade to which he is inclined; and when that is to be done, care is taken, not only by his father, but by the magistrate, that he may be put to a discreet and good man; and if, after a person has learned one trade, he desires to acquire another, that is also allowed, and is managed in the same manner as the former. When he has learned both, he follows that which he likes best, unless the public has more occasion for the other.

The chief, and almost the only, business of the Syphogrants is to take care that no man may live idle, but that every one may follow his trade diligently; yet they do not wear themselves out with perpetual toil from morning to night, as if they were beasts of burden, which as it is indeed a heavy slavery, so it is everywhere the common course of life

---

flax /flæks/ *n.* **a.** a plant that has blue flowers and that is grown for its fiber and its seed; **b.** the fiber of the flax plant

masonry /ˈmesənri/ *n.* **a.** the stone, brick, or concrete used to build things; **b.** work done using stone, brick, or concrete

descent /dɪˈsent/ *n.* **a.** a way of going down something; **b.** a downward slope, path, etc.

magistrate /ˈmædʒɪstreɪt/ *n.* a local official who has some of the powers of a judge

discreet /dɪˈskriːt/ *n.* **a.** used to suggest that someone is being careful about not allowing something to be known or noticed by many people; **b.** not likely to be seen or noticed by many people

perpetual /pəˈpetʃuəl/ *adj.* **a.** continuing forever or for a very long time without stopping; **b.** happening all the time or very often

toil /tɔɪl/ *n.* work that is difficult and unpleasant and that lasts for a long time; *v.* **a.** to work very hard for a long time; **b.** to move slowly and with a lot of effort

amongst all mechanics except the Utopians: but they, dividing the day and night into twenty-four hours, appoint six of these for work, three of which are before dinner and three after; they then sup, and at eight o'clock, counting from noon, go to bed and sleep eight hours: the rest of their time, besides that taken up in work, eating, and sleeping, is left to every man's *discretion*; yet they are not to abuse that interval to luxury and idleness, but must employ it in some proper exercise, according to their various inclinations, which is, for the most part, reading. It is ordinary to have public lectures every morning before daybreak, at which none are obliged to appear but those who are marked out for literature; yet a great many, both men and women, of all ranks, go to hear lectures of one sort or other, according to their inclinations: but if others that are not made for contemplation, choose rather to employ themselves at that time in their trades, as many of them do, they are not hindered, but are rather commended, as men that take care to serve their country. After supper they spend an hour in some *diversion*, in summer in their gardens, and in winter in the halls where they eat, where they entertain each other either with music or discourse. They do not so much as know dice, or any such foolish and mischievous games. They have, however, two sorts of games not unlike our chess; the one is between several numbers, in which one number, as it were, consumes another; the other resembles a battle between the virtues and the vices, in which the *enmity* in the vices among themselves, and their agreement against virtue, is not unpleasantly represented; together with the special opposition between the particular virtues and vices; as also the methods by which vice either openly *assaults* or secretly undermines virtue; and virtue, on the other hand, resists it. But the time appointed for labor is to be narrowly examined, otherwise you may imagine that since there are only six hours appointed for work, they may fall under a scarcity of necessary *provisions*: but it is so far from being true that this time is not sufficient for supplying them with plenty of all things, either necessary or convenient, that it is rather too much; and this you will easily apprehend if you consider how great a part of all other nations is quite idle. First, women generally do little, who are the half of mankind; and if some few women are diligent, their husbands are idle: then consider the great company of idle priests, and of those that are called religious men; add to these all rich men, chiefly those that have estates in land, who are called noblemen and gentlemen, together with their

---

discretion /dɪˈskreʃn/ *n.* **a.** the right to choose what should be done in a particular situation; **b.** the quality of being careful about what you do and say so that people will not be embarrassed or offended

diversion /daɪˈvɜːʃn/ *n.* **a.** the act of changing the direction or use of something; **b.** something that takes attention away from what is happening

enmity /ˈenməti/ *n.* a very deep unfriendly feeling

assault /əˈsɔːlt/ *n.* the crime of trying or threatening to hurt someone physically; *v.* to violently attach (someone or something)

provision /prəˈvɪʒn/ *n.* **a.** the act or process of supplying or providing something; **b.** something that is done in advance to prepare for something else

families, made up of idle persons, that are kept more for show than use; add to these all those strong and lusty beggars that go about pretending some disease in excuse for their begging; and upon the whole account you will find that the number of those by whose labors mankind is supplied is much less than you perhaps imagined: then consider how few of those that work are employed in labors that are of real service, for we, who measure all things by money, give rise to many trades that are both vain and superfluous, and serve only to support riot and luxury: for if those who work were employed only in such things as the conveniences of life require, there would be such an abundance of them that the prices of them would so sink that tradesmen could not be maintained by their gains; if all those who labor about useless things were set to more profitable employments, and if all they that languish out their lives in sloth and idleness (every one of whom consumes as much as any two of the men that are at work) were forced to labor, you may easily imagine that a small proportion of time would serve for doing all that is either necessary, profitable, or pleasant to mankind, especially while pleasure is kept within its due bounds: this appears very plainly in Utopia; for there, in a great city, and in all the territory that lies round it, you can scarce find five hundred, either men or women, by their age and strength capable of labor, that are not engaged in it. Even the Syphogrants, though excused by the law, yet do not excuse themselves, but work, that by their examples they may excite the industry of the rest of the people; the like exemption is allowed to those who, being recommended to the people by the priests, are, by the secret suffrages of the Syphogrants, privileged from labor, that they may apply themselves wholly to study; and if any of these fall short of those hopes that they seemed at first to give, they are obliged to return to work; and sometimes a mechanic that so employs his leisure hours as to make a considerable advancement in learning is eased from being a tradesman and ranked among their learned men. Out of these they choose their ambassadors, their priests, their Tranibors, and the Prince himself, anciently called their Barzenes, but is called of late their Ademus.

And thus from the great numbers among them that are neither suffered to be idle nor to be employed in any fruitless labor, you may easily make the estimate how much may be done in those few hours in which they are obliged to labor. But, besides all that has been already said, it is to be considered that the needful arts among them are managed with less labor than anywhere else. The building or the repairing of houses among us employ many hands, because often a thriftless heir suffers a house that his

lusty /ˈlʌstɪ/ *n.* full of strength and enemy
superfluous /suːˈpɜːfluəs/ *n.* **a.** beyond what is needed; **b.** not necessary
languish /ˈlæŋgwɪʃ/ *v.* to continue for a long time without activity or progress in an unpleasant or unwanted situation
suffrage /ˈsʌfrɪdʒ/ *n.* the right to vote in an election
thriftless /ˈθrɪftlɪs/ *adj.* careless of the future

father built to fall into decay, so that his successor must, at a great cost, repair that which he might have kept up with a small charge; it frequently happens that the same house which one person built at a vast expense is neglected by another, who thinks he has a more delicate sense of the beauties of architecture, and he, suffering it to fall to ruin, builds another at no less charge. But among the Utopians all things are so regulated that men very seldom build upon a new piece of ground, and are not only very quick in repairing their houses, but show their foresight in preventing their decay, so that their buildings are preserved very long with but very little labor, and thus the builders, to whom that care belongs, are often without employment, except the hewing of timber and the squaring of stones, that the materials may be in readiness for raising a building very suddenly when there is any occasion for it. As to their clothes, observe how little work is spent in them; while they are at labor they are clothed with leather and skins, cut carelessly about them, which will last seven years, and when they appear in public they put on an upper garment which hides the other; and these are all of one color, and that is the natural color of the wool. As they need less woolen cloth than is used anywhere else, so that which they make use of is much less costly; they use linen cloth more, but that is prepared with less labor, and they value cloth only by the whiteness of the linen or the cleanness of the wool, without much regard to the fineness of the thread. While in other places four or five upper garments of woolen cloth of different colors, and as many vests of silk, will scarce serve one man, and while those that are nicer think ten too few, every man there is content with one, which very often serves him two years; nor is there anything that can tempt a man to desire more, for if he had them he would neither be the, warmer nor would he make one jot the better appearance for it. And thus, since they are all employed in some useful labor, and since they content themselves with fewer things, it falls out that there is a great abundance of all things among them; so that it frequently happens that, for want of other work, vast numbers are sent out to mend the highways; but when no public undertaking is to be performed, the hours of working are lessened. The magistrates never engage the people in unnecessary labor, since the chief end of the constitution is to regulate labor by the necessities of the public, and to allow the people as much time as is necessary for the improvement of their minds, in which they think the happiness of life consists.

Cultural Notes

1. **Thomas More** (1478—1535)—known to Roman Catholics as Saint Thomas More, was an English lawyer, social philosopher, author, statesman and noted Renaissance humanist. He was an important councilor to Henry VIII

and Lord Chancellor from October 1529 to 16 May 1532. More wrote *Utopia*, published in 1516, was about the political system of an ideal and imaginary island nation.

2. **Syphogrant**—It is the ancient name of the lower magistrate in Utopia, the ideal land invented and described by Thomas More in his book *Utopia*.

Comprehension Exercises

I. Answer the following questions based on the text.

1. What do most people do during their spare time?
2. What games do people like to play?
3. What do people do with the house they inherited from their father?
4. What do people wear when they are at work?
5. What philosophy does the author advocate in the Utopia?

II. Write T for true and F for false in the brackets before each of the following statements.

1. (   ) Men and women share the same work in the Utopia.
2. (   ) People all do some sports during their spare time.
3. (   ) People like to gamble a lot as their entertainment.
4. (   ) People spend a little money or effort maintaining their house instead of rebuilding it.
5. (   ) People in the Utopia don't care much about fashion in clothes.

III. Select the most appropriate word or phrase and use its proper form to complete each of the following sentences.

abuse	assault	incline	descent	discreet
discretion	diversion	diligent	enmity	languish
magistrate	masonry	mischievous	oblige	perpetual
superfluous	suffrage	tempt	thriftless	undermine

1. More and more countries in Europe are beginning to _____ towards some form of socialism.
2. The marriage was considered especially ignominious since she was of royal _____.
3. Then ask as many trustworthy and _____ people as you can to come up with appropriate ways to respond.
4. The two sides are now working _____ to resolve their differences.

5. He and his wife would be compelled to live _____ as second-class citizens.
6. There was no evidence of _____ or trafficking of the drug in the United States.
7. A skillful cook, who understands how to _____ his guests, will contrive to make it as expensive as they please.
8. Their _____ appearance belies their status as one of Britain's top predators.
9. The state dropped two counts each of murder, felony murder and aggravated _____.
10. The President's enemies are spreading rumors to _____ his authority
11. The crowd was so well-behaved that the police presence was _____.
12. There will be pockets of success, but the vast majority on this planet are going to _____ in misery and deprivation
13. An increasing number of states granted white manhood _____ during his administration.
14. The forbearance of the _____ in these instances was certainly wise and just.
15. These negative moods continue to _____ alcoholics to return to drinking long after physical withdrawal symptoms have abated.

IV. Paraphrase the underlined words or expressions in each sentence.

1. Besides agriculture, which is so common to them all, every man has some peculiar trade to which he applies himself; such as the manufacture of wool or flax, masonry, smith's work, or carpenter's work; for there is no sort of trade that is <u>in great esteem</u> among them.

   _____
   _____

2. The chief, and almost the only, business of the Syphogrants is to take care that no man may <u>live idle</u>, but that every one may follow his trade diligently; yet they do not <u>wear themselves out</u> with <u>perpetual toil</u> from morning to night...

   _____
   _____

3. ...but if others that are not made for <u>contemplation</u>, choose rather to employ themselves at that time in their trades, as many of them do, they are <u>not hindered, but are rather commended</u>, as men that take care to serve their

country.

4. But the time appointed for labor is to be narrowly examined, otherwise you may imagine that since there are only six hours appointed for work, they may fall under a scarcity of necessary provisions...

5. ...then consider how few of those that work are employed in labors that are of real service, for we, who measure all things by money, give rise to many trades that are both vain and superfluous, and serve only to support riot and luxury...

V. Discuss with your partner about each of the following statements and write an essay in no less than 200 words about your understanding of one of them.

1. And thus, since they are all employed in some useful labor, and since they content themselves with fewer things, it falls out that there is a great abundance of all things among them...

2. The magistrates never engage the people in unnecessary labor, since the chief end of the constitution is to regulate labor by the necessities of the public, and to allow the people as much time as is necessary for the improvement of their minds, in which they think the happiness of life consists.

3. And thus from the great numbers among them that are neither suffered to be idle nor to be employed in any fruitless labor, you may easily make the estimate how much may be done in those few hours in which they are obliged to labor.

VI. List four websites where we can learn more about Utopia and provide a brief introduction to each of them.

1.

2. _____.

3. _____.

4. _____.

Twenty Minutes' Reading

You are required to read the following sections within 20 minutes.

 **SECTION A**

Biologically, there is only one quality which distinguishes us from animals: the ability to laugh. In a universe which appears to be utterly devoid of humor, we enjoy this supreme luxury. And it is a luxury, for unlike any other bodily process, laughter does not seem to serve a biologically useful purpose. In a divide world, laughter is a unifying force. Human beings oppose each other on a great many issues. Nations may disagree about systems of government and human relations may be plagued by ideological factions and political camps, but we all share the ability to laugh. And laughter, in turn, depends on that most complex and subtle of all human qualities: a sense of humor. Certain comic stereotypes have a universal appeal. This can best be seen from the world-wide popularity of Charlie Chaplin's early films. The little man at odds with society never fails to amuse no matter which country we come from. As that great commentator on human affairs, Dr. Samuel Johnson, once remarked, "Men have been wise in very different modes; but they have always laughed in the same way."

A sense of humor may take various forms and laughter may be anything from a refined tingle to an earth quaking roar, but the effect is always the same. Humor helps us to maintain a correct sense of values. It is the one quality which political fanatics appear to lack. If we can see the funny side, we never make the mistake of taking ourselves too seriously. We are always reminded that tragedy is not really far removed from comedy, so we never get a sided view of things.

This is one of the chief functions of satire and irony. Human pain and suffering are so grim; we hover so often on the brink of war; political realities are usually enough to plunge us into total despair. In such circumstances, cartoons and satirical accounts of somber political events redress the balance. They take the wind out of pompous and arrogant politicians who have lost their sense of proportion. They enable us to see that many of our most profound actions are merely comic or absurd. We laugh when a great satirist like Swift writes about war in Gulliver's Travels. The Lilliputians and their neighbors attack each other because they can't agree which end to break an egg. We laugh because we meant to laugh; but we are meant to weep too. It is too powerful a weapon to be allowed to flourish in totalitarian regimes.

The sense of humor must be singled out as man's most important quality because it is associated with laughter. And laughter, in turn, is associated with happiness. Courage, determination, initiative, these are qualities we share with other forms of life. But the sense of humor is uniquely human. If happiness is one of the great goals of life, then it is the sense of humor that provides the key.

1. The most important of all human qualities is _____.
   A. a sense of humor   B. a sense of satire
   C. a sense of laughter   D. a sense of history
2. The author mentions about Charlie Chaplin's early films because _____.
   A. they can amuse people
   B. human beings are different from animals
   C. they show that certain comic stereotypes have a universal appeal
   D. they show that people have the same ability to laugh
3. One of the chief functions of irony and satire is _____.
   A. to show absurdity of actions
   B. to redress balance
   C. to take the wind out of politicians
   D. to show too much grimness in the world
4. What do we learn from the sentence "it is too powerful a weapon to be allowed to flourish in totalitarian regimes"?
   A. It can reveal the truth of political events with satire.
   B. It can arouse people to riot.
   C. It shows tragedy and comedy are related.
   D. It can make people laugh.
5. Who is Swift?
   A. A novelist.   B. A poet.
   C. A dramatist.   D. An essayist.

SECTION B

Pop stars today enjoy a style of living which was once the prerogative only of Royalty. Wherever they go, people turn out in their thousands to greet them. The crowds go wild trying to catch a brief glimpse of their smiling, colorfully dressed idols. The stars are transported in their chauffeur driven Rolls-Royces, private helicopters or executive aeroplanes. They are surrounded by a permanent entourage of managers, press agents and bodyguards. Photographs of them appear regularly in the press and all their comings and goings are reported, for, like Royalty, pop stars are news. If they enjoy many of the privileges of Royalty, they certainly share many of the inconveniences as well. It is dangerous for them to make unscheduled appearances in public. They must be constantly shielded from the adoring crowds which idolize them. They are no longer private individuals, but public property. The financial rewards they receive for this sacrifice cannot be calculated, for their rates of pay are astronomical.

And why not? Society has always rewarded its top entertainers lavishly. The great days of Hollywood have become legendary: famous stars enjoyed fame, wealth and adulation on an unprecedented scale. By today's standards, the excesses of Hollywood do not seem quite so spectacular. A single gramophone record nowadays may earn much more in royalties than the films of the past ever did. The competition for the title "Top of the Pops" is fierce, but the rewards are truly colossal.

It is only right that the stars should be paid in this way. Don't the top men in industry earn enormous salaries for the services they perform to their companies and their countries? Pop stars earn vast sums in foreign currency often more than large industrial concerns and the taxman can only be grateful for their massive annual contributions to the exchequer. So who would begrudge them their rewards?

It's all very well for people in humdrum jobs to moan about the successes and rewards of others. People who make envious remarks should remember that the most famous stars represent only the tip of the iceberg. For every famous star, there are hundreds of others struggling to earn a living. A man working in a steady job and looking forward to a pension at the end of it has no right to expect very high rewards. He has chosen security and peace of mind, so there will always be a limit to what he can earn. But a man who attempts to become a star is taking enormous risks. He knows at the outset that only a handful of competitors ever get to the very top. He knows that years of concentrated effort may be rewarded with complete failure. But he knows, too, that the rewards for success are very high indeed: they are the recompense for the huge risks involved and if he achieves them, he has certainly earned them. That's the essence of private enterprise.

6. The sentence "Pop stars' style of living was once the prerogative only of Royalty" means_____.
    A. their life was as luxurious as that of royalty
    B. they enjoy what once only belonged to the royalty
    C. they are rather rich
    D. their way of living was the same as that of the royalty
7. What is the author's attitude towards top stars' high income?
    A. Approval.   B. Disapproval.
    C. Ironical.   D. Critical.
8. It can be inferred from the passage_____.
    A. there exists fierce competition in climbing to the top
    B. people are blind in idolizing stars
    C. successful Pop stars give great entertainment
    D. the tax they have paid are great
9. What can we learn from the passage?
    A. Successful man should get high-income repayment.
    B. Pop stars made great contribution to a country.
    C. Pop stars can enjoy the life of royalty.
    D. Successful men represent the tip of the iceberg.
10. Which paragraph covers the main idea?
    A. The first.   B. The second.
    C. The third.   D. The fourth.

Unit Ten

Text A   **How to Escape out of Thought Traps?**
Anonymous

每个人都会面临精神和思维的困境,在当今社会如何脱离它尤其成为人们研究和论争的焦点问题,本文通过对于困境的分析试图找出一条对症的解决办法。

Have you ever been really sure about something, only to find out you were mistaken? Did you notice how you operated "as if" you were correct? You may have even seen, heard, touched, tasted, or smelled the world in a way to support your <u>stance</u>. And perhaps you felt you had solid logic to support this position.

So how did the possibility of an opposite opinion make its way through your logic and basically the reality as you knew it, to get you to change your mind? Did you fight hard to stay where you were? Did you go through so called "denial"? Did you lock in to your position, and build up a wall to prevent entry of any contrary thought?

Now the question I have for you is, "Were you keeping them out or were you trapping yourself in?"

In sales, a prospect may be dead-set in his view about a particular product or service. Now the <u>sales rep</u> may know that the prospect does not have all the facts yet, so he sets out trying to convey this to the prospect.

One of two things can result. One the prospect tightens the grip on his view or two he begins to shift his perception. Now this of course depends on the <u>rapport</u> and sales strategy used by the sales professional to enter

stance /stæns/ *n.* **a.** a way of standing or being placed, posture; **b.** intellectual or emotional attitude
sales rep means "sales representative", whose job is to sell some product to customers
rapport /ræˈpɔː/ *n.* relation; esp. relation marked by harmony, conformity, accord, or affinity

176

into the prospect's "thought blockade" and free him from that "one" perspective. Listen to the conversations around you, perhaps even the words coming out of your own mouth, are you building your own thought blockade or "thought trap"?

If so, how do you get out? Then (If so desired!) how do you get others out?

Recognize The Traps!

Let's start by looking at the traps of the intellectual mind, the one who weaves such wonderful webs of logic that leaves us feeling good while keeping us quite stuck.

> **blockade** /blɒˈkeɪd/ *n.* **a.** the isolation by a warring nation of an enemy area (as a harbor) by troops or warships to prevent passage of persons or supplies; broadly a restrictive measure designed to obstruct the commerce and communications of an unfriendly nation; **b.** sth that blocks
> **congruent** /ˈkɒŋgruənt/ *adj.* **a.** being in agreement, harmony, or correspondence; **b.** conforming to the circumstances or requirements of a situation, appropriate
> **intellect** /ˈɪntɪlekt/ *n.* **a.** the power of knowing as distinguished from the power to feel and to will, the capacity for knowledge; **b.** the capacity for rational or intelligent thought esp. when highly developed; **c.** a person with great intellectual powers
> **validate** /ˈvælɪdeɪt/ *v.* **a.** to support or corroborate on a sound or authoritative basis; **b.** to recognize, establish, or illustrate the worthiness or legitimacy of
> **validation** *n.* an act, process, or instance of validating

Trap One: Being Right

I often tell the couples I work with, "Do you want to be happy or do you want to be right?" Surprisingly, I see quite a lot of incongruent responses. It is like they know they should say "be happy" and (that's why they do), but in fact, they really want to say "be right". Now the real interesting thing is that the intellect wants to be right, regardless of you being right or not. Confused?

Then let's make an important distinction.

You are not your intellect! You the being (soul) are much, much more! The intellect's limitations are not your limitations to the degree that you can separate your "self" (soul) from the intellect. Recognizing these traps and how to avoid them will help in that separation process.

Trap Two: Validation

The intellect seeks constant validation. It is constantly saying recognize me, notice me, "Hey! I'm over here!" Whether it is validation from authorities or peers, this need for validation becomes a crucial trap to avoid. Kids learn this early on. A child comes Home with their report card in hand and an eager look of anticipation, waiting for those few key words, "Oh honey, you did great!" Yeah! The kids can now feel worthy. Now imagine what happens when this is compounded over a few decades. Pretty soon we are all looking for validation in every direction.

Trap Three: Sharing

I've just got to tell you about this one. Oh you won't believe it. The intellect likes to share things. Through sharing it can feel more validated and of course be right. Ever felt like crap and wanted to let others know that you felt that way? Did you hope they would sympathize with your story and tell you how right you are in feeling this way? Hoping they would validate your stance? If so, then you fell into another trap to feed the intellect while starving your real self.

Trap Four: Safety

As the intellect spins its logic, forming a thought blockade, it is also creating a sense of safety. If it constructs well-thought-out logic that sounds reasonable, it is safe from any challenges. So what happens when a contrary idea comes knocking on the door? The intellect's internal safety procedure is kicked in. You may have seen the behaviors that go along with such an internal process if you have ever challenged someone's "sacred cow."

A woman called me up a few weeks back and wanted me to see her son because he was very messy. She asked if I could hypnotize him to always clean up after himself. I told her that it certainly was possible; however I wanted to know a few things first. So I asked her what happens to her when she sees that he hasn't cleaned up after himself? She replied with great tension in her voice, "Well that just makes my blood boil!" So I asked if it always made her blood boil. She stammered, "Yes!"

Then I asked her what she thought about her response she had to his messiness. I asked her what kinds of effects she thinks this may be having on her own body, her health. I continued by saying, what if she could see a messy room and her blood not boil. Talk about running full force right into a sacred cow. (Moooove!)

crap /kræp/ n. a. (usually vulgar) feces; b. (usually vulgar) the act of defecating; c. (sometimes vulgar) nonsense rubbish
sacred cow one that is often unreasonably immune from criticism or opposition
messy /'mesi/ adj. a. marked by confusion, disorder, or dirt; b. lacking neatness or precision; c. extremely unpleasant or trying
hypnotize /'hɪpnətaɪz/ v. a. to induce hypnosis in; b. to dazzle or overcome by or as if by suggestion
tension /'tenʃən/ n. a feeling of nervous anxiety, worry, pressure
make one's blood boil make someone greatly and suddenly angry
stammer /'stæmə/ v. to make involuntary stops and repetitions in speaking

Her intellect's safety alerts kicked in immediately. She got very defensive and went on tirade about how she was right, and no one could see all that she went through day in and day out, raising three kids while working, and if her blood didn't boil she would become just as lazy as her son, and the whole house would be a wreck. Then she ended the call by saying that she was perfectly fine, and it was her son who had the problem.

> **tirade** /taɪˈreɪd/ *n.* a long very angry scolding speech
> **retort** /rɪˈtɔːt/ *n.* a quick, rather angry, often amusing answer
> **external** /ɪkˈstɜːnl/ *adj.* **a.** capable of being perceived outwardly; **b.** of, relating to, or connected with the outside or an outer part
> **externalize** *v.* to make external
> **manifest** /ˈmænɪfest/ *v.* to make evident or certain by showing or displaying
> **seductive** /sɪˈdʌktɪv/ *adj.* having alluring or tempting qualities

Now how many of you identified with her story, sympathized with her stance? Did you get sucked into the trap? Did you let her logical retort validate your own stance?

Go back and read it again. What did she do? How did she trap herself? Her intellect screamed bloody murder the moment we came up on her sacred cow of cleanliness.

It started by building a logical argument around why she was right and he (or me, for challenging her) was in the wrong. She used that along with the lack of validation and recognition from everyone else to validate her logic. And finally, she felt compelled to share it with me to externalize the trap and manifest it into reality.

By sharing, the logic is not just a construct in her mind anymore. Adding voice and breath to it begins to give it a life of its own. This is where the pointing begins. And remember whenever there is one finger pointing outwards, there are three fingers pointing back to the person doing the pointing.

Getting Out of the Trap

Now that you know what to look out for, you can begin using the tools below to stay out as well as help others to stay out of those thought traps. Remember this takes practice. The hardest step is to recognize it. The moment you do recognize it you are in a sense already on your way out. But then it is about freeing yourself from the logic that the intellect has spun around the trap. Even then you may find it is easier to spot other people's traps quicker than your own. And the reason for that is because your own logic is most seductive to you not to others. So while they may be seduced by their logic, you can clearly see through it. And it certainly works the other way around as well. So go slowly with this at first. You don't want to find yourself at the end of the week with no friends because you challenged all their sacred cows without maintaining rapport.

Cultural Notes

sacred cow—Figuratively, it refers to anything that is beyond criticism. For example, "That housing project is a real sacred cow: the city council won't hear of abandoning it." It's an English-language formulation of the Hindu principle of the sanctity of all life, including animal life and especially that of the cow, which is accorded veneration. In India, followers of Hinduism consider cows sacred and do not eat them because they believe the animals contain the souls of dead persons.

Comprehension Exercises

I. Answer the following questions based on the text.

1. How do you understand "prospect" in the fourth paragraph?
2. How do you know you are building a thought blockade for yourself?
3. What is the purpose of the author to mention the woman and her son?
4. What is "sacred cow", according to your understanding?
5. What did the author suggest us to do to stay out of a thought blockade?

II. Write T for true and F for false in the brackets before each of the following statements.

1. (　　) Even what you are sure about may turn out to be incorrect in reality.
2. (　　) If you fight hard against whatever thought contrary to you, you may get stuck in a thought trap.
3. (　　) The being of a person cannot be separated from the intellect although they are often inconsistent with each other.
4. (　　) Children suffer from more thinking traps than adults.
5. (　　) The intellect needs to share feeling with others so as to validate the person's stance.
6. (　　) A woman visited the author and complained a lot about her son's messiness.
7. (　　) The internal safety procedure shelters one from one's own defects.
8. (　　) You should never point your fingers at others no matter how angry you are.

9. (　　) Once you know what the traps are, you'll easily escape out of them.
10. (　　) You should point out the others' thought traps as soon as you've found them.

III. Select the most appropriate word or phrase and use its proper form to complete each of the following sentences.

anticipation	convey	crap	crucial	denial
externalize	hypnotize	incongruent	intellect	messy
perception	rapport	retort	sympathize	stammer
seductive	spin	tension	trap	validation

1. The equality of one class of human beings cannot be purchased by the _____ of the equality of another.
2. One should learn from past mistakes so as to avoid falling into the same old _____ again.
3. We distributed thousands of leaflets to _____ the message that taking a dip could never ever wash away one's sins.
4. Visual illusions are defined by the dissociation between the physical reality and the subjective _____ of an object or event.
5. The subsequent _____ between the two principals assisted the transition process.
6. The midlevel and corps ensemble is full of strong dancers, but sometimes looks ragged or stylistically _____.
7. Again the human _____ is what separates us from animals and confers us with a significant advantage.
8. Some senior professors say the process has brought them _____ and appreciation.
9. Another _____ factor may be the existence of large fund-management firms, whose portfolios are diversified across the globe.
10. But at this time of year, many parents of college-bound students approach their mailboxes with great _____.
11. Although he pretended to _____, he was laughing in his sleeve.
12. Nonetheless, very few managers look forward to dealing with "_____" declining performance situations.
13. This is perhaps the proper place to relate the history of Grandet's _____ and deafness.
14. Emitters of greenhouse gases _____ the true costs of their contribution to climate change.

15. The ability to tweak well-known characters for modern times makes fairy tales particularly _____.

IV. Paraphrase the underlined words or expressions in each sentence.

1. Let's start by looking at the traps of the intellectual mind, the one who <u>weaves such wonderful webs of logic</u> that leaves us feeling good while <u>keeping us quite stuck</u>.

2. If so, then you fell into another trap to <u>feed the intellect while starving your real self</u>.

3. Did you let her <u>logical retort validate your own stance</u>?

4. Her intellect <u>screamed bloody murder</u> the moment we came up on her <u>sacred cow of cleanliness</u>.

5. And finally, she <u>felt compelled to</u> share it with me to <u>externalize the trap</u> and manifest it into reality.

V. Discuss with your partner about each of the following statements and write an essay in no less than 200 words about your understanding of one of them.

1. You are not your intellect! You the being (soul) are much, much more!

2. The intellect's need for validation is a crucial trap to avoid.

3. You may find it is easier to spot other people's traps quicker than your own.

VI. List four websites where we can learn more about logical argument and provide a brief introduction to each of them.

1. _____
   _____
   _____.
2. _____
   _____
   _____.
3. _____
   _____
   _____.
4. _____
   _____
   _____.

Text B

Motivated by All the Wrong Reasons
Teresa Franklyn

这是一种"反其道"的论述，但是揭示了生活中的真理：我们并不是只受正面因素的影响，而如何利用和对待负面影响是每个人都应该重视的。

Sometimes trying to be spiritual holds us back from actually living the spiritual life we want. In our quest to live such spiritual and good lives, we often avoid the stuff that makes us seem unspiritual, even if that very stuff can move us toward our own spiritual growth.

Spiritual seekers are well aware of the power of intention. We know that it is the thought behind the action that is more important than the action itself. We know if we are motivated by fear and take action based on that fear, the results can be limiting and work against us.

Because of this, we try to align our intentions with that of love, abundance and wholeness. Unfortunately, for many of us, when we go within to explore our motivation, seeking that deeper answer to why we want something, we sometimes end up no deeper than where we began. We might tell ourselves we really want to do or get

quest /kwest/ *n.* an act or instance of seeking
motivate /ˈməʊtɪveɪt/ *v.* to provide with a motive, impel
align /əˈlaɪn/ *v.* **a.** to bring into line or alignment; **b.** to array on the side of or against a party or cause

something in order to help humanity or some other noble reason to make us feel better about ourselves, but in reality, we may simply be motivated by money, greed, fame, power, etc.

Upon discovering this, we then sit around telling ourselves we don't want to do something unless we are doing it for the right reasons. So we sit, and sit, and sit. Years pass and we're still sitting, waiting for that right reason to come, that spiritual, pure and noble reason.

While it is noble to want to act out of the right reasons, sometimes the wrong reasons can be just the catalyst we need in order to take action and find the right reasons.

It is through the process of pursuing our destiny that we create our destiny and discover who we truly are and what we're all about. If we sit around waiting to be noble and whole before we act toward nobility and wholeness, we will never get there.

When I was 19, I dated a recovering alcoholic. He was in Alcoholics Anonymous and suggested that I go to Al-Anon (for family & friends of alcoholics) to better understand him. He also knew that my father happened to drink quite a bit and thought it would be good for me to understand more about alcoholism in general. For no other reason than to please him and be a "good" girlfriend, I went. I certainly didn't think I needed to go, not for me, for him, or for my father.

Now we all know that people-pleasing, an ego-driven motive, is not a spiritually good reason to do something. But was it the right reason for me? Yes. And here's why.

In those meetings, I learned about the true nature of alcoholism. I learned that I am not to blame for my father's drinking (I didn't even know I had been blaming myself). I learned that I am worthy, valuable and important. I learned to trust in a Higher Power, have faith that the Universe is in order and most importantly, I learned to trust and

catalyst /ˈkætlɪst/ *n.* **a.** a substance that enables a chemical reaction to proceed at a usually faster rate or under different conditions (as at a lower temperature) than otherwise possible; **b.** an agent that provokes or speeds significant change or action

destiny /ˈdestɪni/ *n.* **a.** sth to which a person or thing is destined, fortune; **b.** a predetermined course of events often held to be an irresistible power or agency

alcoholic /ˌælkəˈhɒlɪk/ **a.** *adj.* of, relating to, or caused by alcohol; **b.** *adj.* affected with alcoholism; **c.** *n.* a person affected with alcoholism

anonymous /əˈnɒnɪməs/ *adj.* **a.** not named or identified; **b.** of unknown authorship or origin

ego /ˈiːɡəʊ/ *n.* the self, esp. as seen in relation to other selves or to the outside world

believe in myself.

All of this came out of my ego's desire to please someone else, to make them think that I am a "good" girlfriend and therefore, a "good" person.

Had I refused to go because my intentions weren't pure and spiritually driven, who knows how many more years I would have lived in blame, shame and denial.

My point is, don't sit around and wait for the right reasons to motivate you. Sometimes the right reasons come disguised as the wrong reasons. If greed is the only thing that will motivate you to get up off that couch and take action toward your dreams, I say go for it! Use whatever you have currently available to you, right or wrong, good or bad, to start the process.

If you have searched within and cannot seem to find the right reasons, use those "wrong" reasons to catapult you into action toward fulfilling your life's purpose. Somewhere along the way, the right reasons will emerge and make themselves very clear to you. Often we think we want something for a certain reason and when we get it, or while in the process of getting it, we discover the true meaning behind our motivations. Or our reasons change, our intentions and motivation changes as we learn and grow.

I have a friend who started a business years ago strictly to make money. Her husband left her and she had to find a way to not only support herself, but also to prove to him that she didn't need him. It was part necessity, part revenge. Actually, to be quite honest, it was mostly revenge. She could have easily taken an office job to support herself since her previous employer before she married had offered her old job back. But she refused. She wanted to make lots of money and become a successful Business woman to spite her ex-husband.

Two years into the business, she discovered that she loved working for herself. She loved the independence and satisfaction that creating her own income generated inside her. Her business transformed as she transformed. She found

denial /dɪˈnaɪəl/ *n.* refusal to satisfy a request or desire

disguise /dɪsˈgaɪz/ *v.* **a.** to change the customary dress or appearance of; **b.** to furnish with a false appearance or an assumed identity

catapult /ˈkætəpʌlt/ *v.* to throw or launch by or as if by a catapult

fulfill /fʊlˈfɪl/ *v.* **a.** to put into effect, execute; **b.** to meet the requirements of (a business order)

revenge /rɪˈvendʒ/ *n.* action taken in return for an injury or offense

spite /spaɪt/ *v.* annoy, offend

joyous /ˈdʒɔɪəs/ *adj.* joyful
embrace /ɪmˈbreɪs/ *v.* **a.** to clasp in the arms, hug; **b.** cherish, love; **c.** encircle, enclose; **d.** to take up esp. readily or gladly
martyrdom /ˈmɑːtədəm/ *n.* the suffering of death on account of adherence to a cause and esp. to one's religious faith
sainthood /ˈseɪnthʊd/ *n.* the quality or state of being a saint

that she loved seeing her customers happy and began focusing a big part of her Business toward customer satisfaction. She discovered that she had a lot of strength and courage and didn't need to depend on anyone else for her well-being.

Motivated initially by revenge, she soon learned that it didn't matter what he thought. In fact, to this day, she has no idea if he knows about her success and she could care less. She is happy, confident and leads a joyous and full life. She is no longer motivated by revenge, spite or ego-driven desires.

Like me, had she not taken action and instead sat around waiting for more noble intentions, it is uncertain where she would be today.

So go out and live your dreams. Lead your spiritual life by accepting and embracing seemingly unspiritual things. Go after your goals, no matter how unspiritually motivated they may be. If this is the only way to get you moving, it doesn't matter if you are doing it for money, revenge, greed, power, attention, glory, martyrdom, sainthood or any other ego-driven desire. Along the way, you'll find your true self and all those "wrong" reasons will fall away and be replaced by more pure and noble reasons. If it takes a wrong reason to turn your life around toward wholeness, it must not be so "wrong" after all.

Cultural Notes

Al-Anon—Al-Anon offers understanding and support for families and friends of problem drinkers, whether the alcoholic is still drinking or not. Alateen, a part of Al-Anon, is for young people aged 12—17 (inclusive) who have been affected by someone else's drinking, usually that of a parent. The parents, children, wives, husbands, friends and colleagues of alcoholics could all be helped by Al-Anon and Alateen whether or not the drinker in their lives recognises that a problem exists. At Al-Anon group meetings members receive comfort and understanding and learn to cope with their problems through the exchange of experience, strength and hope. The sharing of problems binds individuals and groups together in a bond that is protected by a policy of anonymity. Members learn that there are things they can do to help themselves and indirectly to help the problem drinker. Changed attitudes, which come from greater understanding of the illness, may result in the drinker seeking help. Al-Anon is self-supporting through members' voluntary contributions and the sale of its literature. The groups are non-professional and have no religious or other affiliations and no opinions on outside issues. Al-Anon is based on the Twelve Steps and Twelve Traditions adapted from Alcoholics Anonymous; it is non-professional, self-supporting, non-religious, non-political and multi-racial.

Comprehension Exercises

I. Answer the following questions based on the text.

1. What is the meaning of "spiritual" in the first paragraph?
2. How can the wrong reasons be the catalyst we need to find the right ones?
3. How do you understand "wrong reasons" in the text?
4. How did the author convey her idea to us?
5. What is the main idea of the text?

II. Write T for true and F for false in the brackets before each of the following statements.

1. (   ) We are always in the quest of noble motivations for doing things.
2. (   ) Only when we act out of right reasons can we live spiritual lives.
3. (   ) Most of us are deceitful to say that we want to get something in order to help humanity.
4. (   ) We should sit around waiting for the coming of the right reasons.
5. (   ) The author's father had been in Al-Anon for some years.
6. (   ) The author regretted having been to the meetings of Al-Anon in order to please her boyfriend.
7. (   ) The right reasons may come in disguise of the wrong ones.
8. (   ) Mostly for the sake of money, the author's friend started her own business after being deserted by her husband.
9. (   ) The woman leads a joyous life in the revenge of her ex-husband.
10. (   ) The writer was not sure whether her friend, without a noble intention, should take action or not.

III. Select the most appropriate word or phrase and use its proper form to complete each of the following sentences.

abundance	alcoholic	align	anonymous	blame
catapult	catalyst	destiny	denial	disguise
ego	embrace	joyous	martyrdom	motivate
quest	spiritual	spite	valuable	worthy

1. They were always moving from place to place in _____ of a cheap situation, and always spending more than they ought.
2. And you know what they are going to _____ me and I'll probably do better if they're booing me every day.
3. Hawks and golden eagles soar over the prairies, swooping down to dine on an _____ of prey, catching even speedy jackrabbits.
4. The workers' demand for better conditions was a _____ for social change.
5. They wanted our seal to be an allegory representing the _____ of the new nation.
6. An _____ fermentation by yeasts is an essential step in the production of raised breads.
7. Companies are using an old legal tool, the subpoena, to expose _____ posters on Internet discussion boards
8. Avoid having your _____ so close to your position that when your position falls, your ego goes with it.
9. For decades, community colleges have tried to shift the _____ for low transfer rates to the four year colleges.
10. The _____ of human rights to any individual is against the constitution.
11. I had learned her whole character, which was without mystery or _____.
12. Josef Krips at the State Opera hired her in _____ of the fact that she had never sung on stage.
13. There is nothing more _____ than the arrival of a new baby.
14. Taiwan will return to the _____ of the motherland; the whole country must be united. This is the general trend of development and the common aspiration of the people.
15. The researchers concluded that cattle do generally _____ themselves in a north-south direction.

IV. Paraphrase the underlined words or expressions in each sentence.

1. Sometimes trying to be spiritual <u>holds us back</u> from actually living the spiritual life we want.

2. Because of this, we try to <u>align our intentions with</u> that of love, abundance and wholeness.

3. <u>For no other reason than to please him</u> and be a "good" girlfriend, I went.

4. <u>People-pleasing</u>, an <u>ego-driven motive</u>, is not a spiritually good reason to do something.

5. If you have searched within and cannot seem to find the right reasons, use those "wrong" reasons to <u>catapult you into action toward</u> fulfilling your life's purpose.

V. Discuss with your partner about each of the following statements and write an essay in no less than 200 words about your understanding of one of them.

1. It is the thought behind the action that is more important than the action itself.

2. When we go within to explore our motivation to actions, we sometimes end up no deeper than where we began.

3. Sometimes the right reasons of doing things come in disguise of the wrong ones.

VI. List four websites where we can learn more about motivation and provide a brief introduction to each of them.

1. _____
_____
_____.

2. _____
_____
_____
_____.

3. _____
_____
_____
_____.

4. _____
_____
_____
_____.

Twenty Minutes' Reading

You are required to read the following sections within 20 minutes.

SECTION A

Public speaking fills most people with dread. Humiliation is the greatest gear; self-exposure and failing to appeal to the audience come a close second. Women hate it most, since girls are pressurized from an early age to be concerned with appearances of all kinds.

Most people have plenty of insecurities, and this seems like a situation that will bring them out. If you were under pressure to be perfect, you are terrified of failing in the most public ways.

While extroverts will feel less fear before the ordeal, it does not mean they will necessarily do it better. Some very shy people manage to shine. When I met the British Julian Clary, he was shy and cautious, yet his TV performances are perfect.

In fact, personality is not the best predictor of who does it well. Regardless of what you like in real life, the key seems to be to act yourself. Actual acting, as in performing the scripted lines of a character other than you, does not do the job. While politicians may limit damage by having carefully rehearsed, written scripts to speak from, there is always a hidden awareness among the audience that the words might not be true.

Likewise, the incredibly perfect speeches of many American academics are far from natural. You may end up buying their book on the way out, but soon afterwards, it is much like fast food, and you get a nameless sense that you have been cheated.

Although, as Earl Spencer proved at his sister Princess Diana's funeral, it is possible both to prepare every word and to act naturally. A script rarely works and it is used to help most speakers. But, being yourself doesn't work either. If you spoke as if you were in your own kitchen, it would be too authentic, too unaware of the need to communicate with the audience.

I remember going to see British psychiatrist R.D. Laing speak in public. He behaved like a seriously odd person, talking off the top of his head. Although he was talking about madness and he wrote on mental illness, he seemed to be exhibiting rather than explaining it.

The best psychological place from which to speak is an unselfconsciousness, providing the illusion of being natural. Studies suggest that this state of "flow", as psychologists call it, is very satisfying.

1. Women hate public speaking most mainly because of _____.
   A. their upbringing very early on
   B. their inability to appeal to the audience
   C. their sense of greater public pressure
   D. their sense of greater humiliation
2. In the second paragraph, "this" refers to _____.
   A. insecurity   B. sense of failure
   C. public speaking   D. pressure
3. What is the author's view on personality?
   A. Personality is the key to success in public speaking.
   B. Extroverts are better public speakers.
   C. Introverts have to learn harder to be good speakers.
   D. Factors other than personality ensure better performances.
4. The author implies that while speaking R. D. Laing _____.
   A. was both too casual and authentic
   B. was acting like a performer
   C. was keeping a good balance
   D. was aware of his audience
5. In the last paragraph the author recommends that _____.
   A. you forget about your nervousness
   B. you feel natural and speak naturally

C. you may feel nervous, but appear naturally

D. you may imagine yourself to be natural

SECTION B

As you all know, the United States is a country on wheels. Nearly eight million new cars are made each year; four households out of five own at least one car, and more than a quarter have two each. Yet you'll be surprised to learn that some of the car-owners even suffer from malnutrition.

In 1968, a nation-wide survey of malnutrition was made for the first time. It found that 10 million people are suffering in health through inadequate feeding; the causes of their plight(困境)were varied. Unemployment over a long period should be considered as the main factor. And unemployment, strange to say, nine times out of ten results from automation, both in industrial and agricultural areas. For example, in the rural South when a cotton plantation suddenly cuts its force from 100 people to three, the problem to help the displaced arises. So is the case with industrial automation. In fact, probably 2 million jobs are made unnecessary each year in the whole country as a result of the automation process, thus making unemployment a chief social concern. According to government statistics, the number of people unemployed was over 5 percent for the period from 1958 to 1963. In July 1981, it rose to 7.8 percent. As a matter of fact, it has long been known that even during the most prosperous periods there have been people without enough to eat. So I think that's why President Kennedy said in his inauguration speech in 1961, if the government did not help the poor, it could not save the rich.

In 1966, the Social Security Administration calculated that a family of four needed an income of $3,355 a year to be above the line of poverty. And in 1977, the average poverty line of the country was slightly more than $6,200 annual income for a non-farm family of four. According to the Social Security Act, families of that size below poverty line are eligible to receive benefits from the special welfare program. The average weekly payment of benefits now is equivalent to 36 percent of the worker's normal wage. And the number of people who receive government benefits is increasing. In 1973, social insurance payments by governments, mainly to old age pensioners and people who had lost their jobs or were off work through illness, amounted to $86,000 million. Those not fully qualified for insurance payments received $29,000 million in public aid.

But problems still exist. Many people are not reached by the anti-poverty program, because local authorities and agencies do not want to play their part or do not gave the resources to do so. Some poor people will not accept help for various reasons. Of course, there are some more important factors which lie in the structure of the society, but I don't consider it necessary to dig into them here. Yet we will perhaps agree that social welfare programs have solved to some extent the problems of feeding, clothing and housing those below the poverty line. On the whole, it perhaps might be said that American people are living a better life than people in most other countries.

6. The United States is called a country on wheels because _____.
   A. about one-fourth Americans own two cars
   B. a bit over one out of four households are the owners of two cars
   C. nearly 8 million new cars drive in the country every year
   D. 80% Americans have at least one car
7. According to a 1968 survey, ten million Americans found themselves in a difficult health situation chiefly due to _____.
   A. inadequate feeding   B. malnutrition
   C. unemployment   D. automation
8. The author uses "the displaced" (Para. 2) to refer to those who are _____.
   A. unemployed   B. disabled
   C. sick   D. poor
9. The word "eligible" (Para.3) is synonymous with "_____".
   A. necessary   B. urgent
   C. needed   D. worthy
10. Americans are living a better life than those in most of other countries because, to some degree, _____.
    A. many Americans receive benefits from the special welfare program
    B. some poor people can receive help for some reason or other
    C. there is the anti-poverty program in the U.S.
    D. social welfare programs have some measures to settle the problems of those below the poverty line

Unit Eleven

Text A

On Life
Percy Bysshe Shelley

Life and the world, or whatever we call that which we are and feel, is an astonishing thing. The mist of familiarity obscures from us the wonder of our being. We are struck with admiration at some of its transient modifications, but it is itself the great miracle.

What are changes of empires, the wreck of dynasties, with the opinions which supported them; what is the birth and the extinction of religious and of political systems to life? What are the revolutions of the globe which we inhabit, and the operations of the elements of which it is composed, compared with life? What is the universe of stars, and suns, of which this inhabited earth is one, and their motions, and their destiny, compared with life? Life, the great miracle, we admire not, because it is so miraculous. It is well that we are thus shielded by the familiarity of what is at once so certain and so unfathomable, from an astonishment which would otherwise absorb and overawe the functions of that which is its object.

If any artist, I do not say had executed, but had merely conceived in his mind the system of the sun, and the stars, and planets, they not existing, and had painted to us in

obscure /əbˈskjʊə/ **a.** *adj.* dark; hidden; not clearly seen or understood; **b.** *adj.* not well known; **c.** *v.* make obscure
transient /ˈtrænziənt/ **a.** *adj.* lasting for a short time only; brief; **b.** (*US*) guest (in a hotel, boarding house, etc.) who is not a permanent resident
modification /ˌmɒdɪfɪˈkeɪʃən/ *n.* change or alteration
extinction /ɪksˈtɪŋkʃən/ *n.* **a.** making, being, becoming extinct; **b.** act of extinguishing.
religious /rɪˈlɪdʒəs/ **a.** *adj.* of religion; **b.** *adj.* (of a person) devout; god fearing; **c.** *adj.* of a monastic order; **d.** *adj.* scrupulous; conscientious; **e.** *n.* person bound by monastic vows; monk or nun
shield /ʃiːld/ *n.* **a.** piece of armor (metal, leather, wood) carried on the arm, to protect the body when fighting; representation of a shield, e.g. carved on a stone gateway, showing a person's coat of arms; **b.** (*fig.*) person or thing that protects.
unfathomable /ʌnˈfæðəməbl/ *adj.* so deep that can not be reached; (*fig.*) too strange or difficult to be understood
overawe /ˌəʊvərˈɔː/ *v.* awe completely; awe through great respect, etc.
execute /ˈeksɪkjuːt/ *v.* **a.** carry out (what one is asked or told to do); **b.** (*legal*) give effect to; **c.** (*legal*) make legally binding; **d.** carry out punishment by death on (sb); **e.** perform on the stage, at a concert, etc.

words, or upon canvas, the spectacle now afforded by the nightly cope of heaven, and illustrated it by the wisdom of astronomy, great would be our admiration. Or had he imagined the scenery of this earth, the mountains, the seas, and the rivers; the grass, and the flowers, and the variety of the forms and masses of the leaves of the woods, and the colours which attend the setting and the rising sun, and the hues of the atmosphere, turbid or serene, these things not before existing, truly we should have been astonished, and it would not have been a vain boast to have said of such a man, Non merita nome di creatore, se non Iddio ed il Poeta. But now these things are looked on with little wonder, and to be conscious of them with intense delight is esteemed to be the distinguishing mark of a refined and extraordinary person. The multitude of men care not for them. It is thus with Life—that which includes all.

canvas /ˈkænvəs/ n. strong, coarse cloth used for tents, sails, bags, etc. and by artists for oil-painting
spectacle /ˈspektəkl/ n. a. public display, procession, etc, esp. one with ceremony; b. sth seen; sth taking place before the eyes, esp. sth fine, remarkable or noteworthy
astronomy /əˈstrɒnəmɪ/ n. science of the son, moon, stars and planets
turbid /ˈtɜːbɪd/ adj. a. (of liquids) thick; muddy; not clear; b. (fig.) disordered, confused
non merita nome di creatore, se non Iddio ed il Poeta none deserves the name of Creator but God and the Poet
fragment /ˈfrægmənt/ a. n. part broken off; separate or incomplete part; b. v. break into fragments
commencement /kəˈmensmənt/ n. a. beginning; b. (in US universities, and at Cambridge and Dublin) ceremony at which degrees are conferred
abstraction /æbˈstrækʃən/ n. a. abstracting or being abstracted; b. absent-mindedness; c. visionary idea; idea of a quality apart from its material accompaniments
convict /kɒnˈvɪkt/ n. person convicted of crime and undergoing punishment

What is life? Thoughts and feelings arise, with or without our will, and we employ words to express them. We are born, and our birth is unremembered, and our infancy remembered but in fragments; we live on, and in living we lose the apprehension of life. How vain is it to think that words can penetrate the mystery of our being! Rightly used they may make evident our ignorance to ourselves, and this is much. For what are we? Whence do we come? and whither do we go? Is birth the commencement, is death the conclusion of our being? What is birth and death?

The most refined abstractions of logic conduct to a view of life, which, though startling to the apprehension, is, in fact, that which the habitual sense of its repeated combinations has extinguished in us. It strips, as it were, the painted curtain from this scene of things. I confess that I am one of those who are unable to refuse my assent to the conclusions of those philosophers who assert that nothing exists but as it is perceived.

It is a decision against which all our persuasions struggle, and we must be long convicted before we can be convinced that the solid universe of external things is 'such stuff as dreams are made of.' The shocking absurdities of the popular philosophy of mind and matter, its fatal consequences in morals, and their violent dogmatism concerning the source of all things, had early conducted me to materialism. This materialism is a seducing system to young and superficial minds. It allows its disciples to talk, and dispenses them from thinking. But I was discontented with such a view of things as it afforded; man is a being of high aspirations, 'looking both before and after,' whose 'thoughts wander through eternity,' disclaiming alliance with transience and decay; incapable of imagining to himself annihilation; existing but in the future and the past; being, not what he is, but what he has been and shall be. Whatever may be his true and final destination, there is a spirit within him at enmity with nothingness and dissolution. This is the character of all life and being. Each is at once the centre and the circumference; the point to which all things are referred, and the line in which all things are contained. Such contemplations as these, materialism and the popular philosophy of mind and matter alike forbid; they are only consistent with the intellectual system.

It is absurd to enter into a long recapitulation of arguments sufficiently familiar to those inquiring minds, whom alone a writer on abstruse subjects can be conceived to address. Perhaps the most clear and vigorous statement of the intellectual system is to be found in Sir William Drummond's *Academical Questions*.

After such an exposition, it would be idle to translate into other words what could only lose its energy and fitness by the change. Examined point by point, and word by word, the most discriminating intellects have been able to discern no train of thoughts in the process of reasoning, which does not conduct inevitably to the conclusion which has been stated.

What follows from the admission? It

dogmatism /ˈdɔːgmətɪzəm/ *n.* the quality of being dogmatic; being dogmatic
disciple /dɪˈsaɪpəl/ *n.* follower of any leader of religious thought, art, learning, etc.
dispense /dɪsˈpens/ *v.* **a.** deal out; distribute; administer; **b.** mix; prepare, give out (medicines); **c.** do without; **d.** render unnecessary
disclaim /dɪsˈkleɪm/ *v.* say that one does not own, that one has no connection with
alliance /əˈlaɪəns/ *n.* **a.** association or connection; **b.** union of persons, families, e.g. by marriage, or states (by treaty)
transience /ˈtrænzɪəns/ *n.* lasting for a short time only; briefness
annihilation /əˌnaɪəˈleɪʃən/ *n.* complete destruction (of military or naval forces etc.)
dissolution /dɪsəˈluːʃən/ *n.* breaking up; undoing or ending (of a marriage, partnership etc.)
circumference /səˈkʌmfərəns/ *n.* line that marks out a circle or other curved figure; distance round sth
contemplation /ˌkɒntəmˈpleɪʃən/ *n.* deep thought; intention; expectation
consistent /kənˈsɪstənt/ *adj.* (of a person, his behavior, principles, etc.) confirming to a regular pattern or style; regular
recapitulation /riːkəpɪtjʊˈleɪʃ(ə)n/ *n.* repeating; going through again the main points of sth (that has been told, discussed, argued about, etc.)
abstruse /əbˈstruːs/ *adj.* whose meaning or answer is hidden or difficult to understand; profound
vigorous /ˈvɪɡərəs/ *adj.* strong; energetic
discriminating /dɪˈskrɪmɪneɪtɪŋ/ *adj.* **a.** able to see or make small differences; **b.** giving special or different treatment to certain people, countries, etc.; **c.** differential

establishes no new truth, it gives us no additional insight into our hidden nature, neither its action nor itself. Philosophy, impatient as it may be to build, has much work yet remaining, as pioneer for the overgrowth of ages. It makes one step towards this object; it destroys error, and the roots of error. It leaves, what it is too often the duty of the reformer in political and ethical questions to leave, a vacancy.

It reduces the mind to that freedom in which it would have acted, but for the misuse of words and signs, the instruments of its own creation. By signs, I would be understood in a wide sense, including what is properly meant by that term, and what I peculiarly mean. In this latter sense, almost all familiar objects are signs, standing, not for themselves, but for others, in their capacity of suggesting one thought which shall lead to a train of thoughts. Our whole life is thus an education of error.

Let us recollect our sensations as children. What a distinct and intense appreh-ension had we of the world and of ourselves! Many of the circumstances of social life were then important to us which are now no longer so. But that is not the point of comparison on which I mean to insist. We less habitually distinguished all that we saw and felt, from ourselves. They seemed as it were to constitute one mass. There are some persons who, in this respect, are always children. Those who are subject to the state called reverie, feel as if their nature were dissolved into the surrounding universe, or as if the surrounding universe were absorbed into their being. They are conscious of no distinction. And these are states which precede, or accompany, or follow an unusually intense and vivid apprehension of life. As men grow up this power commonly decays, and they become mechanical and habitual agents. Thus feelings and then reasonings are the combined result of a multitude of entangled thoughts, and of a series of what are called impressions, planted by reiteration.

The view of life presented by the most refined deductions of the intellectual philosophy, is that of unity. Nothing exists but as it is perceived. The difference is

---

vacancy /ˈveɪkənsi/ *n.* **a.** condition of being empty or unoccupied; **b.** unoccupied space; blank; **c.** lack of ideas or intelligence; **d.** position in business, etc. for which sb is needed

sensation /senˈseɪʃən/ *n.* **a.** ability to feel; feeling; **b.** (instance of sth that causes a) quick and excited reaction

constitute /ˈkɒnstɪtjuːt/ *v.* **a.** give (sb) authority to hold (a position, etc.); **b.** establish; give legal authority to (a committee, etc.); **c.** make up (a whole); amount to; be the components of

reverie /ˈrevəri/ *n.* **a.** (instance/occasion of a) condition of being lost in dreamy, pleasant thoughts; **b.** piece of dreamy music

entangle /ɪnˈtæŋɡəl/ *v.* **a.** catch in a snare or among obstacles; **b.** (*fig.*) put or get into difficulties, in unfavorable circumstances

reiteration /riːˌtəˈreɪʃən/ *n.* **a.** act of reiterating; **b.** instance of repetition

deduction /dɪˈdʌkʃən/ *n.* taking away (an amount or a part)

merely nominal between those two classes of thought, which are vulgarly distinguished by the names of ideas and of external objects. Pursuing the same thread of reasoning, the existence of distinct individual minds, similar to that which is employed in now questioning its own nature, is likewise found to be a delusion. The words I, YOU, THEY, are not signs of any actual difference subsisting between the assemblage of thoughts thus indicated, but are merely marks employed to denote the different modifications of the one mind.

> **nominal** /ˈnɒmɪnəl/ *adj.* **a.** existing in name or word only, not in fact; **b.** of little importance or value; **c.** (gram) of a noun or nouns; **d.** of, or bearing a name
> **vulgarly** /ˈvʌlɡəli/ *adv.* ill mannered, in bad taste
> **subsist** /səbˈsɪst/ *v.* exist; be kept in existence on
> **assemblage** /əˈsemblɪdʒ/ *n.* bringing or coming together; assembly (now the usual word)

Cultural Notes

1. **Percy Bysshe Shelley** (1792—1822)—Percy Bysshe Shelley was one of the major English Romantic poets and is widely considered to be among the finest lyric poets of the English language. He is perhaps most famous for such anthology pieces as Ozymandias, Ode to the West Wind, To a Skylark, and The Masque of Anarchy. However, his major works were long visionary poems including Alastor, Adonais, The Revolt of Islam, Prometheus Unbound and the unfinished The Triumph of Life.

   Percy Bysshe Shelley, born at Field Place near Horsham in 1792, was the son of Sir Timothy Shelley, the M.P. for New Shoreham. Shelley was educated at Eton and Oxford University. At university Shelley began reading books by radical political writers such as William Godwin. He also wrote The Necessity of Atheism, a pamphlet that attacked the idea of compulsory Christianity. Oxford University was shocked when they discovered what Shelley had written and on 25th March 1811, he was expelled. Shelley eloped to Scotland with Harriet Westbrook, a sixteen-year-old daughter of a coffeehouse keeper. Shelley moved to Ireland where he made revolutionary speeches on religion and politics. He also wrote a political pamphlet A Declaration of Rights, on the subject of the French Revolution, but it was considered to be too radical for distribution in Britain. Percy Bysshe Shelley returned to England where he became involved in radical politics. In 1817 he wrote the pamphlet A Proposal for Putting Reform to the Vote Throughout the United Kingdom. In the pamphlet Shelley suggested a national referendum on electoral reform and improvements in working class education.

In 1822, Shelley moved to Italy with Leigh Hunt and Lord Byron where they published the journal The Liberal. By publishing it in Italy the three men remained free from prosecution by the British authorities. The first edition of The Liberal sold 4,000 copies. Soon after its publication, Percy Bysshe Shelley was lost at sea on 8th July, 1822, while sailing to meet Leigh Hunt.

2. **Sir William Drummond**—He is a distinguished scholar and philosopher. The date of his birth seems not to be ascertained, nor does any memoir of which we are aware, describe his early education. In 1805, his Academical Questions appeared, the first work in which he put forward claims to be esteemed a metaphysician. Although in this work he talks of the dignity of philosophy with no little enthusiasm, and gives it a preference to other subjects, more distinct than many may now admit; yet his work has certainly done more for the demolition of other systems than for instruction in any he has himself propounded. He perhaps carried the skeptical philosophy of Hume a little beyond its first bounds, by showing that we cannot comprehend the idea of simple substance.

Comprehension Exercises

I. Answer the following questions based on the text.

1. Do you think life is a miracle compared with the planets and stars of the universe? Are you satisfied with your own life?
2. In what does the greatness of life lie since it is of such transience?
3. The text suggests that nothing exists but as it is perceived. Is it against your own belief?
4. How can we understand that all familiar objects are only signs, standing not for themselves but for others?
5. I, You, and They are only different modifications of one mind. What does this sentence mean?

II. Write T for true and F for false in the brackets before each of the following statements.

1. (　　) According to the text, when people get into closer connection with each other, the familiarity will get rid of the mist between each other.

2. (　　) People think the world we are in is a great wonder and they look on it with awe and intense delight.

3. (　　) Thoughts and feelings arise with our will as we are human beings.

4. (　　) The author agrees with the conception that nothing exists except what is perceived.

5. (　　) In a sense, our life is made up of the past and future, the being is so transient and impossible to catch.

6. (　　) Everybody has definitely one life, and he could choose to have his life in the center—and then it would be in the center only.

7. (　　) As the text suggests, many of the circumstances of social life were then important to people but not all the way so.

8. (　　) Reverie is a state in which people feel as if they were dissolved into the surrounding universe because the universal beauty is so intense.

9. (　　) People are aware that they are different and that everything around is distinguished with its own characteristics.

10. (　　) Entangled thoughts combine to produce feelings and reasonings and impressions.

III. Select the most appropriate word or phrase and use its proper form to complete each of the following sentences.

abstruse	abstraction	assent	convict	dispense
entangle	eternity	execute	extinction	fragments
infancy	iraculous	obscure	overawe	penetrate
reiteration	shield	spectacle	subsist	transient

1. There are more _____ poems written and printed every year than clear ones.

2. The necessary consequence is a great number of _____ and clandestine connections.

3. We shall simply be resigning ourselves to _____ unless we carry on the four modernizations.

4. Living cells have extremely efficient and near-_____ devices for transforming energy.

5. The Court's desire to _____ "quasi judicial" officers from executive domination has obvious appeal.

6. The entire metropolitan center possessed a high and mighty air calculated to _____ and abash the common applicant.

7. The Windows allows a computer user to _____ multiple programs simultaneously.

8. The _____ of Xerxes's defeat tremendously reinforced the traditional conviction that pride goes before a fall.
9. The production of commodities, in other words, production for sale, was still in its _____.
10. When the archaeologists reconstructed the _____, they were amazed to find that the goddess turned out to be a very modern-looking woman.
11. A sufficiently energetic particle can _____ the entire stack of parallel plates.
12. After the _____ of the juice from the orange, only a tasteless pulp was left.
13. He has refused his _____ to Laws, the most wholesome and necessary for the public good.
14. The warden's clock ticked, the young _____'s pen scratched busily in the big book.
15. Indeed, agencies enjoy considerably wider power to _____ with formal proof than the courts do.

IV. Paraphrase the underlined words or expressions in each sentence.

1. The most refined abstractions of logic conduct to a view of life, which, though <u>startling to the apprehension</u>, is, in fact, that which the habitual sense of its repeated combinations has extinguished in us.

2. It <u>reduces the mind to that freedom</u> in which it would have acted, but for the misuse of words and signs, <u>the instruments of its own creation</u>.

3. We less habitually distinguished all that we saw and felt, from ourselves. They seemed as it were to <u>constitute one mass</u>.

4. It leaves, what it is too often the duty of the reformer in political and ethical questions to leave, a <u>vacancy</u>.

5. Thus feelings and then reasonings are the combined result of a multitude of <u>entangled thoughts</u>, and of a series of what are called impressions, <u>planted by reiteration</u>.

V. Discuss with your partner about each of the following statements and write an essay in no less than 200 words about your understanding of one of them.

1. We are becoming more and more lost in life though we thought we are more understanding and seeing more thoroughly the nature.
   _____
   _____

2. The philosophical state of our existence is that we see less about what we think most familiar to us.
   _____
   _____

3. Different people interpret life differently. Some think it is like wine, but some think life is suffering.
   _____
   _____

VI. List four websites where we can learn more about life and provide a brief introduction to each of them.

1. _____
   _____.

2. _____
   _____.

3. _____
   _____.

4. _____
   _____.

The Rhythm of Life
Alice Meynell

If life is not always poetical, it is at least metrical. **Periodicity** rules over the mental experience of man, according to the path of the

periodicity /ˌpɪərɪəˈdɪsɪti/ *n.* the quality, state, or fact of being regularly recurrent or having periods

orbit of his thoughts. Distances are not gauged, ellipses not measured, velocities not ascertained, times not known. Nevertheless, the recurrence is sure. What the mind suffered last week, or last year, it does not suffer now; but it will suffer again next week or next year. Happiness is not a matter of events; it depends upon the tides of the mind. Disease is metrical, closing in at shorter and shorter periods towards death, sweeping abroad at longer and longer intervals towards recovery. Sorrow for one cause was intolerable yesterday, and will be intolerable to-morrow; today it is easy to bear, but the cause has not passed. Even the burden of a spiritual distress unsolved is bound to leave the heart to a temporary peace; and remorse itself does not remain—it returns.

Gaiety takes us by a dear surprise. If we had made a course of notes of its visits, we might have been on the watch, and would have had an expectation instead of a discovery. No one makes such observations; in all the diaries of students of the interior world, there have never come to light the records of the Kepler of such cycles. But Thomas e Kempis knew of the recurrences, if he did not measure them. In his cell alone with the elements—"What wouldst thou more than these? for out of these were all things made"—he learnt the stay to be found in the depth of the hour of bitterness, and the remembrance that restrains the soul at the coming of the moment of delight, giving it a more conscious welcome, but presaging for it an inexorable flight. And "rarely, rarely comest thou," sighed Shelley, not to Delight merely, but to the Spirit of Delight.

Delight can be compelled beforehand, called, and constrained to our service—Ariel can be bound to a daily task; but such artificial violence throws life out of metre,

orbit /ˈɔːbɪt/ *n.* path followed by a heavenly body, e.g. a planet, the moon, or a manmade object
gauge /ɡeɪdʒ/ *n.* **a.** standard measure; extent; **b.** distance between rails; **c.** thickness of wire, sheet-metal, etc.; diameter of a bullet, etc.; **d.** instrument for measuring, e.g. rainfall, strength of wind, size, diameter, etc., of tools, wire, etc.
ellipse /ɪˈlɪps/ *n.* regular oval
velocity /vɪˈlɒsɪti/ *n.* **a.** speed; quickness; **b.** rate of motion
ascertain /ˌæsəˈteɪn/ *v.* find out (in order to be certain about)
interval /ˈɪntəvəl/ *n.* **a.** time (between two events or two parts of an action); (esp.) time between two acts of a play, two parts of a concert, etc.; **b.** space between (two objects or points); **c.** (*music*) difference of pitch between two notes on a given scale
intolerable /ɪnˈtɒlərəbəl/ *adj.* that cannot be tolerated or endured
temporary /ˈtempərəri/ *adj.* lasting for, designed to be used for, a short time only
remorse /rɪˈmɔːs/ *n.* **a.** deep, bitter regret for wrongdoing; **b.** compunction
gaiety /ˈɡeɪəti/ *n.* **a.** being gay; cheerfulness; **b.** merrymaking; joyful, festive occasions
interior /ɪnˈtɪərɪə/ *adj.* **a.** situated inside; of the inside; **b.** inland; away from the coast; **c.** home or domestic (contrasted with foreign)
presage /ˈpresɪdʒ/ *n.* (*formal*) presentiment; sign looked upon as a warning
inexorable /ɪnˈeksərəbəl/ *adj.* relentless; unyielding
constrain /kənˈstreɪn/ *v.* make sb do sth by using force or strong persuasion

and it is not the spirit that is thus compelled. THAT flits upon an orbit elliptically or parabolically or hyperbolically curved, keeping no man knows what trysts with Time.

It seems fit that Shelley and the author of the "Imitation" should both have been keen and simple enough to perceive these flights, and to guess at the order of this periodicity. Both souls were in close touch with the spirits of their several worlds, and no deliberate human rules, no infractions of the liberty and law of the universal movement, kept from them the knowledge of recurrences. Eppur si muove. They knew that presence does not exist without absence; they knew that what is just upon its flight of farewell is already on its long path of return. They knew that what is approaching to the very touch is hastening towards departure. "O wind," cried Shelley, in autumn,

O wind,

If winter comes can spring be far behind?

They knew that the flux is equal to the reflux; that to interrupt with unlawful recurrences, out of time, is to weaken the impulse of onset and retreat; the sweep and impetus of movement. To live in constant efforts after an equal life, whether the equality be sought in mental production, or in spiritual sweetness, or in the joy of the senses, is to live without either rest or full activity. The souls of certain of the saints, being singularly simple and single, have been in the most complete subjection to the law of periodicity. Ecstasy and desolation visited them by seasons. They endured, during spaces of vacant time, the interior loss of all for which they had sacrificed the world. They rejoiced in the uncovenanted beatitude of sweetness alighting in their hearts. Like them are the poets whom, three times or ten times in the course of a long life, the Muse has approached, touched, and forsaken. And yet

---

elliptically /ɪˈlɪptɪkəli/ *adv.* omitting from a sentence of words needed to complete the construction or meaning

parabolically /ˌpærəˈbɒlɪkəli/ *adv.* of, like, a parabola (a plane curve formed by cutting, a cone on a plane parallel to its side, so that the two arms get father away from one another)

hyperbolically /ˌhaɪpəˈbɒlɪkli/ *adv.* using exaggerated statements

tryst /traɪst/ *n.* (*archaic*) (time and place for, agreement to have, a) meeting, esp. between lovers

infraction /ɪnˈfrækʃən/ *n.* **a.** breaking of a rule, law, etc; **b.** instance of this

Eppur si muove this is what Galileo is alleged to have said on going into house arrest: "but it does move."

flux /flʌks/ *n.* continuous succession of changes

reflux /ˈriːflʌks/ *n.* flowing back; ebb

impetus /ˈɪmpɪtəs/ *n.* **a.** force with which a body moves; **b.** impulse; driving force

subjection /səbˈdʒekʃən/ *n.* getting or being brought under control

desolation /ˌdesəˈleɪʃən/ *n.* making or being desolated

rejoice /rɪˈdʒɔɪs/ *v.* **a.** make glad; cause to be happy; **b.** feel great joy; show signs of great happiness

uncovenanted /ʌnˈkʌvənəntɪd/ opposite of "covenanted" (meaning promised, pledged)

beatitude /bi(ː)ˈætɪtjuːd/ *n.* great happiness; blessedness

forsaken /fəˈseɪkən/ *v.* give up; break away from; desert

docile /ˈdəʊsaɪl/ adj. easily trained or controlled
irrevocable /ɪˈrevəkəb əl/ adj. final and unalterable; that cannot be revoked
irrigate /ˈɪrɪgeɪt/ v. supply with water
Indo-Germanic /ˈɪndəʊʒəːˈmænɪk/ relevant with India and German
lapse /læps/ n. a. slight error in speech or behavior; slip of the memory; tongue or pen; b. falling away from what is right; c. (of time) passing away; interval; (legal) ending of a right, etc. from failure to use it or ask for its renewal
ebb /eb/ v. a. (of the tide) flow back from the land to the sea; b. grow less; become weak or faint; c. the flowing out of the tide; d. (fig.) low state; decline or decay
cumulative /ˈkjuːmjʊlətɪv/ adj. increasing in amount by one addition after another
audacious /ɔːˈdeɪʃəs/ adj. a. daring; bold; b. foolishly bold; c. impudent
rhythmic /ˈrɪðmɪk/ adj. marked by rhythm; having rhythm
maternity /məˈtɜːnɪti/ n. being a mother

hardly like them; not always so docile, nor so wholly prepared for the departure, the brevity, of the golden and irrevocable hour. Few poets have fully recognized the metrical absence of their muse. For full recognition is expressed in one only way—silence.

It has been found that several tribes in Africa and in America worship the moon, and not the sun; a great number worship both; but no tribes are known to adore the sun, and not the moon. On her depend the tides; and she is Selene, mother of Herse, bringer of the dews that recurrently irrigate lands where rain is rare. More than any other companion of earth is she the Measurer. Early Indo-Germanic languages knew her by that name. Her metrical phases are the symbol of the order of recurrence. Constancy in approach and in departure is the reason of her inconstancies. Juliet will not receive a vow spoken in invocation of the moon; but Juliet did not live to know that love itself has tidal times—lapses and ebbs which are due to the metrical rule of the interior heart, but which the lover vainly and unkindly attributes to some outward alteration in the beloved. For man—except those elect already named—is hardly aware of periodicity. The individual man either never learns it fully, or learns it late. And he learns it so late, because it is a matter of cumulative experience upon which cumulative evidence is long lacking. It is in the after-part of each life that the law is learnt so definitely as to do away with the hope or fear of continuance. That young sorrow comes so near to despair is a result of this young ignorance. So is the early hope of great achievement.

Life seems so long, and its capacity so great, to one who knows nothing of all the intervals it needs must hold—intervals between aspirations, between actions, pauses as inevitable as the pauses of sleep. And life looks impossible to the young unfortunate, unaware of the inevitable and unfailing refreshment. It would be for their peace to learn that there is a tide in the affairs of men, in a sense more subtle—if it is not too audacious to add a meaning to Shakespeare—than the phrase was meant to contain. Their joy is flying away from them on its way home; their life will wax and wane; and if they would be wise, they must wake and rest in its phases, knowing that they are ruled by the law that commands all things—a sun's revolutions and the rhythmic pangs of maternity.

Cultural Notes

1. **Alice Meynell** (1847—1922)—Alice Meynell was an English writer, editor, critic, and suffragist, now remembered mainly as a poet. Alice Meynell was born in Barnes of wealthy parents and was educated privately by her father. She spent much of her early life in Italy and converted to Catholicism on reaching her majority. She married Wilfrid Meynell in 1877, working with him on his periodical, Merry England. In addition to writing numerous poems and critical essays, Alice Meynell was one of the leading literary figures of her era, editing anthologies and opening her home for literary gatherings. She was twice nominated as Poet Laureate. Her poems, most of which are fairly short, display a purity and sensitivity reflecting her strong religious beliefs. Preludes (1875) was her first poetry collection.

2. **Kepler** (1571—1630)—Kepler was a German astronomer who discovered how the planets move around the sun. These principles are known as Kepler's Laws, and they greatly influenced the work of Sir Isaac Newton.

3. **Thomas e Kempis** (1380—1471)—Thomas e Kempis was a German monk who is believed to have written The Imitation of Christ.

4. **Selene**—She was an archaic lunar deity and the daughter of the titans Hyperion and Theia. In Roman mythology the moon goddess is called Luna, Latin for "moon". Like most moon deities, Selene plays a fairly large role in her pantheon. However, Selene was eventually largely supplanted by Artemis, and Luna by Diana. In the collection known as the Homeric hymns, there is a Hymn to Selene (xxxii), paired with the hymn to Helios; in it Selene is addressed as "far-winged", an epithet ordinarily applied to birds. The etymology of Selene is uncertain, but if the word is of Greek origin, it is likely connected to the word selas, meaning "light". In post-renaissance art, Selene is generally depicted as a beautiful woman with a pale face, riding a silver chariot pulled by a yoke of oxen or a pair of horses. Often, she has been shown riding a horse or bull, wearing robes and a half-moon on her head and carrying a torch. Essentially, Selene is the moon goddess but is literally defined as "the moon".

5. **Herse**—She is a figure in Greek mythology, daughter of Cecrops (or, according to Pausanias, of Actaeus), sister to Aglaulus and Pandrosus. According to Apollodorus, when Hephaestus unsuccessfully attempted to rape Athena, she wiped his semen off her leg with wool and threw it on the

ground, impregnating Gaia. Athena wished to make the resulting infant Erichthonius immortal and to raise it, so she gave it to three sisters: Herse, Aglaulus and Pandrosus in a basket and warned them never to open it. Aglaulus and Herse opened the basket which contained the infant and future king, Erichthonius, who was somehow mixed or intertwined with a snake. The sight caused Herse and Aglaulus to go insane and they jumped to their deaths off the Acropolis. Shrines were constructed for Herse and Aglaulus on the Acropolis.

Comprehension Exercises

I. Answer the following questions based on the text.

1. Why does the text insist that if life is not always poetical, it is at least etrical?
2. What does "presence does not exist without absence" mean? Do you think it is contradictive?
3. Why is the famous line about the west wind by Shelley is quoted here?
4. Please tell the reason why several tribes in Africa and in America worship the moon rather than the sun.
5. In what way is man similar to that of nature?

II. Write T for true and F for false in the brackets before each of the following statements.

1. (   ) We could only expect the visit of joy rather than go and find it: it is so indefinite for us human beings.
2. (   ) Happiness is something we can make—for example, we can get more happiness if we earn more money.
3. (   ) Young sorrow and the early hope of great achievement come so near to despair is a result of young ignorance.
4. (   ) The law of periodicity is most deeply rooted in the souls of certain of the saints, singularly simple and single.
5. (   ) Ecstasy and desolation will visit people in turn, just like the rising and falling ides, and different seasons.
6. (   ) Generally speaking, people in their latter life will know better about the truth of it.
7. (   ) Poets could write masterpieces when they have the interval sparkles of gift.
8. (   ) In fact, few people could make a course of notes of the visits of happy moods.

9. (　　) Ordinary men rarely learn periodicity on time, they could only learn it partly or too late.
10. (　　) Poetic souls can be in closer connection with the periodicity of the social world.

III. Select the most appropriate word or phrase and use its proper form to complete each of the following sentences.

constancy	constrain	cumulative	deliberate	desolation
docile	elliptically	flux	gaiety	hyperbolically
impetus	infraction	interval	inexorable	metrical
orbit	periodicity	presage	rejoice	subject

1. His theories concerning _____ modulation and structural logic have engaged the attention of our younger composers.
2. Regular irregularities occur with constant _____ and are usually associated with partial heart block.
3. The _____ of the artificial satellite has an apogee of 200 miles from the earth.
4. In total she spent maybe six minutes away from her station, a reasonable _____ on such a night.
5. Her present _____ sounded to him like laughter heard in the shadow of the pulpit.
6. The transaction is the largest buyout in the for-profit education sector and could _____ a wave of similar deals
7. These ingredients limit the chemical reactions that can happen inside cells and so _____ what life can do.
8. All the other wavelengths will emerge as either _____ or circularly polarized light.
9. She was apparently doing so in a _____ and unimpassioned manner, with a view of making the best of it
10. He was criticized for his _____ of the discipline.
11. Education remains in a state of _____ which will take some time to settle down.
12. Innovation experts and consultants stress repeatedly that innovation isn't a matter of _____ knowledge.
13. The soldiers were grateful and _____, made almost childlike by their wounds.

14. Through love the universe with _____ makes changes all without discord.
15. Like most _____ processes, the problem matured slowly, even after the steep rises in interest rates.

IV. Paraphrase the underlined words or expressions in each sentence.

1. Delight can be <u>compelled</u> beforehand, called, and <u>constrained to our service</u>.

2. <u>It seems fit</u> that Shelley and the author of the "Imitation" should both have been keen and simple enough to <u>perceive these flights</u>.

3. They knew that the <u>flux</u> is equal to the <u>reflux</u>; that to interrupt with <u>unlawful recurrences</u>, out of time, is to <u>weaken the impulse of onset and retreat</u>.

4. <u>Constancy in approach and in departure</u> is the reason of her inconstancies.

5. If we had made <u>a course of notes of its visits</u>, we might have been <u>on the watch</u>, and would have had an expectation instead of a discovery.

V. Discuss with your partner about each of the following statements and write an essay in no less than 200 words about your understanding of one of them.

1. Different people have different attitudes towards the world—though the world itself is same.

2. Sensitive minds have greater possibility to perceive the beauty of the world.

3. What is just upon its flight of farewell is already on its long path of return.

VI. List four websites where we can learn more about poems on life and provide a brief introduction to each of them.

1. _____
   _____.
2. _____
   _____.
3. _____
   _____.
4. _____
   _____.

Twenty Minutes' Reading

You are required to read the following sections within 20 minutes.

 SECTION A

The ancient Greeks were much interested in speculating on the nature of the world about them and consequently succeeded in evolving many fascinating theories.

It was two Greek thinkers, Leucippus of Miletus and Dernocritus of Abdera, who first decided that substances could not be broken up indefinitely, that eventually the particles obtained would be so small they could be divided no farther. They concluded that there were a number of varieties of such particles, each making up a different substance; by combining them in different ways, still other substances would result. The Greek word for "indivisible" is atoms, so they named the theoretically indivisible particles atoms.

Their theory did not win favor among the Greeks, but it was resurrected in 1803 by the British chemist John Dalton. He decided that the facts uncovered by the still new science of chemistry could best be explained by supposing each chemical element to be formed of tiny indivisible particles. Each element thus had its own characteristic type of particle, and by varying the manner of combination of these, all existing substances could be constructed. Following the old Greek theory, Dalton called the particles atoms—and this time the atomic theory met with approval.

In 1896 it was discovered that atoms are not indivisible, that certain complicated atoms break up spontaneously liberating particles far smaller than atoms. Then scientists learned how to break up atoms in the laboratory. Today man's whole future hinges upon the manner in which atoms break up and fuse together. But still the name is atom— "indivisible".

1. The selection shows that the ancient Greeks were interested in the _____.
   A. origin of the world
   B. nature of the universe
   C. nature of the physical world
   D. nature and origin of life
2. Two Greek thinkers developed the idea of atoms from the belief that _____.
   A. only a limited number of substances exist
   B. certain substances are indivisible
   C. new substances can be constructed from existing ones
   D. substances cannot be divided indefinitely
3. The atomic theory won favor _____.
   A. among the Greek theorists' contemporaries
   B. in the twentieth century
   C. after John Dalton resurrected it
   D. among the later Greeks
4. The atomic theory was disproved when _____.
   A. Dalton continued his study of chemistry
   B. scientists learned how to break up atoms
   C. man liberated particles smaller than atoms
   D. man found that some atoms break up spontaneously
5. The author says that man's future hinges on how _____.
   A. atoms break up and fuse together
   B. particles smaller than atoms break up
   C. atoms disintegrate spontaneously
   D. chemical elements fuse into new substances

SECTION B

The scattering of galaxies, the habits of macromolecules, and the astounding abundance of stars are forcing those who ponder such matters to a further adjustment of their concept of the place and function of man in the material universe.

In the history of the evolving human mind, with its increasing knowledge of the surrounding world, there must have been a time when the philosophers of the early tribes began to realize that the world was not simply anthropocentric—centered on man himself. The geocentric concept then became common doctrine. It accepted a universe centered on the earth. This first adjustment was only mildly deflationary to the human ego, for man appeared to surpass all other living forms.

The second adjustment in the understanding of man's relation to the physical universe, that is, the abandonment of the earth-center theory, was not generally acceptable until the sixteenth-century Copernican revolution soundly established the heliocentric concept—the theory of a universe centered on the sun. Man is a stubborn adherent to official dogma; eventually, however, he accepted the sun as the center not only of the local family of planets, but also of the total sidereal（恒星的）assemblage, and he long held that view.

Then, less than forty years ago, came the inescapable need for a third adjustment. This shift has deeply punctured man's pride and self assurance, for it has carried with it the knowledge of the appalling number of galaxies.

The "galactocentric universe" suddenly puts the earth and its life near the edge of one great galaxy in a universe of millions of galaxies. Man becomes peripheral among the billions of stars of his own Milky Way; and according to the revelations of paleontology and geochemistry, he is recent and apparently ephemeral in the unrolling of cosmic time. We cannot restore egocentrism or heliocentrism. And since we cannot go back to the cramped but comfortable past, we go forward and find there is more to the story.

The downgrading of the earth and sun and the elevation of the galaxies is not the end of this progress of scientific pilgrims through philosophic fields. The need for another jolting adjustment now appears—not wholly unexpected by workers in science, nor wholly the result of one or two scientific revelations. Our new problem concerns the spread of life throughout the universe. As unsolicited spokesmen for all the earthly organisms of land, sea and air, we ask the piquant question: are we alone?

6. This article is mainly about _____.
   A. galaxies
   B. the habits of macromolecules
   C. the abundance of stars
   D. the place and function of man in the universe

7. The geocentric concept of the universe became common doctrine _____.
   A. at the very beginning of man's existence
   B. within the past forty years

C. when men realized that the world was not anthropocentric

D. when the theory of evolution was accepted

8. Man's third adjustment was necessitated by the discovery that _____.

    A. the sun was the center of only the local family of planets

    B. the earth is only near the edge of one great galaxy in a universe of uncounted galaxies

    C. there is only one great galaxy

    D. the world is geocentric, not heliocentric

9. The galactocentric theory of the universe affected man by _____.

    A. only mildly deflating his ego

    B. deeply disturbing his pride and self-assurance

    C. once again establishing him as master of all things in the universe

    D. revealing to him that intelligent beings live on other planets

10. Which of the following statement is not true, according to the author?

    A. The heliocentric concept was unknown until the Copernican revolution.

    B. The heliocentric concept is more deflationary to the human ego than is the geocentric concept.

    C. Heliocentrism is no longer generally accepted by astronomers.

    D. Heliocentrism is no more sophisticated than is egocentrism.

Unit Twelve

Text A

Love
Ralf Waldo Emerson

Every promise of the soul has innumerable fulfillments; each of it. Nature, uncontainable, flowing, forelooking, in the first sentiment of kindness anticipates already a benevolence which shall lose all particular regards in its general light. The introduction to this felicity is in a private and tender relation of one to one, which is the enchantment of human life; which, like a certain divine rage and enthusiasm, seizes on man at one period, and works a revolution in his mind and body; unites him to his race, pledges him to the domestic and civic relations, carries him with new sympathy into nature, enhances the power of the senses, opens the imagination, adds to his character heroic and sacred attributes, establishes marriage, and gives permanence to human society.

The natural association of the sentiment of love with the heyday of the blood seems to require, that in order to portray it in vivid tints, which every youth and maid should confess to be true to their throbbing experience, one must not be too old. The delicious fancies of youth reject the least savour of a mature philosophy, as chilling with age and pedantry their purple bloom. And, therefore, I know I incur the imputation of unnecessary hardness and

uncontainable /ˌʌnkənˈteɪməbəl/ *adj.* unable to keep in control
forelooking /fɔːˈlʊkɪŋ/ *n.* foreseeing
sentiment /ˈsentɪmənt/ *n.* **a.** mental feeling, the total of what one thinks and feels on a subject; **b.** (tendency to be moved by) (display of) tender feeling contrasted with reason; **c.** expression of feeling; opinions or points of view
felicity /fɪˈlɪsɪti/ *n.* **a.** (*formal*) great happiness or contentment; **b.** pleasing manner of speaking or writing
enchantment /ɪnˈtʃɑːntmənt/ *n.* being charmed or delighted
civic /ˈsɪvɪk/ *adj.* of the official and affairs of a town or a citizen
enhance /ɪnˈhɑːns/ *v.* add to (the value, attraction, powers, price, etc.)
permanence /ˈpɜːmənəns/ *n.* **a.** state of being permanent; **b.** permanent thing, person or position
permanent /ˈpɜːmənənt/ *adj.* not expected to change; going on for a long time; intended to last
heyday /ˈheɪdeɪ/ *n.* time of greatest prosperity or power
throb /θrɒb/ *v.* (of the heart, pulse, etc.) beat esp. beat more rapidly than usual
savor /ˈseɪvə/ *n.* taste or flavor (of sth); suggestion of a quality
pedantry /ˈpedəntrɪ/ *n.* tiresome and unnecessary display of learning; too much insistence upon formal rules
imputation /ˌɪmpjuː(ː)ˈteɪʃən/ *n.* **a.** considering as the act, quality, or outcome of; **b.** accusation, or suggestion of wrong doing

stoicism from those who compose the Court and Parliament of Love. But from these formidable censors I shall appeal to my seniors. For it is to be considered that this passion of which we speak, though it begin with the young, yet forsakes not the old, or rather suffers no one who is truly its servant to grow old, but makes the aged participators of it, not less than the tender maiden, though in a different and nobler sort. For it is a fire that, kindling its first embers in the narrow nook of a private bosom, caught from a wandering spark out of another private heart, glows and enlarges until it warms and beams upon multitudes of men and women, upon the universal heart of all, and so lights up the whole world and all nature with its generous flames.

formidable /ˈfɔːmɪdəbl/ *adj.* **a.** causing fear or dread; **b.** requiring great effort to deal with or overcome
censor /ˈsensə/ *n.* official with authority to examine letters, books, periodicals, plays, films, etc. and to cut out anything regarded as immortal or in other ways undesirable, or in time of war, helpful to the enemy
multitude /ˈmʌltɪtjuːd/ *n.* **a.** great number (esp. of people gathered together); **b.** greatness of number
adherence /ədˈhɪərəns/ *n.* **a.** sticking fast to; **b.** remaining faithful to; supporting firmly
deface /dɪˈfeɪs/ *v.* spoil the appearance of; make engraved lettering illegible
disfigure /dɪsˈfɪɡə/ *v.* spoil the appearance or shape of
nourishment /ˈnʌrɪʃmənt/ *n.* keeping (sb) alive and well with food; making well and strong; improving (land) with manure, etc.
compunction /kəmˈpʌŋkʃən/ *n.* uneasiness of conscience; feeling of regret for one's action
embitter /ɪmˈbɪtə/ *v.* arouse bitter feelings in
melancholy /ˈmelənkəli/ *n.* **a.** sadness; low spirits; **b.** *adj.* sad; low spirited; causing sadness or low spirits

It matters not, therefore, whether we attempt to describe the passion at twenty, at thirty, or at eighty years. He who paints it at the first period will lose some of its later, he who paints it at the last, some of its earlier traits. Only it is to be hoped that, by patience and the Muses' aid, we may attain to that inward view of the law, which shall describe a truth ever young and beautiful, so central that it shall commend itself to the eye, at whatever angle beholden.

And the first condition is, that we must leave a too close and lingering adherence to facts, and study the sentiment as it appeared in hope and not in history. For each man sees his own life defaced and disfigured, as the life of man is not, to his imagination. Each man sees over his own experience a certain stain of error, whilst that of other men looks fair and ideal. Let any man go back to those delicious relations which make the beauty of his life, which have given him sincerest instruction and nourishment, he will shrink and moan. Alas! I know not why, but infinite compunctions embitter in mature life the remembrances of budding joy, and cover every beloved name. Every thing is beautiful seen from the point of the intellect, or as truth. But all is sour, if seen as experience. Details are melancholy; the plan is seemly and noble. In the actual world—the painful kingdom of time and place—dwell care, and canker, and fear. With thought, with the ideal, is immortal hilarity, the rose of joy. Round it all the Muses sing. But grief cleaves to names, and persons, and the partial interests of today and yesterday. The strong bent of nature is seen in the proportion which this topic of personal relations usurps in the conversation of society.

What do we wish to know of any worthy person so much, as how he has sped in the history of this sentiment? What books in the circulating libraries circulate? How we glow over these novels of passion, when the story is told with any spark of truth and nature! And what fastens attention, in the intercourse of life, like any passage betraying affection between two parties? Perhaps we never saw them before, and never shall meet them again. But we see them exchange a glance, or betray a deep emotion, and we are no longer strangers. We understand them, and take the warmest interest in the development of the romance. All mankind love a lover. The earliest demonstrations of complacency and kindness are nature's most winning pictures. It is the dawn of civility and grace in the coarse and rustic. The rude village boy teases the girls about the school-house door; —but today he comes running into the entry, and meets one fair child disposing her satchel; he holds her books to help her, and instantly it seems to him as if she removed herself from him infinitely, and was a sacred precinct. Among the throng of girls he runs rudely enough, but one alone distances him; and these two little neighbours, that were so close just now, have learned to respect each other's personality. Or who can avert his eyes from the engaging, half-artful, half-artless ways of school-girls who go into the country shops to buy a skein of silk or a sheet of paper, and talk half an hour about nothing with the broad-faced, good-natured shop-boy. In the village they are on a perfect equality, which love delights in, and without any coquetry the happy, affectionate nature of woman flows out in this pretty gossip. The girls may have little beauty, yet plainly do they establish between them and the good boy the most agreeable, confiding relations, what with their fun and their earnest, about Edgar, and Jonas, and Almira, and who was invited to the party, and who danced at the dancing-school, and when the singing-school would begin, and other nothings concerning which the parties cooed. By and by that boy wants a wife, and very truly and heartily will he know where to find a sincere and sweet mate, without any risk such as Milton deplores as incident to scholars and great men.

I have been told, that in some public discourses of mine my reverence for the

hilarity /hɪˈlærɪti/ *n.* noisy merriment; loud laughter
civility /sɪˈvɪlɪti/ *n.* politeness; (*pl.*) polite acts
rustic /ˈrʌstɪk/ **a.** *adj.* (in a good sense) characteristic of country people; unaffected; **b.** rough; unrefined; **c.** of rough workmanship
satchel /ˈsætʃəl/ *n.* small bag for carrying light articles, esp. school books
coquetry /ˈkɒkɪtri/ *n.* **a.** flirting; **b.** instance of this
reverence /revərəns/ *n.* deep respect; feeling of wonder and awe

intellect has made me unjustly cold to the personal relations. But now I almost shrink at the remembrance of such disparaging words. For persons are love's world, and the coldest philosopher cannot recount the debt of the young soul wandering here in nature to the power of love, without being tempted to unsay, as treasonable to nature, aught derogatory to the social instincts. For, though the celestial rapture falling out of heaven seizes only upon those of tender age, and although a beauty overpowering all analysis or comparison, and putting us quite beside ourselves, we can seldom see after thirty years, yet the remembrance of these visions outlasts all other remembrances, and is a wreath of flowers on the oldest brows. But here is a strange fact; it may seem to many men, in revising their experience, that they have no fairer page in their life's book than the delicious memory of some passages wherein affection contrived to give a witchcraft surpassing the deep attraction of its own truth to a parcel of accidental and trivial circumstances. In looking backward, they may find that several things which were not the charm have more reality to this groping memory than the charm itself which embalmed them. But be our experience in particulars what it may, no man ever forgot the visitations of that power to his heart and brain, which created all things new; which was the dawn in him of music, poetry, and art; which made the face of nature radiant with purple light, the morning and the night varied enchantments; when a single tone of one voice could make the heart bound, and the most trivial circumstance associated with one form is put in the amber of memory.

> **celestial** /sɪˈlestɪəl/ *adj.* **a.** of the sky; of heaven; **b.** divinely good or beautiful
> **rapture** /ˈræptʃə/ *n.* ecstatic delight
> **visitation** /ˌvɪzɪˈteɪʃən/ *n.* **a.** visit; esp. one of an official nature or one made by a bishop or priest; **b.** trouble, disaster, looked upon as punishment from God
> **trivial** /ˈtrɪvɪəl/ *adj.* **a.** of small value or importance; **b.** commonplace; humdrum; **c.** (of a person) trifling; lacking seriousness; superficial
> **amber** /ˈæmbə/ *n.* hard, clear yellowish-brown gum used for making ornaments, etc.

Cultural Notes

Ralph Waldo Emerson (1803—1882)—Ralph Waldo Emerson is one of the most famous American essayists, poets and philosophers. He was born on May 25, 1803, the fourth of eight children. Waldo entered Harvard at 14. He began then to keep a journal, a practice he continued for the rest of his life, later calling its volumes—all long since published—his "savings bank". His early writings contain much poetry. In October, 1826, Emerson was licensed to preach by the Middlesex Association of Ministers. In 1836 he published his first book, Nature. He began his career as a Unitarian minister but went on, as an independent man of letters, to become the preeminent lecturer, essayist and philosopher of 19th century America. Emerson was a key figure in the "New England Renaissance", as an author and also through association with the Transcendental Club, many writers, notably Henry David Thoreau, Bronson Alcott and Margaret Fuller, gathered around him at his home in Concord, Massachusetts. Late in life his home was a kind of shrine students and aspiring writers visited, as on a pilgrimage. He and other transcendentalists did much to open Unitarians and the liberally religious to science, eastern religions and a naturalistic mysticism. His main themes are individualism, independent thinking, self-reliance, idealism and the worship of nature. His works include Nature, Self-reliance, American Scholar, Overlord and may other essays and poems.

Comprehension Exercises

I. Answer the following questions based on the text.

1. Do you agree with the author that love is so powerful that it can work a revolution in a person's mind and body?
2. Do you think that it is self-contradictory when the author said that the delicious fancies of youth reject the least savor of a mature philosophy, as chilling with age and pedantry their purple bloom, and that though it (love) begin with the young, yet forsakes not the old?
3. How do you understand the author's opinion when he mentioned that he who paints it at the first period will lose some of its later, he who paints it at the last, some of its earlier traits?
4. Do you agree with Dorothy Parker's saying that love is like quicksilver in the hand, leave the fingers open and it stays; clutch it, and it darts away?
5. Make a comment on the opinion that love has no awareness of merit or demerit; it has no scale. Love loves; this is its nature.

II. Write T for true and F for false in the brackets before each of the following statements.

1. (   ) Only the youth are able to portray love in vivid color, therefore, the old have no such passion.
2. (   ) We want to know of a famous person, while we are not interested in his love stories.
3. (   ) A beauty can last in one's life, and the memory of love can outlast that of other things.

Unit Twelve

4. (   ) According to the author, if a man is asked to recall his love stories, he would like to try to avoid it.
5. (   ) Love is so great that it can cause a man change a lot mentally but not physically.
6. (   ) The author thinks that love is human nature, and that it needs no affectation, but true emotion.
7. (   ) In the author's opinion, a man tends to view himself as one with many errors. He would think of himself with a derogatory impression.
8. (   ) If he is a servant of the strong passion, a man will stay young forever both in mind and body.
9. (   ) Everything is beautiful, seen from the point of the intellect, as truth. But all is sour, if seen as experience. Therefore, experience is no better than truth.
10. (   ) Because of love, a girl is a beauty for his beloved one, although she is very plain.

III. Select the most appropriate word or phrase and use its proper form to complete each of the following sentences.

adherence	amber	avert	celestial	civic
cleave	commend	containable	disparaging	enhance
hilarity	incur	permanence	pledge	reverence
rustic	revise	seemly	sentiment	trivial

1. The present became much more diverse and complex, no longer _____ within a single chronological framework.
2. She upbraided herself for the _____, but could not overcome or lessen it.
3. The mayor has tried to foster _____ pride by having a new public library built in the city.
4. The treaties renounce the use of force and _____ the two countries to co-operation.
5. New economic preservation techniques would _____ the marketing of processed agricultural products.
6. Her parents' marriage had seemed to represent solid contentment, happy _____.
7. An enterprise has to _____ certain costs and expenses in order to stay in business.
8. You can neither blame nor _____ him without some twinge of conscience.
9. Its rulers are not held together by blood-ties but by _____ to a common doctrine.

10. Many consumers are unaware of the high caloric content of _____ ordinary meals, particularly at fast food outlets.

11. His genially acerb colleagues lampoon him mercilessly, but he finds in their own folklore grounds for a measure of _____.

12. Thus the temptation is strong to supplement these few autobiographies by writing biographies of _____ or peasant characters.

13. The surcharge revenue could be used to reduce many of the proposed cuts, or to _____ the worst of them.

14. The team worked for five months, repeating the process again and again as they slowly plotted the course of the _____ bodies.

15. And that serves as a check on publishers, who know that if they _____ too frequently they could end up losing sales.

IV. Paraphrase the underlined words or expressions in each sentence.

1. All mankind love a lover. The <u>earliest demonstrations of complacency and kindness</u> are nature's most <u>winning pictures</u>.

2. For it is to be considered that this passion of which we speak, though it begin with the young, yet <u>forsakes not the old</u>, or rather suffers no one who is truly its servant to grow old.

3. I know not why, but <u>infinite compunctions embitter</u> in mature life the remembrances of budding joy, and cover every beloved name.

4. But <u>be our experience in particulars what it may</u>, no man ever forgot <u>the visitations of that power</u> to his heart and brain.

5. For each man sees his own life <u>defaced and disfigured</u>, as the life of man is not, to his imagination.

V. Discuss with your partner about each of the following statements and write an essay in no less than 200 words about your understanding of one of them.

1. Being loved doesn't necessarily lead to loving others.
   _____
   _____

2. We can observe that love does exist everywhere when and only when we get rid of the negative emotions against others.
   _____
   _____

3. Our life divides at the very moment we take our outlook, both towards life itself and the people around us.
   _____
   _____
   _____

VI. List four websites where we can learn more about the author Emerson and his works and provide a brief introduction to each of them.

1. _____
   _____
   _____.

2. _____
   _____
   _____.

3. _____
   _____
   _____.

4. _____
   _____
   _____.

Text B

Of Friendship
Francis Bacon

IT HAD been hard for him that spake it to have put more truth and untruth together in few words, than in that speech, Whatsoever is delighted in solitude, is either a wild beast or a god. For it is most true, that a natural and secret hatred, and

solitude /ˈsɒlɪtjuːd/ *n.* being without companions; lonely

aversation towards society, in any man, hath somewhat of the savage beast; but it is most untrue, that it should have any character at all, of the divine nature; except it proceed, not out of a pleasure in solitude, but out of a love and desire to sequester a man's self, for a higher conversation: such as is found to have been falsely and feignedly in some of the heathen; as Epimenides the Candian, Numa the Roman, Empedocles the Sicilian, and Apollonius of Tyana; and truly and really, in divers of the ancient hermits and holy fathers of the church. But little do men perceive what solitude is, and how far it extendeth. For a crowd is not company; and faces are but a gallery of pictures; and talk but a tinkling cymbal, where there is no love. The Latin adage meeteth with it a little: Magna civitas, magna solitudo; because in a great town friends are scattered; so that there is not that fellowship, for the most part, which is in less neighborhoods. But we may go further, and affirm most truly, that it is a mere and miserable solitude to want true friends; without which the world is but a wilderness; and even in this sense also of solitude, whosoever in the frame of his nature and affections, is unfit for friendship, he taketh it of the beast, and not from humanity.

A principal fruit of friendship, is the ease and discharge of the fulness and swellings of the heart, which passions of all kinds do cause and induce. We know diseases of stoppings, and suffocations, are the most dangerous in the body; and it is not much otherwise in the mind; you may take sarza to open the liver, steel to open the spleen, flowers of sulphur for the lungs, castoreum for the brain; but no receipt openeth the heart, but a true friend; to whom you may impart griefs, joys, fears, hopes, suspicions, counsels, and whatsoever lieth upon the heart to oppress it, in a kind of civil shrift or confession.

aversation /əˈvɜːʃən/ *n.* = aversion **a.** a feeling of stong dislike or unwillingness; **b.** a person or thing that casues this feeling
sequester /sɪˈkwestə/ *v.* keep sb away or apart from other people; withdraw to a quiet place
solitude /ˈsɒlɪtjuːd/ *n.* being without companions; lonely
aversation /əˈvɜːʃən/ *n.* = aversion **a.** a feeling of stong dislike or unwillingness; **b.** a person or thing that casues this feeling
sequester /sɪˈkwestə/ *v.* keep sb away or apart from other people; withdraw to a quiet place
feignedly /ˈfeɪnɪdli/ *adv.* pretendingly
heathen /ˈhiːðən/ *n.* **a.** one who adheres to the religion of a people or nation that does not acknowledge the God of Judaism, Christianity, or Islam; **b.** such persons considered as a group; the unconverted
hermit /ˈhɜːmɪt/ *n.* person (esp. man in early Christian times) living alone
cymbal /ˈsɪmbəl/ *n.* one of a pair of round brass plates struck together to make chanting sounds
adage /ˈædɪdʒ/ *n.* old and wise saying; proverb
Magna civitas, magna solitudoa (*Latin proverb*) a large city is a great place to be alone
suffocation /ˌsʌfəˈkeɪʃən/ *n.* **a.** causing or having difficulty in breathing; **b.** killing, choking by making breathing impossible
sarza /sarˈsa/ *n.* a kind of prescription in medieval, used to cure rheumatic disease
spleen /spliːn/ *n.* bodily organ in the abdomen which causes changes in the blood
sulphur /ˈsʌlfə/ *n.* light yellow non-metallic element (symbol S)

It is a strange thing to observe, how high a rate great kings and monarchs do set upon this fruit of friendship, whereof we speak: so great, as they purchase it, many times, at the hazard of their own safety and greatness. For princes, in regard of the distance of their fortune from that of their subjects and servants, cannot gather this fruit, except (to make themselves capable thereof) they raise some persons to be, as it were, companions and almost equals to themselves, which many times sorteth to inconvenience. The modern languages give unto such persons the name of favorites, or privadoes; as if it were matter of grace, or conversation. But the Roman name attaineth the true use and cause thereof, naming them participes curarum; for it is that which tieth the knot.

And we see plainly that this hath been done, not by weak and passionate princes only, but by the wisest and most politic that ever reigned; who have oftentimes joined to themselves some of their servants; whom both themselves have called friends, and allowed other likewise to call them in the same manner; using the word which is received between private men.

Certainly, if a man would give it a hard phrase, those that want friends, to open themselves unto, are carnnibals of their own hearts. But one thing is most admirable (wherewith I will conclude this first fruit of friendship), which is, that this communicating of a man's self to his friend, works two contrary effects; for it redoubleth joys, and cutteth griefs in halves. For there is no man, that imparteth his joys to his friend, but he joyeth the more; and no man that imparteth his griefs to his friend, but he grieveth the less. So that it is in truth, of operation upon a man's mind, of like virtue as the alchemists use to attribute to their stone, for man's body; that it worketh all contrary effects, but still to the good and benefit of nature. But yet without praying in aid of alchemists, there is a manifest image of this, in the ordinary course of nature. For in bodies, union strengtheneth and cherisheth any natural action; and on the other side, weakeneth and dulleth any violent impression: and even so it is of minds.

The second fruit of friendship, is healthful and sovereign for the understanding,

hazard /'hæzəd/ **a.** *n.* risk; danger; **b.** *n.* game at dice, with complicated chances; **c.** *v.* take the risk of; expose to danger; **d.** *n.* venture to make

thereof /ðeər'ɒv/ *adv.* (*formal*) of that; from that source

privadoes a Spanish term, referring to a private friend; a confidential friend; a confidant

participes curarum partners of cares

alchemist /'ælkɪmɪst/ *n.* a person who studied or practiced alchemy

manifest /'mænɪfest/ **a.** *adj.* clear and obvious; **b.** *v.* show clearly; **c.** *v.* give signs of; **d.** *v.* (*reflex*) come to light; appear

cherisheth /'tʃɜːmjus/ **a.** *n.* care for tenderly; **b.** *v.* keep alive (hope, ambition, feelings, etc.) in one's heart

sovereign /'sɒvrɪn/ *n.* **a.** (of power) highest; without limit; (of a nation, state, power) having sovereign power; **b.** excellent; effective; **c.** ruler, e. g. a king, queen or an emperor; **d.** British gold coin not in circulation now (face value one pound)

as the first is for the affections. For friendship maketh indeed a fair day in the affections, from storm and tempests; but it maketh daylight in the understanding, out of darkness, and confusion of thoughts. Neither is this to be understood only of faithful counsel, which a man receiveth from his friend; but before you come to that, certain it is, that whosoever hath his mind fraught with many thoughts, his wits and understanding do clarify and break up, in the communicating and discoursing with another; he tosseth his thoughts more easily; he marshalleth them more orderly, he seeth how they look when they are turned into words: finally, he waxeth wiser than himself; and that more by an hour's discourse, than by a day's meditation. It was well said by Themistocles, to the king of Persia, That speech was like cloth of Arras, opened and put abroad; whereby the imagery doth appear in figure; whereas in thoughts they lie but as in packs. Neither is this second fruit of friendship, in opening the understanding, restrained only to such friends as are able to give a man counsel; (they indeed are best;) but even without that, a man learneth of himself, and bringeth his own thoughts to light, and whetteth his wits as against a stone, which itself cuts not. In a word, a man were better relate himself to a statua, or picture, than to suffer his thoughts to pass in smother. Add now, to make this second fruit of friendship complete, that other point, which lieth more open, and falleth within vulgar observation; which is faithful counsel from a friend. Heraclitus saith well in one of his enigmas, Dry light is ever the best. And certain it is, that the light that a man receiveth by counsel from another, is drier and purer, than that which cometh from his own understanding and judgment; which is ever infused, and drenched, in his affections and customs.

tempest /ˈtempɪst/ *n.* violent storm; (*fig.*) violent agitation
clarify /ˈklærɪfaɪ/ make or become clear; make (a liquid, etc.) free from impurities
discourse /ˈdɪskɔːs/ *n.* **a.** speech; lecture; sermon; treatise; **b.** (*formal*) talk preach or lecture upon (usu. at length)
marshalleth /ˈmɑːʃəlɪŋ/ *n.* **a.** an officer of highest rank; official responsible for important public events or ceremonies, e.g. one who accompanies a High Court judge; an officer of the royal household; **b.** *v.* arrange in proper order; **c.** guide or lead (sb) with ceremony
counsel /ˈkaʊnsəl/ *n.* group of persons appointed, elected or chosen to give advice, make rules and carry out plans, manage affairs, etc., esp. of government
whet /wet/ *v.* sharpen (a knife, axe, etc); (*fig.*) sharpen or excite (the appetite; a desire)
smother /ˈsmʌðə/ *v.* **a.** cause the death of, by stopping the breath of or by keeping air from, kill by suffocation; **b.** put out (a fire); keep (a fire) down; **c.** cover; wrap up, overwhelm with
enigma /ɪˈnɪgmə/ *n.* question, person, thing, circumstance, that is puzzling
infuse /ɪnˈfjuːz/ *v.* **a.** (*formal*) put, pour (a quality, etc. into); **b.** pour (hot) liquid on (leaves, herbs, etc.) to flavor it to extract its constituents; **c.** undergo infusion
drench /drentʃ/ *v.* make wet all over, right through
flatter /ˈflætə/ *v.* **a.** praise too much, praise insincerely (in order to please); **b.** give a feeling of pleasure to

So as there is as much difference between the counsel, that a friend giveth, and that a man giveth himself, as there is between the counsel of a friend, and of a flatterer. For there is no such flatterer as is a man's self; and there is no such remedy

preservative /prɪˈzɜːvətɪv/ *n.* subsistence used for preserving

admonition /ˌædməˈnɪʃən/ *n.* (*formal*) warning

pierce /ˈpɪəs/ *v.* **a.** (of sharp-pointed instruments) go into or through; **b.** (fig. of cold, pain, sounds, etc.) force a way into or through; affect deeply; **c.** penetrate

corrosive /kəˈrəʊsɪv/ *adj.* substance that wears away, destroys slowly by chemical action or disease; being worn away thus

absurdity /əbˈsɜːdɪti/ *n.* state of being ridiculous; unreasonableness

against flattery of a man's self, as the liberty of a friend. Counsel is of two sorts: the one concerning manners, the other concerning business. For the first, the best preservative to keep the mind in health, is the faithful admonition of a friend. The calling of a man's self to a strict account, is a medicine, sometime too piercing and corrosive. Reading good books of morality, is a little flat and dead. Observing our faults in others, is sometimes improper for our case. But the best receipt (best, I say, to work, and best to take) is the admonition of a friend. It is a strange thing to behold, what gross errors and extreme absurdities many (especially of the greater sort) do commit, for want of a friend to tell them of them; to the great damage both of their fame and fortune: for, as St. James saith, they are as men that look sometimes into a glass, and presently forget their own shape and favor.

Cultural Notes

1. **Lord Francis Bacon** (1561—1626)—Lord Francis Bacon is the father of experimental philosophy, whose father had been Lord Keeper, and he himself was a great many years Lord Chancellor under King James I. Nevertheless, amidst the intrigues of a Court, and the affairs of his exalted employment (Because of bribery and extortion he was sentenced by the House of Lords to pay a fine of about four hundred thousand French livers, to lose his peerage and his dignity of Chancellor.), was enough to engross his whole time, he yet found so much leisure for study as to make himself a great philosopher, a good historian, and an elegant writer. A more surprising circumstance is that he lived in an age in which the art of writing justly and elegantly was little known, much less true philosophy. Lord Bacon, as is the fate of man, was more esteemed after his death than in his lifetime. His enemies were in the British Court, and his admirers were foreigners.

2. **Epimenides the Candian**—He is a semi-legendary Cretan poet, prophet, and wonder-worker, variously dated to between 600 and 500 BC, and credited with remarkable longevity, with wandering out of the body and with a miraculous sleep of 57 years. He was a Cretan by birth, of the city of Cnossus.

3. **Numa the Roman**—He is the legendary king of Rome, successor to Romulus. His consort, the nymph Egeria, was said to have aided him in his rule. The origin of Roman ceremonial law and religious rites was ascribed to him. Among other achievements, he was supposedly responsible for the pontifices, flamens (sacred priests), vestal virgins, worship of Terminus (the god of landmarks), the building of the temple of Janus, and the reorganization of the calendar into days for business and holidays.

4. **Empedocles the Sicilian** (493 BC—444 BC)—Empedocles is the Greek philosopher, poet, and scientist. He propounded a pluralist cosmological scheme in which fire, air, water, and earth mingled and separated under the compulsion of love and strife. Empedocles was born of a noble family in the Sicilian city of Acragas (modern Agrigento).

5. **Apollonius of Tyana**—He is a Greek philosopher, and he lived in 1st century AD. As a philosopher of the Neo-Pythagorean school, he traveled widely and became famous for his wisdom and reputed magical powers. He was accused of treason by both Nero and Domitian, but escaped by supposedly magical means. A record of his travels, based on the journal of his companion, Damis, and written (216 AD) by Flavius Philostratus, is a mixture of truth and romantic fiction. Some critics have denounced it for its similarity to the Christ story, but others, such as Voltaire and Charles Blount, have championed the doctrines of Apollonius. He died, supposedly at age 100, after setting up a school in Ephesus.

6. **Heraclitus**—Heraclitus, the son of Vloson, was born about 535 BC in Ephesos, the second great Greek Ionian city. Scholars place his death at about 475 BC. He was a man of strong and independent philosophical spirit. Unlike the Milesian philosophers whose subject was the material beginning of the world, Heraclitus focused instead on the internal rhythm of nature which moves and regulates things, namely, the Logos (Rule). Heraclitus is the philosopher of the eternal change. He expresses the notion of eternal change in terms of the continuous flow of the river which always renews itself. Heraclitus accepted only one material source of natural substances, the Pyr (Fire). This Pyr is the essence of Logos which creates an infinite and uncorrupted world, without beginning. It converts this world into various shapes as a harmony of the opposites. The composition of opposites sustains everything in nature. "Good" and "bad" are simply opposite sides of the same thing.

Unit Twelve

Comprehension Exercises

I. Answer the following questions based on the text.

1. Why is friendship so difficult to describe in words?
2. Do you think the kings and emperors can also be true in friendship? What for?
3. What do you think about friendship in your own opinion?
4. What's your opinion on the statement: Whatsoever is delighted in solitude, is either a wild beast or a god?
5. What do you think about the second fruits of friendship mentioned in the text?

II. Write T for true and F for false in the brackets before each of the following statements.

1. (   ) If a person is among the crowds, he will not feel lonely.
2. (   ) The friends in a small town are closer than those in the big cities.
3. (   ) According to the author, people don't understand what solitude is, and what its scope is.
4. (   ) he nature of human beings tends to look for the friendship, which is different from that of the animals.
5. (   ) Nothing can open the heart of a person, but a true friend.
6. (   ) In human history, only the weak and passionate princes would seek for friendship in their subjects and servants.
7. (   ) The kings and monarchs had joined some of their servants to themselves in order to build a solid foundation for their rule.
8. (   ) There are many ways to keep the mind in health, such as taking medicine, reading good books. Of all them the best one is the friend counsel.
9. (   ) Birds of a feather flock together. An evil person can't make friends with a noble man.
10. (   ) Communicating can help to clarify one's mind, make one wiser, therefore, communicating is always far better than meditation.

III. Select the most appropriate word or phrase and use its proper form to complete each of the following sentences.

admonition	attribute	aversion	clarify	counsel
drench	discharge	flatter	hazard	impart
infuse	induce	mere	pierce	reign
remedy	suffocation	sovereign	smother	solitude

1. Perhaps it is the desire for _____ or the chance of making an unexpected discovery that lures men down to the depths of the earth.
2. I underwent _____ therapy for my addiction to smoking.
3. Some cynics say that sport is a _____ instrument of capitalist domination.
4. It precipitates out as iron oxide and can then be recovered and recycled, leaving water pure enough to _____ into a river
5. Foods that have been carefully crafted to _____ pleasurable sensory experiences can also become victims of this truism.
6. Such love will drown him in _____, pain and despair.
7. Only the president's strong control was able to _____ some sense of seriousness to the meeting.
8. As long as your interests and mine were at variance I could give you no _____ on this subject.
9. They have not used this article before, but they are willing to _____ a try.
10. During the _____ of the white terror, many progressives fall victim to the secret police.
11. They often _____ the simplest manifestations of nature to agencies of which they know nothing.
12. Independence and _____ equality among states is a fundamental principle of international law.
13. Trying to do this will help _____ the problem and test the programmer's understanding of it.
14. They tried to _____ up the murder by pretending that her death was accidental.
15. The tea should be allowed to _____ for several minutes.

IV. Paraphrase the underlined words or expressions in each sentence.

1. For a crowd is not <u>company</u>; and faces are but a gallery of pictures; and talk but a <u>tinkling cymbal</u>, where there is no love.

Unit Twelve

2. But we may go further, and affirm most truly, that it is <u>a mere and miserable solitude</u> to want true friends; without which the world is <u>but a wilderness</u>.

3. A principal fruit of friendship, is <u>the ease and discharge of the fulness and swellings of the heart</u>, which passions of all kinds do cause and induce.

4. For there is no man, that imparteth his joys to his friend, but he <u>joyeth the more</u>; and no man that imparteth his griefs to his friend, but he grieveth the less.

5. Reading good books of morality, is a little <u>flat and dead</u>.

V. Discuss with your partner about each of the following statements and write an essay in no less than 200 words about your understanding of one of them.

1. Sometimes we do like praise, but faithful counsel from our close friends is important to all of us.

2. As human beings are the social animals, seeking for true friendship is part of one's life.

3. One's own understanding and judgment is usually influenced by his affections and the customs. It has its own limitations.

VI. List four websites where we can learn more about friendship and provide a brief introduction to each of them.

1. _____

2. _____
_____
_____.

3. _____
_____
_____.

4. _____
_____
_____.

Twenty Minutes' Reading

You are required to read the following sections within 20 minutes.

SECTION A

For me, scientific knowledge is divided into mathematical sciences, natural sciences or sciences dealing with the natural world (physical and biological sciences), and sciences dealing with mankind (psychology, sociology, all the sciences of cultural achievements, every kind of historical knowledge). Apart from these sciences is philosophy, about which we will talk later. In the first place, all this is pure or theoretical knowledge, sought only for the purpose of understanding, in order to fulfill the need to understand what is intrinsic and consubstantial to man. What distinguishes man from animal is that he knows and needs to know. If man did not know that the world existed, and that the world was of a certain kind, that he was in the world and that he himself was of a certain kind, he wouldn't be man. The technical aspects or applications of knowledge are equally necessary for man and are of the greatest importance, because they also contribute to defining him as man and permit him to pursue a life increasingly more truly human.

But even while enjoying the results of technical progress, he must defend the primacy and autonomy of pure knowledge. Knowledge sought directly for its practical applications will have immediate and foreseeable success, but not the kind of important result whose revolutionary scope is in large part unforeseen, except by the imagination of the Utopians. Let me recall a well-known example. If the Greek mathematicians had not applied themselves to the investigation of conic sections, zealously and without the least suspicion that it might someday be useful, it would not have been possible centuries later to navigate far from shore. The first men to study the nature of electricity could not imagine that their experiments, carried on because of mere intellectual curiosity, would eventually lead to modern electrical technology, without which we can scarcely conceive of contemporary life. Pure knowledge is valuable for its own sake, because the human spirit cannot resign itself to ignorance. But, in addition, it is the foundation for practical results that would not have been reached if this knowledge had not been sought disinterestedly.

1. To the author, what is most important to mankind?
    A. Technical applications of knowledge.
    B. Theoretical knowledge.
    C. Natural knowledge.
    D. The biological knowledge.
2. In the paragraph that follows this passage, we may expect the author to discuss _____.
    A. the value of technical research
    B. the value of pure research
    C. philosophy
    D. unforeseen discoveries
3. The author points out that the Greeks who studied conic sections _____.
    A. were mathematicians
    B. were interested in navigation
    C. were unaware of the value of their studies
    D. worked with electricity
4. The title below that best expresses the ideas of this passage is _____.
    A. Technical Progress
    B. A Little Learning Is a Dangerous Thing
    C. Man's Distinguishing Characteristics
    D. Learning for Its Own Sake
5. The practical scientist _____.
    A. knows the value of what he will discover
    B. is interested in the unknown
    C. knows that the world exists
    D. conceives of contemporary life

SECTION B

Stress is a word commonly found in today's vocabulary, and is often used to describe modern working and living patterns, especially in big cities. Yet stress has been a part of daily life since time immemorial. Thus it would be more pertinent to define stress as the way in which the human body deals with all kinds of threatening situations, from confrontations with wild, vicious animals, to struggling through a crowded subway station during the early-morning rush hour: the effects on the body being universal.

When confronted with a stressful situation the body reacts by releasing a hormone known as ACTH from the posterior pituitary gland situated at the base of the brain. The hormone, traveling through the network of arteries that make up the primary blood supply route, reaches the kidneys, or more specifically, glands situated on the peripheries, where it stimulates the release of adrenaline. This has an antagonistic effect on various bodily functions. This is to say it stimulates a response in certain organs, whilst inhibiting actions in others. In other words a type of trade-off is reached, whereby energy saved by shutting down one function is thus used to enhance the performance of a neighbor. In this way, the body can prepare itself fully for the oncoming danger by using, primarily, the same given amount of energy, giving rise to what is known as the fight or flight response.

When the fight or flight response is activated, with the release of adrenaline, blood is directed away from non-vital functions such as the skin and digestion, and redirected to the essential organs such as the brain to facilitate thought, the large muscle groups to facilitate speed, and the lungs to increase the amount of oxygen uptake into the bloodstream, whilst the heart beats faster to pump the blood round the body at an increased rate of speed, and raising the blood pressure. Once the stressful situation has passed the opposite occurs, resulting in what is known as the sympathetic rebound. The heart slows down and blood is redirected away from the lungs, brains and muscles, flowing, once more, to every part of the body, whilst digestion resumes. It is, however, the sympathetic rebound, or more specifically, the effects of the sympathetic rebound that lead to the myriad of modern stress-related diseases.

Stress, in fact, as been linked to many more common diseases, such as cancer and even the common cold. The reason for this is that during the fight or flight response the body's immune system that fights disease is also shut down, leaving the person more vulnerable to illness, and is, indeed, one of the commonest forms of stress-related problems. Unfortunately, however, modern life is packed full of stressful situations, and costs industry, thus the economy, millions of dollars each year in lost revenue. Traveling to work in morning, meeting tight deadlines whilst at work, studying to further one's qualifications, paying the mortgage or children's school fees are but a few. Thus, it transpires that stress is a modern day epidemic that urgently needs addressing.

6. The word "pertinent" in the first paragraph can be replaced by _____.
   A. positive   B. negative
   C. appropriate   D. probable
7. Facing stress, _____ in the brain release a hormone to cope with that situation.
   A. ACTH
   B. the network of arteries
   C. pituitary gland
   D. the peripheries
8. Modern stress-related illnesses are believed to be caused by _____.
   A. being under constant stress
   B. the after effects of stress
   C. modern life styles
   D. the release of adrenaline
9. Which of the following statements is NOT true of the stressful situation in modern life?
   A. To pay the mortgage.
   B. To commute to the office.
   C. To further one's qualifications.
   D. To resume digestion.
10. The best title for this passage is _____.
    A. Stress and the Human Immune System
    B. Stress and the Human Body
    C. Stress and the Illness
    D. Stress and the Response of Immune System